Classic Restaurants

OF

YOUNGSTOWN

THOMAS WELSH & GORDON F. MORGAN
WITH THE MAHONING VALLEY HISTORICAL SOCIETY

AMERICAN PALATE

Published by American Palate
A Division of The History Press
Charleston, SC 29403
www.historypress.net

First published 2014
Second printing 2014

ISBN 978.1.60949.798.9

Library of Congress CIP data applied for.

To Elaine M. Welsh, whose courage and support made this project possible.

Be not forgetful to entertain strangers:
for thereby some have entertained angels unawares.
Hebrews 13:2, KJV

CONTENTS

ACKNOWLEDGEMENTS

This project benefited from the guidance and support of numerous colleagues, friends and relatives. We would like to offer special thanks to H. William Lawson, executive director of the Mahoning Valley Historical Society, for permitting the use of scores of historical images from the organization's vast collection. We would also like to thank Pamela Speis, archivist of the Mahoning Valley Historical Society, who provided invaluable assistance. Mrs. Speis not only tracked down volumes of material related to the history of local restaurants but also assisted in the selection of images that would eventually be included in this volume. Additional images were provided by David Michael Adams, Wendy Aron, Mike Avey, Bob Bakalik, Paula Berndt, Cecelia Bouslough, Nea Bristol, Anthony Cafaro Sr., Carmine Cassese, Vernon Cesta, Joseph Cherol, Nora Chrystal, George and Anna Dubic, James Esposito, Marycarmen Kelly, Lou Kennedy, Solomon "Jack" Kravitz, Morris Levy, George Mager, Mark Marino, Michele Orostin, Greg Petrakos, Anna M. Quaranta, Carlos and Celerina Ramírez, Carole Nudell Sherman, Gregory Speero Jr., Charlie Staples, Laurie Palazzo Sunyog, Janet Umbel and Deanna Vallos. During the early stages of this project, Michael K. Geltz offered assistance as a researcher and contributor. Throughout this process, we benefited from the guidance of Dr. George D. Beelen, retired professor of history at Youngstown State University, and Dr. Paul McBride, emeritus professor of history at Ithaca College. We received further assistance from public historians Joshua Foster, Ben Lariccia, Richard Quinn and Richard S. Scarsella, while Dick Nard provided copies of the wonderful illustrated maps he created of local hot spots in the 1950s and '60s. Also worthy of mention are the many people who agreed to be interviewed regarding their impressions of Youngstown's various restaurants. Interviewees included David Michael Adams, Stacey Adger, Dennis Alexander, Thomas and Florence Alexander, Bernadette Dell'Arco Angle, Wendy Ziegler Aron, Mike Avey, Bob Bakalik, Dr. George D. Beelen, James D. Bennett, Paula Berndt, Beverly Blackshear, JoAnn Blunt, Douglas and Cecilia Bouslough, Sophia Brooks, Anthony Cafaro Sr., Thomas Campana Jr., Honorable Thomas J. Carney, Elder Rosetta Carter, Bob and Mary Lou Casey, Attorney Robert F. Casey, Carmine Cassese, Joseph Cassese, Vernon Cesta, Joseph and Laura Cherol, Sandra Cika, Joseph and Dorothy Courtney, Tim Curtin, Shirley Dangerfield, Gene and Jan DeCapua, Neil Dell'Arco, Sherry DeMar, Bobby DeVicchio, James Gray Doran, Patti Ferraro Druzisky, George and Anna Dubic, Mary Ann Dudzik, Grace Einfelt, Michael and Loretta Ekoniak, Marilyn Abbott Emerick, Jim Esposito, Roberto Faraglia, Chris Palazzo Febinger, Donia Kravitz Foster, Joshua Foster, Attorney Robert S. and Elaine Fulton, Jim Graycar, Dr. Daniel Greenfield, Mary Hake, Jack Hamilton, Father John C. Harris, Jacob Harver, Faith Hodnick, Mervyn Hollander, Honorable Judge Joseph M. Houser, Josephine Houser, Linda Kravitz Kantor, Marycarmel Kelly, Julie Kennedy, Lou Kennedy, Patrick Kerrigan, Phil Kidd, Richard Koker, Rose Kravitz, Solomon "Jack" Kravitz, Dr. Fred Kurz, Connie Kushma, Ben Lariccia, Nick Lavanty, Thomas J. Leventi, Joseph Levy, Morris Levy, Bert Lockshin, Judith Lukin, Robyn Maas, George Mager, Rose Makosky, Dr. Kurt Malkoff, Rich Mamone, Amelia Marinelli, Mark Marino, Robert Marino, Nar Martinez, Dave Mastry, Dr. Paul McBride, James McNicholas, Marcia Melvin, Honorable Harry Meshel, Bill Mettee, Florence Mirkin, Steve Moritz, Carmen Naples, Dick Nard, Father Edward P. Noga, Minerva Nudell, Stan Nudell, Joe Nudo, Nick and Rose Pacalo, Dennis Palazzo, Marty Pallante, Jeff Palusak, George Pavlich, Jim Pernotto, Greg Petrakos, Mark C. Peyko, Judy Phillips, Joseph Planey, Ruth Fletcher Pope, Jim and Debbie Precurato, Tom and Kathy Price, Ann M. Quaranta, Jerry Quaranta, Ron Quaranta, Richard Quinn, Leroy Raffel, Carlos and Celerina Ramírez, Kate Ramunno, Jack Raver Sr., Dr. Regina Rees, Christian Rinehart, Marsha Robinson, Fred and Josephine Ross, Anne Massullo Sabella, Richard S. Scarsella, Chad Scianna, Carol Nudell Sherman, Pearl Berezo Sinistro, Robert "Smitty" Smith, Gregory Speero Jr., Charlie Staples, Laurie Palazzo Sunyog, Betty Swanson, Marilyn Sweeney, Jamie Szmara, John Thomas, B.J. Thompson, Jack Thorne, Bill Umbel, Janet Umbel, Deanna Vallos, William Vallos, Michael and Kanella

Acknowledgements

Varveris, Dave Vasvari, Carmen Vecchione, George Wainio, William Wainio, T. Gordon Welsh, Dr. Frank P. Yanek, Patricia Lyden Yank, Fred and Soo Ja Yanoski, Edna Zaitzew and Roxanne Zoccoli. While conducting general research for this project, we benefited from the assistance of the following individuals: Debbie Bushmire, Sara Churchill, Sally Freaney, Stuart Gibbs, Suzette Hinson, Michele Mellor and Tim Seman, reference librarians at Youngstown's Reuben-McMillan Public Library. We owe a special word of appreciation to Elaine M. Welsh and Jeannette M. Welsh, who served as remarkably patient proofreaders.

Thomas G. Welsh Jr. and Gordon F. Morgan Jr.
January 25, 2014
Youngstown, Ohio

DINING ON THE TOWN

In February 1970, Milt Simon, longtime owner of Youngstown's Mural Room, announced that his iconic restaurant would close after more than twenty years of operation. The news prompted a flurry of tributes from the numerous civic organizations that had used the restaurant as a regular meeting place. Situated near downtown's Vindicator Square, not far from the Art Deco building that housed the city's daily newspaper, the Mural Room had set a standard for elegant dining since 1945.

Over the years, it had become a major venue for holiday banquets, graduation parties and after-prom dinners, and its attractions included an elegant blue-and-green interior featuring murals of woodland scenery along the banks of the Mississippi. The real draw for the restaurant's patrons, of course, was the Mural Room's distinctive fare, which included salt sticks, onion rolls, tortes, chiffon pies and fresh salads featuring homemade dressings.

For decades, local diners had benefited from the expertise of the restaurant's Spanish-born chef, Gabriel Covas, whose succulent entrees ranged from prime rib to frog legs. Meanwhile, its pastry chef, Fred Dell'Arco, produced breads that were virtually unrivaled within the community. Overall, the Mural Room, with its idiosyncratic blend of southern charm and international cuisine, provided patrons with an atmosphere and menu they recognized as the best the city had to offer. Therefore, the restaurant's demise signaled the close of an elegant chapter in the history of downtown Youngstown.

A *Vindicator* article reported that the official reason for the restaurant's closing was the newspaper's decision to build a new production plant on the site of the Mural Room's traditional parking lot. The restaurant's owner, however, described this development as "a blessing in disguise," adding that it freed him from a lease that "still had several years to run." Over the previous two years, Simon admitted, "Night-time dining in downtown Youngstown [had] become a thing of the past except for a few special occasions."[1]

Among those present during the restaurant's final evening of business was Amelia Marinelli, who recalled that the proprietor presented each guest with a small bottle of champagne. Decades later, she described the experience of dining in a full-blown downtown entertainment district. "It was so different to go downtown then, especially on a Saturday," Mrs. Marinelli said. "Ladies would get dressed up. I used to even put my furs on; and then, we would meet somebody for dinner, usually at the Mural Room. It was always a very nice restaurant."

While numerous factors contributed to the restaurant's demise, it was clear to many observers that the growth of Youngstown's suburban communities had come at the expense of the city itself. One year earlier, in 1969, the opening of the Southern Park Mall in neighboring Boardman Township drew scores of area residents who once frequented downtown's glittering retail district as well as the uptown area's fashionable nightclubs and restaurants.

The debilitating effects of suburbanization was compounded in the late 1970s and early '80s, when the collapse of the Mahoning Valley's steel industry deprived Youngstown of its economic backbone. Starting with the 1977 shutdown of Youngstown Sheet & Tube's massive plant in neighboring Campbell, Ohio, the city's narrative became one of inexorable decline. Over the next decade, as other steel plants and satellite businesses closed their operations, the former "Steel Valley"—a region comprising Mahoning and Trumbull Counties as well as portions of western Pennsylvania—lost an estimated forty thousand manufacturing jobs.[2]

In 1970, when the Mural Room closed its doors, the city was home to an estimated 140,509 people, a far cry from its peak population of more than 170,000 in 1930, when it was the third-largest city in Ohio. A decade later, in 1980, the city's population sat at 112,146—a drop of more than 20 percent. The population continued to fall steadily over the next few decades, and in 2011, it was recorded to be a mere 66,982. Not surprisingly, the Mural Room's fate was eventually shared by a host of other urban restaurants and eateries, including the Voyager Motor Inn, Hasti House, the Western Reserve Room, the Hub, Palazzo's, the Mansion and the Colonial House, to name a few. Those that survived were often forced to reinvent themselves amid constantly changing circumstances.

Youngstown, of course, wasn't the only city to be affected by the sweeping trend of deindustrialization. As writer George Packer noted, "It was happening in Cleveland, Toledo, Akron, Buffalo, Syracuse, Pittsburgh, Bethlehem, Detroit, Flint, Milwaukee, Chicago, Gary, St. Louis, and other cities across a region that in 1983 was given a new name: the Rust Belt." Packer added, however, that "it happened in Youngstown first, fastest, and most completely, and because Youngstown had nothing else, no major-league baseball team or world-class symphony, the city became an icon of deindustrialization, a song title, a cliché."[3]

The local impact of deindustrialization was compounded by the fact that Youngstown's economy had once revolved around steel production. In the early 1980s, labor lawyer and activist Staughton Lynd noted that many Youngstown residents had, until recently, viewed the city's steel mills as "permanent fixtures," and it was therefore difficult for them to envision an economic future that did not depend on steel production.[4]

Perhaps the community's most enduring commodity was a distinctive local cuisine—one that reflected the wide variety of immigrant and migrant groups who arrived in the area during the heyday of the steel industry. Although many of the city's upscale restaurants were forced to close, the popularity of local food continues to be reflected in the survival of independent establishments such as Antone's, the Boulevard, Casa Ramirez, Charlie Staples' Bar-B-Que, the Golden Dawn, Kravitz's Delicatessen, the MVR, Scarsella's and the Tokyo House.

"What was really unique about this area was that we had so many nationalities," explained retired restaurateur Douglas M. Bouslough. "At the time we were kids working at the Boulevard Tavern, there weren't any one-star, two-star, three-star, four-star or five-star restaurants in Youngstown," he added. "But on Tuesday, you could go over to the West Side and get the best damned stuffed peppers there ever were. On a Friday, you could go up to the North Side and get calamari, or you could come to the Boulevard and get a great fish dinner."

Food originally presented on the tables of recent arrivals from Austria-Hungary, Southern Italy and the American South eventually found its way into church halls, concession stands, taverns and restaurants. Moreover, in a community that was often plagued by ethnic, racial and religious conflict, the sharing of food often preceded other kinds of interaction. "There are many things that divide this community, but one of the unifying elements in this community is the food," said Mark C. Peyko, publisher of the *Metro Monthly*, a local newspaper. "Food is like music, and music is like food. You can't keep people apart when something is that good. You have people sharing it, regardless of their color or background."

Through his newspaper, as well as a local television program called *Homeplate*, Peyko celebrates what he calls "vernacular foods." These foods include Youngstown's ubiquitous "Brier Hill Pizza," a tasty (though relatively unadorned) form of pizza developed in the last century by Italian American residents of the city's most celebrated working-class neighborhood.

Also on the list are the community's numerous varieties of pierogi (an Eastern European dumpling), which reflect the culinary traditions of regions included in modern-day Poland, Lithuania, Ukraine and Slovakia. Meanwhile, local barbecue lovers owe a debt to the African American migrants who brought with them closely guarded recipes that were developed in the Deep South. With the clear exception of high-end Italian cuisine, many of these food traditions were underrepresented in the city's fine-dining establishments. Yet they were all part of the local culinary experience, and today, many "vernacular foods" remain staples of the city's independent restaurants, taverns and eateries.

These establishments continue to showcase the area's gift for hospitality. "The independent restaurants around here are unique for their family orientation, their hominess, and the way they greet their customers," observed lifelong resident George Wainio. "If you walk into the Boulevard or the MVR, it's just like walking back in time." He added: "These places change, but they don't change. The second or third generations of the families operating these establishments have somehow managed to maintain the warm atmosphere that many people associate with the old days."

Significantly, the establishments included in this narrative range from top-tier dining spots to neighborhood taverns noted for their exceptional food. While a certain amount of space has been devoted to restaurants associated with pizza, this manuscript does not attempt to provide an overview of the community's pizzerias, given their large number and extraordinary variety. Nor does this book focus on businesses specializing in ice cream products, e.g., Handel's and Parker's Frozen Custard. These topics deserve a separate treatment.

Although a large percentage of the establishments highlighted in this book have disappeared, it would be a mistake to characterize the story of

INTRODUCTION

Youngstown's restaurants and eateries as an exclusive narrative of decline and demise. This story also encompasses the positive themes of resilience and continuity—even growth. Indeed, a quiet technological revolution was launched as early as 2000, with the establishment of the Youngstown Business Incubator (YBI), which set out to support business-to-business software companies. As the YBI expanded, it developed and restored a once desolate block of West Federal Street, thereby contributing to what has shaped up as a downtown renaissance.

In 2005, a high-tech convocation center called the Chevrolet Centre (currently known as the Covelli Centre) opened on the site of a vacant steel mill located southeast of Youngstown's Central Square. Then, four years later, in 2009, the *Vindicator* reported that a private developer intended to restore the Realty Building, a historic skyscraper located on Central Square, and transform it into an upscale apartment building. More recently, in 2011, the city announced that a $9 million project would turn the downtown's long-abandoned Erie Terminal into a sixty-five-unit residential complex.

By 2013, a little more than forty years after the closing of the Mural Room, downtown Youngstown hosted a number of thriving restaurants, including Overture, V², O'Donald's and Roberto's Italian Ristorante. Meanwhile, landmark restaurants and eateries elsewhere in the city—including the MVR, the Golden Dawn and the Boulevard—have remained symbols of continuity in rapidly changing neighborhoods. A few businesses, notably Charlie Staples's Bar-B-Que, reemerged dramatically after brief sabbaticals, while others, including Kravitz's Delicatessen, gained a new lease on life after relocating beyond the city's borders.

This attempt to reconstruct a portion of the history of Youngstown's restaurants and eateries, stretching from 1945 to the present, draws upon a range of archival materials, including city directories, newspaper articles, advertisements, menus and personal letters. In addition, we have conducted oral history interviews with former patrons and owners, many of whom were more than happy to share their memories, artifacts and old photographs. Their contributions enriched this project, and we are grateful for their generosity.

Although this narrative moves chronologically, each chapter has been organized around a theme that reflects the dominant trends of the period in question. Chapter One, "Postwar Dining," covers the period stretching from 1945 to 1955, when the baby boom temporarily masked the exodus of urban dwellers to the suburbs and Youngstown's restaurant industry seemed more vibrant than ever. Chapter Two, "A Moveable Feast,"

This 1952 photograph of downtown Youngstown, taken at West Federal and Hazel Streets, captures the community's vitality during the post–World War II era. The crowds that gathered at the city's core fueled a vibrant restaurant industry. *Courtesy of Mahoning Valley Historical Society.*

covers the deceptively stable period between 1956 and 1966, when urban neighborhoods and businesses appeared to hold their own, despite the dramatic expansion of the suburbs. Chapter Three, "Times They Are A-Changin'," describes the period between 1966 and 1976, when local diners turned increasingly to suburban restaurants and suburbanites began to avoid the city altogether.

Chapter Four, "Feast to Famine," covers the challenging period between 1977 and 2000, when the impact of factors including deindustrialization undermined all but the most resilient of Youngstown's restaurants. Finally, Chapter Five, "Recipe for Rebirth," covers the period from 2001 to the present, which has been marked by the gradual redevelopment of Youngstown's restaurant industry, particularly in a refurbished downtown. Each chapter will take into account the unique history and character of the various businesses described, while outlining some of the reasons they prospered or disappeared.

While many of the Youngstown metropolitan area's restaurants are currently located in suburban communities, this book focuses on those that continue to operate within the municipal boundaries and those that began life in the city before their relocation. Notably, we have made a few exceptions to this rule in those cases where restaurants located just beyond the city limits are popularly identified with urban neighborhoods.

The unique businesses described in these pages not only reflect Youngstown's ethnic diversity and tenacious entrepreneurial spirit but also offer evidence of renewal in a city that, for many observers, remains a symbol of the Rust Belt phenomenon. Taken as a whole, the offerings of these restaurants are remarkably diverse and surprisingly affordable. Perhaps the survival of independent restaurants, assisted by a collective commitment to preserve local culinary traditions, has enabled Youngstown to maintain its identity in the face of numerous challenges. In any case, this volume is a long-overdue tribute to Youngstown's resilient tradition of dining out.

Chapter 1

POSTWAR DINING

In 1945, Gregory Speero returned from the U.S. military with more than he anticipated. Apart from life and limb, the young veteran came back to the Mahoning Valley with new skills, which he was determined to transform into a livelihood.

Twenty-eight years old when he entered basic training, Speero was one of three privates who responded to an officer's shouted command: "OK, anybody that can cook, step forward." The three volunteers, including Speero, were hustled aside and asked about their age. "The other guys were younger," explained Speero's son, Gregory Jr., decades later. "So, the officers said to my father, 'OK, you are a staff sergeant, in charge of the kitchen.'"

While Speero had done a little cooking in his time, he was hardly an experienced chef. Over the next few years, he learned to manage a large industrial kitchen, and on the whole, he found little to complain about. He ate regularly and never saw combat. At the same time, though, his duties were carried out in a lonely military outpost in the Alaskan wilderness. So by August 1945, as the war in the Pacific wound down, Speero was relieved to find himself in the familiar bustle of downtown Youngstown, Ohio.

On August 15, Speero was among tens of thousands of Youngstown-area residents who anxiously awaited the official announcement that the war was over. By early evening, thirty thousand people had crammed into Youngstown's Central Square, while hundreds of others gathered at local churches, temples and synagogues.[5] Notably, the crowds surpassed even the turnout for the late

Foster's Lunch, owned by Clifford Aunkst and Gregory Speero, was a popular sandwich shop on Wood Street in the 1940s. When the business was forced to relocate, Speero established his own restaurant, the Wickwood, on Wick Avenue. *Courtesy of Gregory Speer Jr.*

Gregory and Susan Speero, proprietors of the Wickwood, work back to back in the restaurant's tiny kitchen. *Courtesy of Gregory Speero Jr.*

president Franklin D. Roosevelt, whose motorcade had passed through town in October 1940, amid "miles of bunting and flags."[6]

In an apparent move to prevent rioting, city hall ordered the closing of all taverns and beer halls, and other businesses followed suit. "Celebrants searched fruitlessly for a place to quench their thirst," the *Vindicator* reported, adding that one local bartender, in the process of closing down his establishment, had cheerfully informed a prospective customer, "Lady—you couldn't get a drink at any price."[7]

This turned out to be the case for Gregory Speero and his young wife, Susan, who hoped to mark the occasion with a simple toast. "All the damned bars were closed, because people would've gone nuts," said Gregory Jr., drawing on his parents' account of the event. Toward the end of the evening, he said, the couple came across an old bottle of Manischewitz wine, which was rapidly turning into vinegar. "My mother said…they didn't get drunk; they got sick on the wine," Gregory Jr. recalled.

If their celebration of V-J Day proved anticlimactic, the Speeros were more than compensated by the developments of the next few years. Within months of his return to Youngstown, Gregory Speero established a partnership with family friend Clifford Aunkst, and the pair opened an eatery, Foster's Lunch, on Wood Street, a pleasant artery that ran along a bluff overlooking the downtown retail district.

Several years later, when the lease for the Wood Street eatery was discontinued, Speero established his own business in a building located a few blocks to the northeast. With his wife, Susan, he opened a small restaurant called the Wickwood, which stood along the busy thoroughfare of Wick Avenue. Nestled between the city's Masonic Temple and the First Presbyterian Church, the restaurant drew dozens of professors, staff members and students associated with rapidly expanding Youngstown College.

The restaurant's second-floor room, which could be accessed through a side entrance, became a lunchtime destination for prominent local businessmen, including Alex Downie Sr., J.P. Lombard and A.A. Samuels, who often closed the afternoon with a friendly game of pinochle. Other regular patrons were Joseph Vaschak, cofounder of the Vaschak-Kirila Funeral Home, and Stanley Strouss, son of Youngstown retailer Clarence Strouss Sr.

Around the time that Gregory Speero and Clifford Aunkst laid the groundwork for their partnership, several established restaurateurs were resuming interrupted careers. Among them was Harry Malkoff, co-owner of the 20th Century Restaurant and a clutch of lesser-known establishments, including the Griddle, the Gob Shop and the Dixie Kitchen. Harry and his wife, Faye, a remarkably inventive chef and baker, had established the 20th Century in 1941 on the outskirts of the city's North Side. The gleaming Art Deco structure reminded well-traveled patrons of the resort restaurants that dotted Miami Beach.

Yet the Malkoffs' decision to locate the restaurant two miles north of the downtown area ensured that no local bank would risk granting them a business loan, given that few lenders could imagine the subsequent development of the area's quasi-suburban districts. The couple's difficulties were compounded in 1944, when Harry was drafted at the relatively mature age of thirty-six. The news came as a bit of a shock, and decades later, Harry would half-jokingly remark to his son, Kurt, that "somebody on the draft board had it in for him."

During Harry's yearlong absence, the Malkoffs' various businesses were managed by Faye, whose creativity in the kitchen was matched by her formidable business skills. When her gregarious and charismatic husband returned to Youngstown from a military posting in New Guinea, he swiftly resumed his place at the "front end" of the business.

Meanwhile, Jack Raver, the youthful son of local restaurateur Lewis "Lew" Raver Sr., was winding down his tour as a midshipman on a patrol craft in the South Pacific. Jack was the scion of a talented and peripatetic family of partly Scandinavian background, and he had grown up with stories of his relatives' colorful adventures.

His grandfather Allen Thurman Raver had managed a hotel and restaurant for six years at Skiatook, Oklahoma, where the Raver children, including Jack's father, divided their time between helping with the family business and riding horses along the borders of a nearby Indian reservation. One of Jack's aunts, Hazel, proved so skillful at riding bareback that the local Native Americans referred to her as "Quenya" ("Little Pony"), a name that stuck.

After a brief interval in Canada, the Ravers circled back to Youngstown, and by the 1920s, Jack's father, Lewis, was the manager of the dining rooms at the local YMCA. Then, in 1926, Lewis and his father, Allen, established Raver's Tavern (later called Raver's Restaurant) on Central Square, and the family took pride in the fact that the restaurant was listed in Duncan Hines's famous "red book."[8]

While the Ravers supported Jack's decision to enlist in the navy at the age of seventeen, his departure left them shorthanded. During his absence, Jack's duties, which included the management of the two-story restaurant's first floor, fell to Quenya's son, Allen Butcher.

Other returnees from World War II included Carmen and Ralph Naples, the sons of local restaurateur Andrew Naples. Since its establishment in 1934, the Napleses' Golden Dawn Restaurant & Lounge, located on the city's

North Side, had been a magnet for politicians, business leaders, professionals and labor leaders alike. When the war ended, the family was preparing to move the business to its third location—the first of two sites the restaurant would occupy on Logan Avenue, then a venue for high-end car dealerships.

Before he entered the military in 1942, Carmen Naples had been a member of Ohio State University's championship football team, and he recalled that sports often dominated the conversations that percolated along the Golden Dawn's gleaming bar. Some returning veterans, however, had more practical issues in mind when they stopped in for a cold beer and a plate of pasta. More than a few had taken advantage of the Servicemen's Readjustment Act of 1944 (better known as the GI Bill) to further their education, and the Naples family was known for its academic aptitude.

Andrew Naples's eldest son, John, a chemical engineer, had been recruited by the government for the Akron-based synthetic rubber project during World War II, and both of John's younger brothers had attended a university. "Well, Ralph had his degree," ninety-two-year-old Carmen Naples noted. "He had four years of college math, and he was in the air force…If they'd have trouble [with their homework], he said, 'Give it to me,' and he'd be very helpful."

Overall, the postwar era held tremendous opportunities for returning veterans like Gregory Speero, Jack Raver, Kurt Malkoff and the Naples brothers Carmen and Ralph. The five men were reconnecting with a bustling industrial community of nearly 170,000 people, and each would participate in a restaurant industry that continued to thrive, despite the back-to-back crises of the Great Depression and World War II.

Yet the war had clearly taken its toll. Apart from the obvious loss of "manpower" as thousands entered military service, restaurants had faced crippling material shortages. In a 2010 interview, delicatessen owner Rose Kravitz recalled that, even as many of her male relatives were called into military service, her business's "avenue of supply was being cut off, because rationing came in."

The Office of Price Administration (OPA) and the War Production Board (WPB) had appeared almost immediately after the Japanese attack on Pearl Harbor, and both were designed to help the U.S. government meet the needs of the military by rationing and also converting production to military supplies.

Now that the war was finally over, about 16 million GIs were returning to their homes, and the workforce of the continental United States had practically doubled overnight. Moreover, within five years of V-J Day, the country's population would jump to slightly more than 151 million, an increase of 18 million from 1930.

Many Americans of this period emerged as ardent consumers. As historian Kenneth T. Jackson noted, "For more than five years military necessity had taken priority over consumer goods, and by 1945 almost everyone had a long list of unfilled material wants."[9] The apparent growth of Youngstown's economy during the postwar era breathed new life into a restaurant industry that had proven resilient even during the worst of times. The industry's greatest challenge, perhaps, came during the grueling years of the Great Depression.

Depression-Era Dining

Youngstown had been especially hard hit during the first years of the Depression. In the early 1930s, over one-third of the local workforce was unemployed, and the area's steel industry witnessed a 40 percent decline in production. During this period, homelessness became so widespread that Youngstown mayor Joseph F. Heffernan reopened a vacant police station as a shelter, which he called Friendly Inn.[10] Incredibly, however, a number of the city's restaurants not only survived but thrived—a development that probably owed a great deal to the presence of a large industrial elite.

A compelling example was the Star Oyster House, which began life as a "hole-in-the-wall" on West Boardman Street. In 1927, four enterprising Greek American businessmen purchased the tiny establishment, with plans to transform it into a major downtown destination. The original structure held a maximum of twenty-five customers, more than adequate for the restaurant's limited clientele. Hence, the first priority for siblings Harry and Louis Magulas—along with their business partners, Peter Zografides and Harry Stratigos—was to increase volume.

The new proprietors succeeded. "In a few months the little place was doing a land office business, with folks standing in line to be served," the *Vindicator* reported later. The next step was to accommodate the restaurant's growing base of customers. First, the lunch counter was expanded, while more tables were "squeezed" into the dining room. Then, in 1929, partitions were pulled down to make way for a larger dining area. Even the Wall Street crash and subsequent economic depression failed to deter the Star Oyster House's loyal patrons; by 1935, the business partners felt confident enough to spend $25,000 to remodel and enlarge their establishment.[11]

Some observers probably saw the restaurant's remodeled exterior as a jarring departure from the nineteenth-century shop fronts that dominated the

The Star Oyster House, located on West Boardman Street in downtown Youngstown, offered local residents a wide range of fresh seafood dishes. *Courtesy of Mahoning Valley Historical Society.*

downtown. The restaurant's sea green façade featured a stylized underwater scene composed of one-inch squares of ceramic tile. "This panel represents the ocean into which various colored tropical fish and lobsters have been worked, and the company name and bright coral plants have the appearance of growing up from the ocean bed," the *Youngstown Telegram* reported.

The mural was bordered at the top by a light trough, which illuminated the front of the building "through white opal flashed glass," while a large neon sign, "with a lobster and star worked in," jutted at an angle over West Boardman Street.[12]

The Star Oyster House's popularity owed to the fact that it kept its promise to deliver some of the freshest seafood in town. The establishment's blue points were shipped from Long Island Sound, while clams and scallops were harvested along the North Carolina coast. The restaurant's lake trout, white fish, blue pike and perch hailed from the Great Lakes, while red snapper, Spanish mackerel and sea trout were captured in the Gulf of Mexico.

None of these sea creatures was shipped in frozen. "All lobsters and blue points are received here alive," the *Vindicator* reported. "And, believe it or not, the blue points and lobsters are fattened here much the same as chickens." Likewise, jumbo frogs were shipped in live "from Huey Long's domain" of Houma, Louisiana, and co-owner Harry Magulas claimed that the meat was sweeter because "the big croakers live in warm swamps."[13]

Two years later, in 1937, a similar expansion project was carried out at Moore's Tavern, a Youngstown institution that traced back to the Spanish-American War.[14] Founded by local raconteur Johnny Moore, the tavern first opened its doors at Westlake Crossing, a grade crossing at the intersection of West Federal Street and West Rayen Avenue, several blocks west of the downtown area.

The tavern's relocation to Central Square at the turn of the century enabled it to draw a broader range of customers, including the community's steelworkers, who took advantage of the establishment's cheap fare. After Johnny Moore's passing in 1917, his sons, Joseph and Leo, took over the business and, in the wake of Prohibition, turned it into a restaurant. The tavern portion of the business reopened in the early '30s, and in the spring of '37, the proprietors introduced the elegant "Sky Bar" restaurant, based in a second-story addition to the building.

The new space, designed to appeal to younger diners, was decorated with Masonite paneling "ranging from chocolate, old rose and pink through tan." These subdued panels were separated by gleaming strips of stainless steel. The Sky Bar's streamlined tables and chairs were jet black, "with a center all-steel base," and lighting fixtures could "be adjusted to give various shades of colored light through discs of colored glass." This "modernistic" dining room was managed by Mrs. Bertha L. Chambers, a veteran of the local restaurant industry.[15]

Months earlier, in February 1937, the Raver family had unveiled its remodeled restaurant on West Boardman Street, which sat behind the Mahoning National Bank (now Huntington Bank) and had one entrance that looked out on Central Square. At a cost of $50,000, the project drew the admiring attention of the *Vindicator*, which stated that "art in everyday life is vividly exemplified in the gleaming black Carrara glass front, contrasted by the silver-colored aluminum trimmings in the exterior of the newly-reconstructed Raver's Tavern."[16]

The restaurant's remodeled interior also drew praise. "The walls of the first floor dining room are papered in a serene shade of blue broken by recurring white designs," the *Vindicator* reported, adding that the space was suffused with light provided by "[t]wo large octagonal windows trimmed in aluminum." Meanwhile, the second-floor dining room featured "green wall paper with antique designs," and its natural light was "provided by three rectangular windows with horizontally divided panes." Both dining rooms were furnished with small square tables intended to seat 3 or 4 diners, along with larger round tables that could accommodate 12 to 15 guests. Overall, the two-story restaurant could seat 225 people. [17]

Jack Raver recalled the challenges the movers faced when they transported two of the large wooden tables to the second-floor dining room. "These twelve-foot-diameter tables came in, with the top and legs separate," he explained. "As my granddad was standing by the steps, the mover said: 'We can't carry these up the stairs. They're too big.' Well, he went down to the carpenter...and he asked, 'Can I use your hatchet?' and he took the hatchet and cut a swath through the finished ceiling of the stairway, and he said, 'Now I think you can get them up there.'"

Significantly, these downtown establishments weren't the only restaurants to expand operations during the "hard times" of the Depression. In the fall of 1933, the American Restaurant, a downtown fixture, unveiled its refurbished dining room on North Phelps Street. The restaurant's owner, Louis Carvelas, informed the media that his once modest establishment could now seat 125 patrons and offered floor space of 2,500 square feet.[18]

Likewise, the Youngstown Hotel, a landmark on Central Square since 1922, opened a 240-foot addition in the winter of 1936. The Youngstown Hotel Grill & Blue Room, as the new space was called, featured a 20-foot circular bar of Brazilian walnut with an African mahogany top. The new grill opened into a spacious dance floor called the Blue Room, where a local orchestra performed every night, including Saturday evening cocktail hours.[19]

During this period, other restaurants developed along Youngstown's periphery. In 1937, Harry and Faye Malkoff took a gamble on the restaurant business, apparently unfazed by the economic downturn. The couple had recently hit the "bug" (an illegal lottery) for a couple hundred dollars and used the winnings to travel to California. While there, the Malkoffs encountered a curb-service hamburger restaurant, and the concept stuck with them. As their son, Dr. Kurt Malkoff, explained decades later, his parents came home with a plan. "They said, 'OK, we're going into the restaurant business,'" he said.

After reviewing local properties, they settled on a former bicycle shop along Youngstown's southern border, which they reopened as the Griddle. Lacking the funds to advertise, Harry Malkoff engaged in a little subterfuge. "My father convinced all his relatives to park their cars in front of the place and [made it] look like it was busy," Dr. Malkoff observed. The business proved so successful that the couple decided to remodel the building, but the idea of temporarily closing down was anathema to Harry. Instead, Dr. Malkoff explained, "they tore down the bicycle shop and threw the pieces out the window in the middle of winter, and redid the whole restaurant as it was running."

Like many aspiring restaurateurs, the Malkoffs were becoming aware of the trend toward novelty in the U.S. restaurant industry. As food and travel writer John F. Mariani observed, U.S. restaurants came to rely increasingly on the power of "the gimmick." "Lunch wagons, milk bars, diners, drive-ins, speakeasies, restaurants shaped like hot dogs, restaurants designed to look like a pirate's den, restaurants where the waiters sing opera, restaurants with wine lists as thick as family bibles—all are, in their own way, gimmicks to hook crowds," Mariani wrote.[20]

Likewise, Harry and Faye's Malkoff's launching of one of Youngstown's first hamburger restaurants proved an effective "hook" for local customers. Over time, the couple kept an eye on national trends, and most of their ventures succeeded. Among those that failed was the Malkoffs' attempt, in 1950, to establish the glamorous El Morocco restaurant, which replaced the Gob Shop, a more sophisticated version of the Griddle. "The waitresses went around with large trays of food, so you would look at the food," Dr. Malkoff noted. "Well, the concept worked very well in New York, but not in Youngstown." More often than not, however, the Malkoffs showed remarkable prescience when developing businesses—a quality reflected in the success of the 20th Century.

From Dairy to Luncheonette

The power of novelty was reflected in the development of the regional Isaly's dairy chain, whose main plant occupied a spot just west of downtown Youngstown. As historian Brian Butko explained, the chain's primary draw was its signature Skyscraper ice cream cone, whose preparation required such dexterity that clerks who were given the responsibility held "a position of respect."[21]

The Skyscraper cone, introduced in the 1920s, became a favorite among customers. It reminded many of the streamlined Art Deco high-rises of the period, while also offering them more than their money's worth of ice cream. The cone's main purpose, of course, was to draw people into the stores, and Isaly's was able to justify this novelty item as "good business," given that it was dealing in volume to increase its profit margin.

This approach proved effective with other novelty items, including the Klondike, which Isaly's developed in 1922, about the same time that Harry Burt, a Youngstown entrepreneur, introduced the Good Humor Bar. Such novelties helped the chain become a ubiquitous presence in cities like Youngstown, and by 1947, Isaly's had reached its peak, boasting a chain of four hundred stores.[22]

Initially, the concept of the Isaly's dairy store was introduced as a means of selling ice cream. Beyond its sizable dairy-delivery-route business—which included Youngstown by 1918—Isaly's sold dairy products directly to customers from a tiny stand outside its original main plant in Mansfield, Ohio. At some point, William Isaly decided to build on this concept by launching company stores that would offer a range of products.

Isaly believed that, if he could sell his products directly to customers instead of going through middlemen, the stores could operate with narrower margins by creating profits through volume sales. In addition, the stores would benefit from expert merchandising, and a portion of the profits could be used to enhance the quality of the firm's dairy products. The first Isaly's franchise in Youngstown opened in 1918, and many more followed.[23]

Over time, greater care was taken with the design of the Isaly's stores. In 1931, Samuel Isaly (one of William's sons) informed company architect Clyde Schuemacher that he wanted shops that would function as a "natural merchandiser." These outlets, he insisted, should be places "where the poor as well as the well to do would shop and feel at home." Samuel Isaly envisioned the franchises as "the smartest store on the street and different from anything else," and Schuemacher's subsequent efforts produced the "look" that Isaly's retained for decades.

The Isaly's on West Federal Street was among many regional franchises that operated in the Youngstown area. While Isaly's was best known for its Skyscraper ice cream cone, the chain offered a wide menu, and most dishes were prepared from scratch. *Courtesy of Mahoning Valley Historical Society.*

Each store's façade was clothed in white Carrara glass tile, and the streamlined interiors featured stainless steel countertops and aluminum chairs. Moreover, the franchise provided the range of services one would expect to find at a soda fountain, a delicatessen, a convenience store and a restaurant, respectively. The concept worked, and as Butko observed, "While the Depression was closing other businesses, Isaly's reported that every store's sales gained 20 to 42 per cent."[24]

By the time the United States entered World War II, Isaly's stores functioned as social and commercial centers in scores of neighborhoods around Youngstown. As early as 1940, many of these neighborhoods were buoyed by a steep rise in manufacturing designed to assist the United Kingdom as it fought off a relentless German air attack. After Pearl Harbor, Youngstown, which accounted for 10 percent of national steel production, played an invaluable role in the war effort.[25]

Urban Change in the Postwar Era

The postwar era, however, witnessed a dizzying array of changes, some of which threatened the stability of working-class neighborhoods. A key provision of the GI Bill called for the creation of a Veteran's Administration mortgage program, which gave "official endorsement and support to the view that the 16 million GI's of World War II should return to civilian life with a home of their own."[26]

If the new law struck veterans and builders alike as a dream come true, the subsequent construction boom benefited suburban areas almost exclusively, while furthering the decline of cities. "By 1950 the national suburban growth rate was ten times that of central cities," Kenneth T. Jackson noted, "and in 1954 the editors of *Fortune* estimated that 9 million people had moved to the suburbs in the previous decade."[27]

What's more, the absence of a nondiscrimination clause in the VA's mortgage program helped to ensure that postwar suburbs would reflect unprecedented levels of economic and racial homogeneity. As Jackson observed, "What was unusual in the new circumstances was not the presence of discrimination—Jews and Catholics as well as blacks had been excluded from certain neighborhoods for generations—but the thoroughness of physical separation which it entailed."[28]

Downtown Dining

The implications of such trends weren't readily apparent in Youngstown, where regional chains like Isaly's continued to garner huge profits in the central city. Local entrepreneur David Michael Adams noted that, in the years following World War II, downtown retained its position as the bustling hub of the community and was the site of numerous restaurants.

Adams recalled that, as a child, he was often invited to "help out" in the kitchen beneath Stone's Grill, a tavern and restaurant where his father, John Zajac Adams, worked as head chef. Housed in a nineteenth-century building (the current site of First Educators Investment Corporation), Stone's Grill sat at the intersection of West Federal and Hazel Streets. "When you walked out of there at busy times, all the buses would pick up people on the next corner over...and the streets were so crowded you actually had to wait for another bus to come along," he said.

Like many local taverns, Stone's Grill on West Federal Street earned a reputation for fine food. The building's façade, shown in this 1930s photograph, was streamlined in the early 1950s. *Courtesy of Mahoning Valley Historical Society.*

Adams described bus trips he took with his father, who regularly purchased provisions for the restaurant. A typical destination was the Pyatt Street Market, located just off Market Street, a mile south of downtown. Most errands involved the purchase of produce, including the potatoes that Adams often peeled in the restaurant's cavernous kitchen. On other occasions, father and son visited a nearby fish market, and Adams recalled one harrowing journey involving a crateful of hissing lobsters.

At the time that John Zajac Adams worked as a chef at Stone's Grill, the popular restaurant (part of a Columbus-based chain) was concluding an expansion project coordinated by then manager Leon Grown, who had worked at the establishment since the late 1920s.

The restaurant's newest addition was its Plantation Room, which featured coral leather upholstery and bleached mahogany furniture. Designed to

convey "the charm and graciousness of the Old South," the dining room was described in an undated 1940s advertisement as "Youngstown's most superb setting for morning breakfast, lunch, dinner, banquets, afternoon parties, shoppers' tea, five o'clock cocktails or an after-the-theater snack."

The establishment's main dining room was "enhanced by fluorescent lighting and a battery of photo-color-murals of Youngstown of yesteryear and today," while the bar had been "enlarged to twice its former size." Patrons were encouraged to take advantage of the restaurant's Monday and Tuesday lunch specials, which included potted chicken with baked curried rice, fricassee sauce, duchess potatoes and rolls and muffins with butter—all for thirty-nine cents.

Hungrier, or more prosperous, diners could take advantage of the seventy-seven-cent steak dinner, which typically cost one dollar. They often topped off these lunch specials with the grill's signature Singapore Sling, which could be purchased on Mondays and Tuesdays for just twenty-five cents.[29]

Several years later, in 1952, the restaurant saw another renovation, under the supervision of incoming manager Mark Berman and his assistant, Harold Greenspan. The building's exterior and interior were thoroughly revamped, giving the restaurant a streamlined and contemporary look. An advertisement that appeared in the *Vindicator* in August 1952 also indicated that the facility's dining room had been expanded to "provide greater seating."[30]

The attractions of Stone's Grill, of course, were geared to adults, and youngsters like David Adams found more appropriate diversions elsewhere. A favorite destination, Adams recalled, was Jay's Lunch (popularly known as "Jay's Hot Dogs"), an establishment located near the corner of Chestnut and West Federal Streets, just west of the Warner Theater, the current site of the DeYor Performing Arts Center.

Jay's Lunch had been established more than two decades earlier by James Pappas, a resourceful Greek immigrant who arrived in the United States in 1917.[31] The eatery's main attraction was its Coney Island–style sauce, which one local journalist later described as "indigestion-generating, but palate-pleasing."[32] Apart from hot dogs, Jay's served home-style entrées like chili, beef stew and stuffed cabbage.

The fare at Jay's Lunch, for all its culinary appeal, had the further benefit of being cheap. Youngstown native Tom Price recalled that in the 1940s, when

Mark Berman, manager of Stone's Grill, pours a shot of Four Roses as the tavern's well-known chef, John Zajac Adams (right, foreground), looks on. This photograph was taken about 1950. *Courtesy of David Michael Adams.*

Many local restaurants relied on the services of Hollander's Meats. In 1950, Louis Hollander purchased the former Petrakos Grill, which he reopened as Hollander's Grill. The restaurant offered full-course dinners, but local teenagers were drawn to Hollander's marble-topped soda fountain. *Courtesy of Mahoning Valley Historical Society.*

he took lessons at the Strouss' Music Center, his mother, who accompanied him on the bus, often stopped at Jay's Lunch. "My mother would say to my brother and me, 'Do you guys want to get some hot dogs?'" Price explained. "We'd always say, 'Sure.' They'd have ten hot dogs for a dollar, so we'd take them home for supper."

Yet Jay's Lunch held an attraction beyond the price, or even the quality, of the food. "The gentleman that worked the front of the grill, in the window, always drew a crowd," explained area resident Fred Ross. "They would stop and just watch him line his arm with, maybe, ten, twelve hot dogs. He used a paint brush to put the mustard on—and, I mean, he was quick." Ross added, chuckling, "All we would think was, 'This guy's perspiring'—but that didn't deter us from ordering the hot dogs."

By the 1940s, the eatery had secured a liquor license and expanded its schedule to twenty-four hours a day. "We loved to go in there and sit down late at night, just to hear the blonde waitress take orders and yell them out to the cook, who was the fellow with the arm," Ross recalled. "She always closed with the same refrain, and she'd belt it out: '...and a bowl of beans!'"

Some observers suggested that the cook's physical dexterity accounted for the shop's popularity. Retired financial consultant James D. Bennett, however, attributed Jay's success to its secret sauce. He recalled that his father-in-law, Bill Barth, took him to the eatery sometime after Bennett moved from East Liverpool, Ohio. "Bill liked to shock me, and so we were downtown one day, and he said, 'Let's get a sandwich,'" Bennett explained. "He took me over to Jay's...and the smell of beer just woofed out of the place."

Ultimately, Bennett's skepticism was overcome by one taste of Jay's signature Coney Island dog. "It was a great hot dog," he said. "In fact, it was the best hot dog I've ever had. They're still in the area, and to me, they're just as good now as they were then."

Another popular draw—for children and adults alike—was the Petrakos Grill & Tea Room, located on West Federal Street, across from McKelvey's Department Store. The eatery was known for its ice cream products, including the Chocolate Nut Puffee, a combination of cherry almond and chocolate ice cream served with nuts, chocolate sprinkles and whipped cream; the Peach Melba, a blend of peach slices, vanilla ice cream and whipped cream; and the Petrakos Special, which featured half of a banana, chocolate ice cream, marshmallow dressing, nuts and whipped cream.

Those with bigger appetites could choose from the eatery's "Dainty Lunches," such as the Petrakos Club Sandwich, which featured a fried egg, chicken, bacon and tomatoes; the Youngstown Special, a combination of cold pork, cream cheese, pickle and mayonnaise; and the Chaney High, a triple-decker sandwich that included chicken, bacon, tomato, lettuce and dressing.[33]

In the mid-1950s, the eatery was purchased by local meat supplier Louis Hollander, who renamed it Hollander's Grill and shifted the menu's focus to hamburgers, roast beef sandwiches and steak dinners, although he retained the soda fountain and continued to sell ice cream products.

No less popular than the Petrakos Grill & Tea Room was a nearby Isaly's outlet, one of several in the downtown area. Besides the store's signature Skyscraper cone, customers could order sundaes that featured up to ten flavors of ice cream, including hot fudge, chocolate marshmallow, strawberry, orange, butterscotch, tin roof and cherry. Patrons could also choose from sandwiches ranging from conventional corned beef to more exotic Roquefort cheese.[34]

Shop-n-Dine

Downtown shoppers with children in tow found a range of cheap dining options that also appealed to youngsters. Most of the district's department stores and five-and-dime outlets operated lunch counters that provided light fare and the usual range of soda and ice cream products.

The largest of these, perhaps, was maintained by the F.W. Woolworth Company, located on the north side of West Federal Street, not far from the intersection of West Federal and Phelps Streets. "I especially liked the lunch counter at Woolworth's, which could probably seat about one hundred people," recalled Father John C. Harris, a lifelong resident and Anglican priest. "Woolworth's had balloons for the kids, and if you popped one, you might find a coupon for a reduced price for a banana split or a milkshake."

Elder Rosetta Carter, a local community organizer, indicated that it was a "big deal" to sit with her family at Woolworth's lunch counter. "My dad worked in the coke plant at Youngstown Sheet & Tube; every payday, he'd take us downtown, and we'd take a booth at the Woolworth's counter," she recalled. "Now, this was at a time when African Americans didn't feel comfortable anywhere west of Central Square. They served us, but they weren't excited about it."

Shoppers and businesspeople patronized the smaller lunch counters operated by McKelvey's and Strouss' department stores, respectively. Despite the crowds, servers tended to be courteous and efficient. "The Strouss' Grille had a long, serpentine counter that offered plenty of space, and it had tables as well," recalled Attorney Robert S. Fulton. "You would order your

Patrons at McKelvey's lunchroom dine beneath a panoramic image of the steel mills that lined the Mahoning River and produced much of the city's wealth. *Courtesy of Mahoning Valley Historical Society.*

Soda fountains and lunch counters thrived in the city's downtown area. This lunch counter, operated by People's Drug, was located near the corner of West Federal and North Hazel Streets. *Courtesy of Mahoning Valley Historical Society.*

food and get it promptly—no muss, no fuss." Fulton added that Strouss' Department Store also operated a basement eatery that sold hot dogs and chocolate malts, which served as rewards for children who behaved during lengthy shopping expeditions.

Similar lunch counters and eateries were maintained by neighboring five-and-dime stores like McCrory's and S.H. Kresge's, along with pharmacies such as People's Drug. Another economical option was the lunch counter at Oles' Market, located a block west of Central Square. Adding to the counter's popularity was the fact that the market itself could be accessed from West Federal, South Phelps and West Boardman Streets.

"Oles' Market's lunch counter was located on the street floor, and a bakery operated on the third floor," recalled Bert Lockshin, whose family owned the Golden Age Beverage Company. "When I stopped there, I always ordered a cup of coffee and a fresh donut, which was still warm."

Meanwhile, travelers and commuters in search of a convenient meal stopped at the Erie Lunch, an eatery operated by Greek immigrants George and Nick Jianopoulos (widely known as the "Johnson brothers") at the Erie Terminal Building, on the corner of Phelps and Commerce Streets. "They had a terrific business because there was a lot of traffic when the trains stopped there," recalled former Ohio lawmaker Harry Meshel.

Those seeking an affordable sit-down meal also enjoyed options, including the Ringside Café, a tidy establishment on the corner of North Hazel and Commerce Streets that offered Chinese and mainstream American entrées. Youngstown native Ben Lariccia recalled that stopping for Chinese food at the Ringside was a "special treat" after a day of shopping with his mother. "It was kind of exotic to eat Chinese food in Youngstown during that era," Lariccia stated.

He added that his grandmother, an Italian immigrant, was impressed with some of the Chinese food that her relatives brought home. "Grandma appreciated the abundant greens and vegetables in the Chinese dishes her children let her sample," he explained. "She cooked a lot of Italian greens, none of which I ever saw in any restaurant in Youngstown, Italian or otherwise, until the last thirty years."

Area resident Dick Nard took advantage of the Ringside's ninety-nine-cent special, which featured a steaming plate of spaghetti and a bowl of coleslaw. "Inside, it looked like a typical Chinese restaurant, but they served fantastic pasta and the best coleslaw I'd ever had," he recalled. "It really was a meal in itself."

For many local diners, however, the neighboring Italian Restaurant (on North Hazel Street, between Commerce and West Federal Streets) was a preferred destination. "That was as good Italian fare as you could have

Above: The Ringside Café on the corner of West Commerce and North Hazel Streets offered a unique combination of American and Chinese cuisine. *Courtesy of Mahoning Valley Historical Society*.

Left: Owner Frank A. Micchia poses in front of downtown Youngstown's Italian Restaurant, which he operated from 1932 to 1967. *Courtesy of Mahoning Valley Historical Society*.

This menu from the Italian Restaurant reflects its Old World charm. During most of its years of operation, the Italian Restaurant was located on North Hazel Street, across from McKelvey's Grille. *Courtesy of Mahoning Valley Historical Society.*

anywhere, at any time," recalled Dr. George D. Beelen, a retired history professor. "As I remember, they had…waitresses…that were extremely helpful, congenial, sometimes calling you by name, putting your napkin down in front of you on your lap, treating you almost like (better than) family, sometimes, and willing to tell you what's really good today, what the chef made and what he was really proud of today."

The restaurant's "homey" atmosphere was reflected in an informality that many customers found endearing. "We often stopped at the Italian Restaurant, and I remember even being seated in the kitchen," said Patti Ferraro Druzisky, who joined her mother at the restaurant after running errands downtown. "If they were busy, they had a couple of extra tables, right in the corner in the kitchen; and if it was OK with you, they would let you park back there and order your food."

Meanwhile, students who patronized the Italian Restaurant could depend on complimentary servings of freshly baked Italian bread—and, on occasion, an extra helping of an entrée. Fred Ross, who studied to be a beautician after returning home from the military, recalled the kindness of a kitchen worker named Mrs. Abate. "She'd always make it a point to come out of the kitchen, come over to our booth and give us a little something special," Ross observed. "And there were times when I wouldn't be able to go in because I didn't have the bucks. The next time I would come in, she'd question me: 'Where were you?'"

Throughout the 1940s and early '50s, the western portion of the downtown area featured a host of other restaurants and eateries, including the Rainbow Bar, the Master's Grill, the American Bar, the Dutch House Restaurant, Clark's Restaurant, the Colonial Bar, the Dutch Hut, the Sahara Room and the De-Luxe Café.

Some of these dining establishments, including Joseph's Restaurant, were hidden in plain sight. Ensconced above a bowling alley on South Phelps Street, just north of Youngstown City Hall, Joseph's was a dining spot for local professionals, who occasionally spent the afternoon playing cards there.

Florence Mirkin, stepdaughter of proprietor Nick Joseph, shared fond memories of the restaurant. "It wasn't a fancy place, but the food was very good," she recalled. "One of Nicky's specialties was called a 'Knosher Sandwich,' because in Yiddish, a *knosher* is someone who likes to eat a lot."

East End Attractions

Although the western end of downtown offered its share of color and excitement, it was a placid district when compared to the eastern section, a veritable maze of Italian produce markets, Eastern European bakeries, Greek coffee shops, fish markets, poultry shops, discount retail stores, sports bars, furniture outlets and used-car dealerships. The district's dubious status was affirmed by the presence of establishments like the Park Theater (later known as Park Burlesque) and the Hotel Vanier, which provided lodgings to the "artists" who performed next door.

That said, many businesses that ringed the eastern side of Central Square had claims to respectability, even prestige. Such landmarks included the Tod Hotel, the Stambaugh Building, the People's Bank Building (currently the Realty Building) and the Keith-Albee Building, a Neoclassical structure that had graced the square since 1926.

The Keith-Albee Building hosted several businesses, including the Palace Theatre, a popular venue for films and live entertainment. Patrons of the theater were bound to visit at least one of the three dining establishments also housed in the building: the Palace Grill, an upscale tavern; Rodney Ann's, an eatery that offered light fare and ice cream; and Sweetland (formerly Friedman's), a confectionary that occupied the building's north end, at the corner of Commerce Street and Wick Avenue.

The largest of the three was the Palace Grill, which had been established in the mid-1930s by James Vallos, a native of Greece's Arcadia region. The restaurant's spacious L-shaped interior could accommodate more than two hundred customers, who ranged from industrial executives to steelworkers. James Vallos's son, William, recalled that the restaurant had two main entrances: one that faced Wick Avenue and another that looked north to Commerce Street. The latter, situated behind the Sweetland confectionary, was marked with a sign that read, "Theatre Bar."

The signage was appropriate, said James Vallos's daughter, Deanna, who explained that her parents often hosted entertainers who performed at the nearby Palace Theatre. Celebrity patrons included Frank Sinatra, Bob Hope and Jack Benny, who "always ordered the same thing—baked beans," she said. Deanna Vallos recalled that her mother, Ethel, was especially fond of the Andrews Sisters, who promoted war bonds in Youngstown in the early 1940s.

Jack Benny's supposed reliance on baked beans notwithstanding, the Palace Grill's menu offered a range of enticing options. "Their main specialty was prime rib on a hard roll," William Vallos recalled. "They cooked a whole prime rib every day, along with a fresh uncured ham and dozens of short ribs."

The restaurant was also known for its homemade soups, including an "irresistible" split-pea soup. While the tavern did not produce pastries in-house, donuts were brought in every morning from Youngstown's Poloukas Bakery, and pies were purchased from the Limbropoulos family's Homemade Pies Company.

The Palace Grill's centerpiece was a hand-carved walnut bar that ran seventy-five feet along the eastern wall of the restaurant's interior. The bar was supplemented by wooden booths that stretched about sixty feet along the northern and southern walls of the main dining room, along with a dozen large tables and a sizable lunch counter. William Vallos explained that the restaurant's furnishings were "the best money could buy." He added that the bar itself was custom-designed by Youngstown's Yoho & Hooker Lumber Company.

This sleek interior suited the establishment's most reliable patrons, who worked at the executive offices of the Youngstown Sheet & Tube Company, which was then located in the top four floors of the nearby Stambaugh

The Palace Theatre, on the northeastern edge of Central Square, was adjacent to the Palace Grill, whose patrons often stopped in after catching a film or live show at the nearby theater. *Courtesy of Mahoning Valley Historical Society.*

This undated photo, taken at the Palace Grill in the 1940s, shows (left to right) owner Jim Vallos and hostess Rose Tzarnas with Ralph Naples, whose family owned the popular Golden Dawn Restaurant. *Courtesy of Deanna Vallos.*

Building. Other prestigious patrons included local attorneys Joseph Betras and Sam Karam, along with Judge Sidney Riegelhaupt.

Adding to the restaurant's upscale atmosphere was the owner's insistence that staff members dress formally. "My father always wore a fresh white shirt and a bow tie," recalled Deanna Vallos. "The bartenders also wore a shirt and tie, and the waitresses were all dressed properly."

Yet James Vallos also recognized the need to cater to working-class customers. "In a steel town like Youngstown, every self-respecting tavern cashed paychecks and sold work gloves and cheroots behind the counter," observed Youngstown native Tim Cassidy. "Otherwise, they would've gone out of business." The Palace Grill was no exception to this rule.

Teenage Rendezvous

While the Palace Grill attracted professionals, business executives and full-time steelworkers, neighboring establishments like Rodney Ann's and Sweetland served the needs of those on a limited budget, including students. Former patron Mary Ann Dudzik recalled that Rodney Ann's could be accessed from the lobby of the Palace Theatre, and she described it as "a popular hangout for kids."

Sweetland dominated the Keith-Albee Building's northwest corner, and its name was rendered in large gilded letters that hung above the main entrance. Marilyn Sweeney, who patronized the business when it was known as Friedman's, described marble flooring and large display cases "filled with these marvelous chocolates." She added that one section of the interior featured ice cream parlor tables and chairs, where customers could sit and enjoy a soda, ice cream sundae or sandwich.

Another affordable eatery stood within a stone's throw of Sweetland, at the base of the Wick Avenue Bridge. The Williams Diner, later known as the Town Diner, featured a stainless-steel-and-porcelain exterior that stretched more than forty feet along Commerce Street. The diner's mahogany-trimmed interior could accommodate almost fifty customers, and its late-night schedule ensured that it would draw scores of teenagers after weekend sporting events.

At the same time, the Williams Diner was a popular daytime destination. Father Edward P. Noga, pastor of Youngstown's St. Patrick Church, recalled that, as a child, he often met his grandmother at the diner, usually after catching a film at the Palace Theatre. "There [was] basic food, always

Sweetland confectionary and the Town Diner were popular meeting places for teenagers and young adults, many of whom gravitated to downtown's numerous retail outlets and movie houses. *Courtesy of Mahoning Valley Historical Society.*

very busy, because the square was busy," he said. "They would [serve] sandwiches, coffee, soda and all that. But I remember that…because my maternal grandmother was so special to me."

Other family-friendly dining establishments included Pete Parthmos's Central Square Grill and Nick and Gus Zigouras's Boston Grill, located on East Federal Street, between North Walnut and North Watt Streets. In addition, the eastern district of downtown hosted at least two Isaly's franchises, one of which sat on the southeastern corner of the square, between the Central Square Grill and the Strand Theatre.

Cheap fare was also available at the Clock Bar, near the corner of East Federal and Champion Streets. The tavern was known for its chili dogs, French fries and baked beans. "I liked it better than Jay's," recalled Dr. George D. Beelen, who stopped there with his family before catching the "Campbell Hill bus" to nearby Campbell, Ohio.

Meanwhile, diners could choose among dozens of smaller establishments, including the Walnut Room, Rudy's Grill, the Champion Restaurant, the Golden Gate Grill, the Sun Grill, the Steel City Club and Cohen's Kosher Deli. The massive Tod Hotel, which dominated the corner of Market and East Boardman

Streets, maintained its own restaurant, Ye Old Rip Tavern, which was located in the lobby. The restaurant's Dutch-American theme was reflected in a narrative mural that depicted scenes from Washington Irving's story "Rip Van Winkle."

Family-Friendly Taverns

At the time, several taverns that dotted the eastern end of downtown were popular family dining spots. Joseph Planey recalled that, when his mother took him downtown on weekends, they often stopped to eat at a tavern called the Blue Ribbon Grill. "One of the things I remember was that they would have a roast beef, or a ham, hanging in the front window, with a heat lamp that highlighted it and kind of whetted your appetite," he added.

Lou Cimmento was a welcoming presence at downtown's Blue Ribbon Grill. In his youth, Cimmento fought professionally under the name "Young Billy Wallace," and relatives claim he once squared off against future actor Jack Palance. *Courtesy of George Mager.*

Located on East Federal Street, not far from Central Square, the Blue Ribbon Grill was one of scores of taverns owned by New Castle, Pennsylvania–based entrepreneur Jacob Raffel, whose sons, Forrest and Leroy, later established the Arby's fast food chain. "I remember the décor was composed of hundreds of bottles of whiskey, which lined the back of the bar," Leroy Raffel recalled. "There was a cage in the back where they cashed paychecks for steelworkers, and the food was incredibly cheap." He added that it wasn't uncommon to see entire families dining at the tavern.

Also popular among working-class families was the Brass Rail, which stood on East Federal Street, between Cross's drugstore and the Public Market. The tavern's varied menu included entrées ranging from "roast young turkey with cranberry sauce and dressing" to "wieners with spaghetti." A menu dating back to November 29, 1933, offers a glimpse of the Brass Rail's inexpensive fare during the Depression. In the early 1930s, customers could order a T-bone steak for forty cents, while sandwiches (including the signature "Brass Rail Tasty Barbecue") sold for ten cents apiece. Similarly, baked short ribs with potatoes were available for twenty-five cents, and fried oysters with coleslaw and mashed potatoes cost just thirty-five cents.[35] While these prices had certainly risen by the mid- to late 1940s, the restaurant remained a popular destination for diners seeking hearty food at a reasonable price.

During the postwar era, tavern operators throughout the city recognized that families on a budget would be drawn by cheap food, and many took steps to make their businesses "kid-friendly." On the city's East Side, for instance, the DeMain brothers' Royal Oaks Tavern compensated for a limited menu by selling "pink ladies," concoctions of cherry pop and ginger ale that delighted the children of adult patrons. "So many people will come in here and say, 'I remember coming here, and Daddy would sit at the bar, and all of Daddy's friends would keep sending us pink ladies and chili dogs,'" observed Lou Kennedy, current co-owner of the Royal Oaks. "Kids loved coming here, and everybody has a memory of that."

In 1947, the Boulevard Tavern, on the city's South Side, introduced Friday evening fish dinners, which became popular with local families. This "experiment" began when owners Ange and Joe Petrella purchased ten pounds of Great Lakes whitefish from seafood purveyor Tony Aulisio at the Public Market. "They whipped up some cole slaw from fresh cabbage, slivered potatoes for French fries and cut thick slabs of Italian bread," a later *Vindicator* article noted. "The price of a dinner was 60 cents."[36]

A similar development occurred at the Mahoning Valley Restaurant (known as "the MVR"), which sat in the midst of Smoky Hollow, a

The Brass Rail was open to the public twenty-four hours a day, and local industrial workers, fresh from the night shift, often stopped in for an early morning breakfast. This ashtray promotes the restaurant's role as a community meeting place. *Courtesy of Mahoning Valley Historical Society.*

Founded by six of the DeMain brothers in 1934, the Royal Oaks emerged as a popular bar and eatery on the city's East Side. This 1945 photograph shows (from left to right) Henry, Joe, Ralph, John, Albert and Tony DeMain. *Courtesy of Lou Kennedy.*

neighborhood just north of downtown Youngstown. While the MVR was known mainly as a "shot-and-beer joint" for industrial workers, it gradually expanded its kitchen to accommodate a more diverse clientele. Decades later, it emerged as one of the city's most enduring Italian American restaurants.

High-End Dining

Some local diners, however, wanted more than a good bargain, and their rarified tastes fueled the rise of downtown's fine-dining establishments. At the upper end of the scale was the Mural Room, which sat on West Boardman Street, not far from the main offices of the *Youngstown Vindicator*. The restaurant, housed in a building that once served as "the scene of boxing and wrestling matches," occupied the structure's entire basement.

At some point, the building, designed as a facility for the Moose Club, was purchased by a local chapter of the Veterans of Foreign Wars, and in 1945, the VFW "opened the lovely rooms with their large mural photographs of river woodland and cherry blossom scenes." Within four years, the Mural Room's proprietor, Joseph Rango, sold the restaurant to a group of businessmen led by entrepreneur Milton Simon and meat supplier Louis Hollander.[37]

Simon and Hollander evidently played a role in the development of the restaurant's old South theme, which was reflected in a series of murals that depicted scenes along the banks of the Mississippi River. As patrons descended a staircase that led to the restaurant's main entrance, they encountered a stylized painting of a riverboat paddling toward the horizon. "The place had a kind of southern charm, and I can still recall those elegant linen tablecloths," said Bernadette Angle, whose father, Fred Dell'Arco, was the restaurant's celebrated pastry chef. "You felt like you were in a tranquil, welcoming environment; everyone was so friendly," she added.

While the staff's warmth and hospitality contributed to an atmosphere many customers associated with the American South, the Mural Room's menu had a decidedly international flavor. Gabriel Covas, the restaurant's head chef, was a Spanish immigrant, and he was widely admired for his skill and versatility. "He was known for a few specifically Spanish dishes, like Spanish rice, or as we called it *paella*, but he also had a reputation as *the* chef in town," recalled Pearl Berezo Sinistro, who grew up as a part of the city's small but vibrant Spanish American community.

The Mural Room near Vindicator Square set a local standard for dining elegance. The restaurant's pastoral murals depicted scenes along the banks of the Mississippi River. *Courtesy of Mahoning Valley Historical Society.*

Dr. Kurt Malkoff, whose parents were close friends of Louis Hollander and his wife, Florence, spent many pleasant hours in the Mural Room, and he described the entrées and baked goods as achieving a "different level—New York, LA levels of food." Likewise, Louis Hollander's son, Mervyn, recalled amenities that transcended local standards. "As soon as you sat down, the waiters provided appetizers like sauerkraut balls, creamed herring and a basket of rolls," he said. "These were all offered free of charge to make sure you came back for more."

For Edna Zaitzew, the Mural Room "was one of those places you went if you had a particularly nice date," and she was drawn to one of the restaurant's seafood specialties. "When I went there, I would always order the frog's legs, because they had big, fat frog's legs," she recalled. "They were really the best in town."

Gabriel Covas's succulent entrées were preceded by Fred Dell'Arco's bread basket, a generous assortment of baked goods that included the Mural Room's famous "salt sticks." "The salt sticks looked like croissant rolls, but they were dipped in butter and baked to a crispy light brown," Bernadette Angle explained. "They would literally melt in your mouth." She added that customers were also drawn to her father's six-layer cakes, which included almond and Black Forest cherry chocolate. These impressive cakes were often featured at weddings catered by the Mural Room.

A souvenir matchbook from the Mural Room reflects the restaurant's old South theme. The riverboat on the matchbook resembles a large painting that graced the restaurant's main entrance. *Courtesy of Mahoning Valley Historical Society.*

Indeed, catering was a large part of the Mural Room's business. Beyond the main dining room, the restaurant maintained private rooms and a ballroom that could accommodate large crowds. At some point, the Mural Room's cool blue interior was enhanced by local artist and designer Victor Kosa, who developed a method of injecting liquid plastic into panels that were affixed to the ceiling in order to create large organic patterns. Decades later, Kosa's nephew, Dr. George D. Beelen, recalled that the technique created the effect of "huge leaves and branches throughout the entire ceiling."

Adding to the restaurant's aura of sophistication was the presence of full-time organist-pianist Joe Baumgartner, whose blindness didn't prevent him from being attentive to the children who gathered around him during performances. Baumgartner kept a cardboard "treasure box" nearby, and children were encouraged to select any toy that caught their eye.

The Mural Room wasn't the only upscale dining establishment on West Boardman Street, which ran parallel and to the south of West Federal Street, the site of Youngstown's glistening retail outlets. If West Boardman Street was less opulent than its northern neighbor, it nevertheless functioned as the city's corridor of power. City hall and the municipal police and fire departments all claimed spots along its narrow perimeters, and the city's ultimate symbol of legal authority, the Mahoning County Courthouse, stood

The Ohio Hotel (later called the Pick-Ohio) featured a buffet restaurant, an upscale bar and a sandwich shop called the Purple Cow. The building, which currently houses the Youngstown Metropolitan Housing Authority, stands a few blocks west of the city's Central Square. *Courtesy of Mahoning Valley Historical Society.*

at the intersection of West Boardman and Market Streets, just beyond the southwestern edge of Central Square.

While the street was relatively narrow, it boasted more than its share of large buildings, which had the unintended effect of blocking out the sun, thereby underscoring the gray, institutional nature of the surrounding architecture. A refreshing departure from this pattern was the Hotel Pick-Ohio, which, along with Raver's Tavern, imbued the street with a touch of glamour—even as the Star Oyster House, with its brightly colored ceramic façade, offered an unexpected dash of Coney Island.

Built in 1911, in the Neoclassical Revival style, the twelve-story Hotel Pick-Ohio was first known as the Ohio Hotel. Twenty-eight years later, in 1939, the hotel was purchased by the Albert Pick Hotels Corporation, and the name Hotel Pick-Ohio came into common usage. The building was a landmark in every sense of the word. Its twelfth-floor ballroom was a popular venue for organizational banquets, and after 1946, its lobby featured a sprawling mural by well-known American artist Louis Grell.

Diners who visited the Hotel Pick-Ohio tended to gravitate to the Crystal Room, known for its steaming Sunday buffet. "The chefs wore the big tall hats, and the atmosphere was extremely elegant," recalled Father John C. Harris, a longtime proponent of the city's downtown area. "I remember being there as a kid, and the only thing that I can think of that compares is the William Penn Hotel in Pittsburgh."

Ruth Pope Fletcher became aware of the restaurant because her aunt, Mary Martinko Kanetsky, worked there as a waitress. "All I can remember about the interior of the Crystal Room is that it had beautiful cloth drapery, and there were linen tablecloths and napkins," she recalled. "They always had some well-known guests, including Esther Hamilton, who wrote a regular column for the *Vindicator*." Mrs. Fletcher noted that the columnist was "easy to pick out because she always wore a brown suit and a hat."

Many years later, as a college student, Mrs. Fletcher herself worked as a member of the Crystal Room's waitstaff, and she recalled that even the most mundane tasks were executed with flair. "When the guest would leave," she explained, "I would use a silver tray and feather-whisk broom to sweep bread crumbs off the table."

Among the Crystal Room's specialties was Welsh rarebit, a cheddar fondue served over toasted bread. The restaurant, however, offered a full menu, ranging from "steaks and chops" to Continental entrées such as chicken française. "The kitchen was immense, and the chefs wore tall white hats," Mrs. Fletcher recalled. "They had several chefs, including a head chef, a sous-chef and a pastry chef, and I recall that the pastry chef was from either France or Belgium." For some residents of Youngstown, the Crystal Room offered a taste of the luxurious atmosphere enjoyed by diners in metropolitan centers like New York City.

Underworld Watering Holes

Several floors below, on the hotel's busy street level, a different sort of eating establishment operated. The Purple Cow Sandwich Shop was part of a chain of eateries hosted by the Albert Pick Hotels, and its whimsical mascot was evidently inspired by Gelett Burgess's nineteenth-century ditty: "I never saw a purple cow/I never hope to see one;/But I can tell you, anyhow,/I'd rather see than be one!"

The eatery provided entrées ranging from "cooked butt steak" to grilled pork chops, all served with "Italian salads." Modestly priced specialties included the forty-cent Purple Cow Hamburger, described as "finely ground" beef on a bun, served with sweet relish and fried onions. Another favorite was the sixty-cent Big Purple, described as "a mild sweet onion slice cooked between two juicy burgers on a toasted bun, with a dill pickle or sweet pickle relish." Patrons seeking lighter fare had the option of ordering the thirty-cent Purple Calf, a tasty blend of grape juice and ice cream.[38]

In many ways, the eatery seemed a benign presence. Its customers included couples winding down an evening at the theater and high school students fresh from a dance or football game. That said, the Purple Cow's policy of remaining open twenty-four hours a day ensured that its clientele would be eclectic—and during the early hours of the morning, local underworld figures were known to drop in for a cup of coffee and a snack.

The Purple Cow's reputation as a "mob hangout" was crystallized by a widely reported "fracas" that occurred in the early hours of December 31, 1947. The main player in the drama was Joseph "Fats" Aiello, a racketeer who owned the 115 Club, a gambling joint located on East Federal Street on the other side of Central Square. Aiello's wiry frame rendered his childhood moniker meaningless, and the confusion arising from this situation was compounded by his insistence on pronouncing his family name as "AY-LEE-OH," as opposed to "I-YEL-LOH."

Sometime after midnight in the early hours of December 31, one of Aiello's associates escorted two disruptive teenagers to the club's ground-floor exit, where they "kicked out the glass in the elevator safety door." A policeman standing nearby "nabbed" the youths, handcuffed them and prepared to transport them to the police station. "Before he could get to a call box to summon the patrol wagon, one of Aiello's henchmen appeared on the scene [and] asked the policeman to release the boys," a *Vindicator* article reported. "He said the management would pay for the expense. The boys were released."

Whatever Aiello's motive for giving the youths a "break," he soon had reason to regret the move. A few hours after the disturbance, Aiello closed his club for the evening, and in the company of several other underworld figures (including Sandy Naples and Joseph DeCarlo), he stopped at the Purple Cow, where the teenagers confronted the mobsters. An argument ensued, "wherein 'Fats' shot a wild bullet at 17-year-old Lou Bogash and his gang administered a pistol-beating and brutal kicking to Bogash's companion, a man known as Jack the Ripper."

Any public concern over the incident was heightened by the fact that none of the participants had been called in for questioning. "About the only

Nestled between the Masonic Temple and First Presbyterian Church, the Wickwood restaurant was a popular dining spot for students and faculty at Youngstown College. *Courtesy of Gregory Speero Jr.*

known concrete action in investigations so far has been that of Del Courtney, manager of the Pick-Ohio," the *Vindicator* reported. Courtney apparently suspended several hotel staff members "on charges of gross neglect of duty" over their failure to report the incident to local police.

Notably, the community's easygoing attitude toward organized crime was reflected in the article's headline, which read, "Aiello's Aid Saves Boys from Jail," an odd way to frame a story about a gangster who took a "wild" shot at one teenager and was involved in the pistol-whipping of another.[39] It would appear that mobsters like Aiello were occasionally viewed as guardians of public order.

Gregory Speero Jr., whose family operated the Wickwood restaurant, recalled that his relatives were positively reassured by the presence of local mobsters, which gave them a feeling of security. "At one time, the restaurant was open twenty-four hours, and my grandfather worked the night shift," Speero explained. "Well, at night, the gangsters would come in and drink coffee and eat, and you were as safe as though you were in your mother's arms."

Speero went on to describe an incident involving two adolescent "punks" who began to "hassle" his grandfather, an elderly Greek immigrant. "As Grandpa told me, 'The next thing I know, three guys picked them up by the scruff of their necks, punched them out and threw them out the door,'"

Speero recalled. "He told me that one of the guys said: 'Old man, when we're in here, ain't nobody going to bother you. We don't want no problems, and we're going to make sure there are no problems.'"

Further evidence of public—and official—tolerance for organized crime was reflected in the informal downtown "taxi service" organized by the Jungle Inn, an infamous casino in nearby Liberty Township. Historian Joshua Foster noted that the Paddock & Horseshoe Bar (West Federal Street) and the Hickory Grill (South Phelps Street) served as "pickup spots" for the casino. The Paddock played this role between the late 1930s and 1942, while the Hickory Grill did so between 1947 and 1949, the same year law enforcement closed the Jungle Inn.

"The casino hired regular drivers who transported people back and forth between Liberty and downtown Youngstown," Foster observed. "Once customers had finished gambling at a casino that kept late hours, they had the option of returning to Youngstown, where they could enjoy food, drink and entertainment at a nightclub that also remained open until the early hours of the morning."

These symbiotic relationships owed much to the fact that Dominic "Moosey" Caputo, co-owner of the Paddock & Horseshoe Bar, was a partner in the Jungle Inn. At the same time, Charles Sedore, proprietor of the Hickory Grill, was an ex-partner in the casino who had also served as "mayor" of Halls Corners, a tiny municipality established to protect the casino from "dry" laws in surrounding Trumbull County.

Public tolerance for organized crime had its limits, however. By 1948, the lawlessness that prevailed under the administration of Mayor Ralph W. O'Neill inspired voters to elect a reformist candidate, Charles P. Henderson, who led a ferocious crackdown on gambling and other illicit activities. Henderson's efforts gained national recognition, and in the 1950s, President Dwight D. Eisenhower appointed him to the Commission of Intergovernment Relations. These developments would have a significant—albeit short-lived—impact on the policies and practices of certain local nightclubs and restaurants.

Postwar Nightlife

During the postwar era, notoriety attached itself to yet another local nightclub, though for reasons that had nothing to do with gambling and everything to do with the provocative nature of the entertainment provided. The Club Lido, located on Market Street about a mile south of the city's downtown area, drew top musical and stage talent from around the country, including a number of cutting-edge acts that challenged the boundaries of acceptable entertainment.

In an August 1948 edition of *The Spotlite*, a Youngstown-based entertainment guide, columnist "Jimmie Gee" noted that the club offered "[s]omething different and something enjoyable" in its newest headliners, which he described as "3 of the country's top male mannequins of female fashion."[40] The column was followed by a centerfold advertisement that included a large photograph of female impersonators Sunny West, Gene Darling and Joe Dayre. The ad explained that the trio would be accompanied by "Max Brown and His Hi-Hatters," while encouraging patrons to take advantage of the establishment's supper club.

Significantly, cross-dressing had long been a feature of vaudeville and, later, burlesque entertainment, and it was often employed to comic effect. Acts such as the "male mannequins," however, struck a nerve among those already concerned about the changing moral climate of the postwar era. Therefore, it isn't surprising to learn that, in 1950, Club Lido saw its liquor license revoked for, among other things, "indecent entertainment."[41]

Meanwhile, nightclub patrons in search of more mainstream entertainment had a wide range of options, and venues included the Ritz Bar & Supper Club, located on the East Side; the Cotton Club, on downtown's eastern end; and the Club Merry-Go-Round, based on Youngstown's West Side. All were known to draw top national talent to the area.

The Ritz Bar & Supper Club had been an East Side landmark since the 1930s, when founder William M. Cafaro, a foreman at Truscon Steel Company, purchased a vacant shop on the corner of Wilson Avenue and Shehy Street and turned it into a tavern and nightclub. "Prohibition ended by 1934, and my father started selling drink tickets and meal tickets for a place called the Ritz Bar: a business that did not yet exist," noted his son, Anthony Cafaro Sr., retired president and CEO of the Cafaro Corporation.

Anthony Cafaro explained that his father's position as a foreman in Truscon Steel's quality-control department enhanced his ability to sell the tickets. "The guys wanted to secure their jobs, and they were more than willing to spend 5 cents or 10 cents on these tickets," he said. "So, over a period of a year or so, he put together $1,500. That was his nest egg, and that's what made it possible for him to establish the Ritz Bar."

Soon after, William Cafaro formed a business partnership with his brother, John, and the pair gradually expanded the building, until it occupied an

The Ritz Bar & Supper Club drew top national entertainers to Youngstown in the 1940s and '50s. Music performed at the club was regularly broadcast by local radio station WKBN. *Courtesy of Anthony Cafaro Sr.*

entire city block. The Ritz drew increasingly large crowds for breakfast, lunch and dinner, Anthony Cafaro observed. "It went from a bar to a supper club over a period of years," he added. "I'm sure that transformation was complete by the beginning of the war years."

Throughout the 1940s, the Ritz Bar hosted national acts, including the Glenn Miller Band and Tommy Dorsey Band, whose popular vocalist, Frank Sinatra, would soon launch an independent career. The tavern's spacious bar, which featured one of the earliest commercially produced television sets, abutted a sizable dining area and dance floor, where WKBN held remote radio broadcasts.

For adventurous East Side teenagers like future Ohio lawmaker and state Democratic chairman Harry Meshel, the Ritz Bar was a "last stop" before wrapping up a tour of local entertainment vistas. "We would walk to the Elms Ballroom from the East Side, and then, we'd walk downtown to Stone's Grill for a few minutes," Meshel recalled. "Then, we walked over to the Ritz Bar, and by the time we got over there, we were hungry."

The Ritz Bar offered a wide range of Italian entrées, along with standard steaks and chops, but the nightclub was best known for its zesty red sauce. "They would sometimes mix chicken into the sauce; and when they made the spaghetti sauce, they would add hocks and bones with beef and pork to enrich it," Meshel recalled. "They would simmer it for an hour or two in the pot, and they ended up with this terrific Italian sauce."

The nightclub's kitchen was managed by William and John Cafaro's mother, Flora Diana Cafaro, whose sister, Lena Diana Bell, became the driving force behind Youngstown's Belleria Pizza, a business established on the East Side by two of her daughters, Phyllis Frasco and Rose Liberato, in the early 1950s.

While the city had a number of popular African American nightclubs in the 1940s and early '50s, the most prominent of these was the Cotton Club, located on East Federal Street. "The night life was when the blacks and whites got together," recalled the club's former manager, Isadore Blakeny, in a 1999 interview. "We had several top black clubs when I was in college. I managed the finest club in town called the Cotton Club."

Blakeny noted that top entertainers—including Ella Fitzgerald, the Ink Spots and Tony Bennett—often stopped at the Cotton Club in the early morning hours, usually after performing at white-owned nightclubs. "That's [where] the integration was," he recalled. "All the musicians would come down there. They appreciated playing with each other. The saxophones and trumpets would have jam sessions and play all night long."[42]

The Cotton Club's close rival was the Black and Tan Club, located to the southwest of Westlake Crossing on the city's North Side. "Instead of going up on West Federal Street, you would go right up that street across the tracks, and back in there was…one of the best African American clubs in town," recalled Harry Meshel. "I used to go there all the time…They had some tough guys in there, but if they knew you were up to no wrong, they'd embrace you."

Meanwhile, the Club Merry-Go-Round operated on Salt Springs Road, a winding thoroughfare that offered a clear view of Youngstown's sprawling steel plants. Based in a working-class neighborhood on the West Side, the Club Merry-Go-Round stood a few blocks north of the spot where Salt Springs Road intersected with (and terminated) Steel Street, a venue for bustling shot-and-beer joints.

Despite its gritty surroundings, the nightclub gained a reputation for drawing top acts, and its interior exuded an unexpected elegance and glamour. The walls of the dining room featured delicate bas-reliefs of mermaid-like creatures, which reflected, once again, the skill and vision of

Souvenir Program Card

1283 Salt Springs Road
Youngstown, Ohio

Club Merry-Go-Round

PLANTER'S PUNCH
1 oz. lemon or lime juice, 1 teasp. sugar, 1 jigger Jamaica rum. Shake well with fine ice and pour unstrained into 10 oz. glass. Decorate with slice of orange, lemon, cherry and sprig fresh mint.

GIN RICKEY
Juice and rind of ½ lime. Cube of ice. 1 jigger of gin. Fill with club soda.

SLOE GIN FIZZ
1½ oz. lemon juice, 1 teasp. sugar, 1 jigger sloe gin. Shake well with cracked ice and strain into highball glass. Fill with ice-cold soda.

MINT JULEP
In 10-oz. glass muddle few sprigs fresh mint with 1 teasp. sugar and splash of soda. Fill glass with fine ice and pour in 1½ oz. of bourbon. Set glass into container and pack tightly with fine ice. Stir mixture briskly for minute to freeze ice to outside of glass. Lift out and decorate with 2 sprigs mint, slice of orange, lemon and a cherry. Fine powdered sugar dusted over mint adds to frosted appearance of drink.

SINGAPORE SLING
1 oz. lemon juice, ½ teasp. sugar, 1 oz. gin, 1 oz. cherry brandy. Shake well with cracked ice and pour unstrained into 10-oz. glass. Decorate with slice of orange, lemon and a cherry.

TOM AND JERRY
1 whole egg, 1 teasp. sugar, 1 pinch salt. Mix by hand or electric mixer. Add 1 jigger of rum. Pour mixture into glass mug. Add boiling water slowly while stirring to prevent egg from curdling. Sprinkle nutmeg on top.

HOT TODDY
In glass mug place the following: 1 lump sugar, 1 stick cinnamon, 3 cloves stuck into slice of lemon, 1 jigger of rum, whisky or brandy. Leave silver spoon in glass to prevent heat from cracking it. Add boiling water.

SIDE CAR
½ oz. lemon juice, ¾ oz. brandy, ¾ oz. Cointreau or triple sec. Shake well with cracked ice and strain into cocktail glass.

OLD FASHIONED
1 lump sugar saturated with bitters, splash of soda, muddle. 1 cube of ice, 1 slice of orange, lemon and a cherry. Over this pour 1 jigger of rye, bourbon or Scotch whisky.

MANHATTAN
½ sweet vermouth, ⅔ rye or bourbon whisky, bitters if desired. Stir with cracked ice and strain. Serve with cherry.
DRY MANHATTAN:
Dry instead of sweet vermouth.

SHERRY FLIP
1 whole egg, 1 teasp. sugar, 1 jigger sherry. Shake well with cracked ice and strain into Delmonico glass. Sprinkle nutmeg on top. Brandy or port may be used instead of sherry.

EGGNOG
1 whole egg, 1 teasp. sugar, 5 oz. milk, 1 jigger liquor (brandy, whisky, rum or sherry mostly used). Shake with cracked ice and strain. Sprinkle grated nutmeg on top.

FROZEN DAIQUIRI
½ oz. lemon or lime juice, ½ teasp. sugar, dash maraschino liqueur, 1½ oz. white rum. Mix with fine cracked ice on electric mixer or shake well by hand. Pour unstrained into champagne "saucer" Top with a cherry.

DAIQUIRI
½ oz. lemon or lime juice, ½ teasp. sugar, 1 jigger white rum. Shake well with cracked ice and strain.

DUBONNET COCKTAIL
1 oz. gin, 1½ oz. Dubonnet. Stir with cracked ice and strain. Top off with a twist of lemon peel.

This cocktail menu for the Club Merry-Go-Round reflects the nightclub's glamorous atmosphere. Known for its spirits and fine food, the club drew top-line entertainers such as Ella Fitzgerald, Vic Damone and Ethel Waters. *Courtesy of Mahoning Valley Historical Society.*

The Club Merry-Go-Round's most distinctive feature was a circular bar that slowly revolved over the course of the evening. *Courtesy of Joseph Cherol.*

designer Victor Kosa. Other highlights included the club's revolving bar and clamshell stage, which hosted legendary performers such as Nat King Cole, Vic Damone, Ella Fitzgerald, the Mills Brothers, Ethel Waters, Frankie Laine and Patti Page.[43]

During an intermission at the club in 1948, Vic Damone graciously agreed to give an impromptu performance to graduating seniors of Youngstown College during a "Post-Exam Hop" at the North Side's Elms Ballroom. "I told him: 'We have people who will buy records,' and 'Kids have called here, and they like you,'" recalled Harry Meshel. "So Vic Damone did it. He got off at the West Side, came over to the Elms and the crowd got a free show featuring a nationally known singer."

In the late 1940s, the Club Merry-Go-Round even played a role in a small piece of U.S. entertainment history. On Monday, December 1, 1947, Ella Fitzgerald and her trio—Hank Jones, Ray Brown and Charlie

The elegant Torch Club, located on Youngstown's West Side, eventually gave way to the Club Merry-Go-Round, a nightclub that flourished in the 1940s. *Courtesy of Joseph Cherol.*

Smith—opened a two-week engagement at the nightclub.[44] Fitzgerald and her fiancé, Ray Brown, the bassist for the Dizzie Gillespie Band, took advantage of the opportunity to get married in downtown Youngstown's Central Tower Building.[45]

For all its notoriety, the Club Merry-Go-Round enjoyed a surprisingly short run, closing at the end of the 1940s. The club proved to be a brief epoch in the larger story of the Cherols, a family of Italian immigrants who established a market and delicatessen on the city's West Side in 1917. By 1933, the family had relocated the business from Waverly Street to Salts Springs Road, and by the 1940s, they expanded it to include the Torch Club, the elegant predecessor of the Club Merry-Go-Round, which was operated by entrepreneur Nicky Constantino.

Upon his return from the U.S. Navy after World War II, Joseph Cherol took advantage of the GI Bill and earned a business degree from the University of Pittsburgh. In the early 1950s, he took over the family business and maintained the former site of the Club Merry-Go-Round as a tavern and banquet center. He married his wife, Laura, in 1952, and the couple continued to run the business for more than five decades. "She is a wonderful cook," said Joseph Cherol, referring to his wife. "People still stop me on the street to compliment the food."[46]

The Draw of the Suburbs

Neighborhood businesses like Cherol's and the Ritz Bar became less common, given that postwar zoning regulations restricted businesses from operating in newer residential areas. Over time, more restaurateurs and tavern owners were drawn by the allure of urban areas that abutted the "dry" townships surrounding the city. Given that liquor sales in suburban communities were mostly restricted to state stores, taverns and restaurants benefited from the business of suburbanites in search of food and entertainment closer to home.

James Palazzo was among those who recognized this trend early on. In 1955, Palazzo's Restaurant, located on Midlothian Boulevard, was among the earliest businesses on the border of Boardman Township to serve alcoholic beverages—a development that fueled the establishment's growth. Before long, Palazzo added a small coffee shop to the facility, while extending the dining area to accommodate 250 people. Meanwhile, his wife, Mary, an excellent cook, introduced authentic Italian dishes.

Palazzo embarked on his entrepreneurial career in 1941, when he and his wife established a small meat and produce outlet called the Erie Street Market. During this period, he continued to work at Republic Steel, assisting his wife at the store during his time off. In 1947, the couple opened a small tavern, the Oasis Bar, on Market Street, just below the Market Street Bridge.

Three years later, in 1950, Palazzo relocated the business to downtown Youngstown, where it occupied the lobby of the Earle Hotel, a landmark on the corner of West Federal Street and Belmont Avenue, across from the current site of the Youngstown Fire Department. While the Oasis Bar was a relatively modest affair, its customers included notable figures like entertainer Patti Page and future Ohio governor Michael DiSalle.

The chance to hobnob with celebrities and political figures wasn't enough for James Palazzo, however. Decades later, his son, Dennis, recalled that his father was "really itching" to open a full-fledged restaurant, one less dependent on the sale of alcohol. An avid sportsman and gambler, James Palazzo was drawn to an undeveloped stretch of land just north of Boardman Township, and the grocery store and tavern were eventually sold off to make way for Palazzo's Restaurant.

Ultimately, James Palazzo and his family were part of a small trickle of entrepreneurs who gravitated to the sparsely populated districts of the lower South Side and beyond. These business owners were among the first to respond to the reality that the suburbs were growing more quickly than

The Oasis Bar, operated by James and Mary Palazzo, was based at the Earl Hotel, on the corner of West Federal Street and Belmont Avenue. The bar's food and atmosphere drew well-known patrons like entertainer Patti Page and Ohio governor Michael DiSalle. The couple later established Palazzo's Restaurant on the city's South Side. *Courtesy of Laurie Palazzo Sunyog.*

the city, even though the urban core seemed vibrant. As early as 1954, the *Vindicator* reported that the city's population had risen modestly to 168,330, a gain of just 610 from a decade earlier. During the same period, the neighboring suburbs of Boardman and Austintown saw their respective populations virtually double.[47]

After World War II, local businessman and developer Edward J. DeBartolo shrewdly anticipated this trend and set out to build subsidized homes for returning veterans in neighboring Boardman Township. In the 1950s, the developer followed up with the construction of a modern strip plaza in the township—one that detractors labeled as "DeBartolo's fourteen stations of the cross."[48] DeBartolo, however, took such criticism in stride, recalled former restaurateur Jack Raver, who knew the developer as a "regular" at his downtown restaurant in the 1950s.

By this time, Raver's had moved to its final location on the corner of South Phelps and West Front Streets. "Eddie ate breakfast there every morning," Raver said. "At six o'clock we opened up, and at one minute to six, Eddie DeBartolo always came in and met his attorney there." He

Raver's Restaurant, established in the 1920s, had several downtown locations over the years. The Raver family took pride in the fact that the establishment was listed in Duncan Hines's "red book" of outstanding restaurants. *Courtesy of Mahoning Valley Historical Society.*

recalled that his staff was delighted by DeBartolo's habit of meeting business associates at the restaurant, given that the developer routinely left a five-dollar tip for a seventy-cent meal. "He'd hang out and meet people," Raver said.

After one such meeting, Raver claimed, DeBartolo called him over to his table and gestured out a window. "You know, Jack, you're going to see grass grow down Federal Street," the developer said. Surprised by the comment, Raver asked, "Why is that?" After a short pause, DeBartolo went on to predict that Boardman would eventually become the community's retail and entertainment center. "Well, that's exactly what happened," Raver noted.

Chapter 2
A MOVEABLE FEAST

At the close of the nineteenth century, Ohio lawmaker William R. Stewart promoted legislation to launch the construction of Youngstown's Market Street Bridge, which connected the city's downtown area to the then semirural South Side. This move had far-reaching consequences, given that a portion of the neighborhood located to the south of the bridge would eventually blossom into a retail and entertainment area known as "the Uptown District."

Stewart himself turned out to be one of those anomalous figures whose career was largely forgotten by subsequent generations. An African American attorney who learned his craft by helping Civil War veterans secure their pensions, Stewart went on to serve two terms as a state lawmaker between 1895 and 1899. As state senator for an overwhelmingly white community, he sponsored legislation to provide pensions to civil servants, secured tax support for a local hospital and promoted a bill that advocated tough measures against vigilantism.[49]

The lawmaker's most notable legacy, however, was the development of the city's South Side. By the time Stewart completed his second term in 1899, an extended public transportation program had contributed to the growth of Fosterville, a former mining center that emerged as one of the South Side's most important neighborhoods.

"With the completion of the trolley line and the opening of Terminal Park, later known as Idora Park, at the terminus of the line, the south side began to grow in earnest," noted local historian Sean Posey. The amusement park's opening in 1899 coincided with the completion of the Market Street Bridge, he added, stressing that these developments coalesced to fuel the expansion of other neighborhoods such as Lansingville.[50]

In a fast-paced industrial center like Youngstown, however, few people had time to reflect on the community's storied past. By the late 1950s, the South Side's economic vitality was taken for granted by most area residents, whose attitudes were informed by the optimism of the postwar era.

Bustling Market Street

In 1956, Market Street, between Ridge Avenue and Midlothian Boulevard, was studded with no fewer than 250 businesses. They included restaurants, nightclubs, car dealerships, banks, furniture stores, appliance outlets, jewelry stores, pharmacies, clothing outlets, bridal shops, florists, dry cleaners, car washes, automobile supply outlets and many others. Indeed, by the late 1950s, the Uptown District was rapidly outstripping downtown as a major destination for local diners and shoppers.

Almost a dozen restaurants, taverns and eateries were located in the short space of five blocks that separated the Market Street Bridge from Myrtle Avenue. They included the Elite Restaurant, the Green Gables Tavern, the Farmer's Daughter, the Ma-Fe Club, the Rex Tavern, the Oak Glen Restaurant, the Shangri-La and a small bar operated by the Ancient Order of Hibernians, an Irish American fraternal organization.

Many of these establishments were remnants of an earlier time, and most were relatively modest affairs. Veteran diners, however, knew better than to be taken in by nondescript or dilapidated facilities. James D. Bennett learned this lesson under the tutelage of his father-in-law, Bill Barth, a seasoned traveler who prided himself on his ability to find good food in unpromising venues. "He would find the worst-looking places in the world to take somebody in order to shock them," Bennett recalled.

One of his father-in-law's favorite Italian restaurants was Carosella's, located on the corner of Market Street and Myrtle Avenue. "On the outside, it wasn't impressive at all, and the entrance had a screen door," Bennett explained. "I remember that I was pleasantly surprised when we went inside...The food was great; it was clean." At the same time, Bennett conceded that "it was the kind of place that, if you were a stranger driving through town, you probably wouldn't have stopped there."

Out-of-town visitors would have been even less encouraged by the appearance of Ding Ho's, a Chinese restaurant located cater-corner from Carosella's, in the middle of a crowded block bordered by Pyatt Street and East Myrtle Avenue. "The canopy was always looking like it was ready to fall off," recalled Father Edward P. Noga, who often visited his grandmother on the city's South Side. "But Ding Ho's was very good Asian food."

The restaurant's limited size ensured that it would depend heavily on its carryout trade, but patrons who chose to dine on the premises faced challenges beyond cramped seating. "Whenever you went to Ding Ho's, you needed to be patient," recalled former Mahoning County commissioner Thomas Carney. "Everything was prepared fresh, so you might wait for your food for an hour or so. The food was very good, but it certainly wasn't fast in coming."

For most customers, though, the food was worth the wait. Donia Kravitz Foster, whose parents operated Youngstown's Elm Street Delicatessen, often accompanied her father on weekend trips to Ding Ho's to pick up carryout. "We would always sit in the booth, and everybody would come and talk to us," she recalled. "To have someone, an owner, recommend something and then bring out something special…was a wonderful feeling." Ms. Foster was particularly fond of specialties like Peking duck.

Meanwhile, those in search of authentic Italian cuisine weren't limited to the fare at Carosella's. They could also stop at an eatery operated by Luigi and Mary Grace Scarsella on the corner of Pyatt and Market Streets. "It was very small," recalled Connie Kushma, the Scarsellas' granddaughter. "We only had four booths, one small table and a dozen stools at the bar." She added, however, that the menu included a range of traditional dishes, including pasta fagioli, braciole and chicken cacciatore.

At the time, Mary Grace Scarsella wasn't far removed from the culinary traditions of Italy's Abruzzo region. More than two decades earlier, in the 1930s, she had traveled to Fagnano Alto to assist her husband's elderly parents, who owned a large farm in the region, and she was trapped there after the outbreak of World War II. "She was in Italy thirteen years," explained Mrs. Kushma. "She raised three daughters there." During that time, Mrs. Scarsella developed many of her signature recipes, as she cooked for the laborers in her father-in-law's fields.

Other restaurants and eateries in the neighborhood included the Star Dinette, the Tropics Lounge, Bedell's and the Château Tavern. By the late 1950s, a Brown Derby restaurant also operated on Market Street, on the block bordered by East Myrtle and Williamson Avenues, although it would eventually relocate to South Avenue.

Established in Los Angeles in the 1920s, Brown Derby had been introduced to northeastern Ohio in 1941 by Akron-based entrepreneur Gus Girves, and local diners were drawn to the restaurant's steak dinners, zesty soups and signature Cobb salad, purportedly developed by the California-based chain's cofounder, Robert H. Cobb.[51]

In contrast to the Brown Derby, with its linen tablecloths and uniformed waitstaff, most of the establishments that lined the blocks between Williamson and Indianola Avenues were relatively informal. The Palm Gardens, the Manila Grill, the Evergreen, the Carlton, the Zanzibar and the Atomic Bar were essentially taverns that served food.

Among these, the Atomic Bar, managed by Gene Abbott, gained a citywide reputation for novelty foods such as "Jo-Jo" potatoes (breaded and deep-fried potato wedges), "broasted" chicken and a rich, cheesy pizza. "Our pizza was regularly served at the Idora Park ballroom and the Town Tavern on the West Side," recalled Gene Abbott's daughter, Marilyn Abbott Emerick. "We used a combination of Swiss cheese, Longhorn cheese and freshly grated Parmesan cheese; and our dough was baked down the street at Kling's Bakery—absolutely delicious."

No less welcoming to the casual diner were the Glen-Mar Restaurant, the Barbecue Pit, the Plaza Grill, Eddie's Donut Shop, Tom Burton's Bar & Grill and Gene's Restaurant, which was owned and operated by a member of the Isaly family. "They used to fry donuts every morning at Gene's," recalled South Side native Bob Casey. "When you went there in the morning and ordered a donut, it would still be warm."

Local families often gravitated to the Dinner Bell, a tiny restaurant located between Indianola and Hylda Avenues. "When I graduated from South High School in 1948, that's where I celebrated with my mother and father," recalled South Side native Marilyn Sweeney. "It was modest, but very nice, and I'd usually order something along the lines of baked chicken with gravy and dressing."

Meanwhile, businesspeople and others in search of a convenient meal depended on Mr. Wheeler's, a diner with two locations on Market Street—one on the corner of East Indianola Avenue and the other between Boston and East Avondale Avenues.

Shirley Dangerfield, who managed the second location, recalled that her customers were "mostly businesspeople, car dealers and funeral directors." She pointed out that Mr. Wheeler's served the thickest milk shakes in town and was also known for its burgers, chili, soups and macaroni and cheese. "I'm not sure why the macaroni and cheese was so good, but it was the best I've had," she added.

Boardman Township native and attorney Robert S. Fulton was fond of Mr. Wheeler's largest hamburger, a stuffed sandwich with a quarter pound of beef that was known as "the Topper." His wife, Elaine Fulton, recalled that Mr. Wheeler's was known for its home-style pies, and she especially enjoyed the restaurant's cherry, apple and pumpkin pies.

Rise of the Uptown District

By the late 1950s, the district abutting Indianola Avenue, a main artery that spanned the city's South Side, hosted a handful of restaurants that challenged downtown's monopoly on fine dining. The first to appear on the scene was the Colonial House, which opened in 1949. The two-story Colonial Revival structure, with its stately columns and paneled interior, set a new standard for weekend dining in the Youngstown area.

"That was where I took my wife, Josephine, to her first big dinner out," recalled Fred Ross, who was married several years before the business opened. "She was so impressed by the environment that she had trouble eating the food." That evening, the Rosses had their first taste of valet parking. "Overall, it was an impressive experience," Ross observed.

By the mid-1950s, the Colonial House was managed by Carl Rango, who had formed a partnership with co-owners Frank Fetchet and Vince DeNiro. When it came to the establishment's furnishings and amenities, the partners spared no expense.

Ray Whalen, who patronized the restaurant in the 1960s, offered a detailed description of its main dining room. "It was a warm, beautiful interior," Whalen said. "They had wooden floors, wooden beams in the ceiling and wooden columns; and I can remember nice wallpaper and chandeliers… There was a long staircase with wooden banisters that led to the second floor, where they had beautiful private rooms."

While the restaurant's regular customers included professionals, business leaders and political powerbrokers, it also became a destination for families marking special occasions and teens enjoying after-prom dinners. Patrons, regardless of background, appreciated the Colonial House's wide menu, which included entrées ranging from broiled filet mignon to sautéed jumbo Louisiana frog legs served on toast points.

In 1959, the Colonial House was joined by another fine-dining establishment, Cicero's, located a few storefronts to the north. The new

The Colonial House was an elegant presence on the city's South Side for decades. With its hand-carved bar, gleaming woodwork and distinctive furnishings, the restaurant was a natural venue for formal celebrations. *Courtesy of Mahoning Valley Historical Society.*

The interior of the Colonial House offered diners a pleasant combination of comfort and style. *Courtesy of Mahoning Valley Historical Society.*

restaurant's co-owners included racketeer Vince DeNiro, who had pulled out of the Colonial House in the mid-1950s and subsequently focused on the development of the Sans Souci, a Las Vegas hotel and casino.

However, within three years of the Sans Souci's 1957 grand opening, which featured a performance by vocalist Rudy Vallee, the owners were forced to close the casino portion of the business. As the Sans Souci faltered, DeNiro pursued other projects.

After establishing a business partnership with contractor Edward Cochran (also involved in the Sans Souci) and businessman Dominic Frank, DeNiro set out to make Cicero's the most luxurious restaurant in Youngstown. Unlike the Colonial House, whose designers aimed for classical elegance, Cicero's embodied the glitz and glamour of Las Vegas.

Patrons who entered the restaurant found themselves in a dramatic multilevel interior that reflected the unique vision of designer Victor Kosa. The centerpiece of Cicero's was a streamlined bar that was illuminated by gilded pendant lights and lined with molded upholstered chairs. Each dining area was partitioned with wrought-iron filigree, and the restaurant's various levels were bordered with brick planters that brimmed with foliage.

The main dining area featured a suspended coffered ceiling, which was bathed in the glow of recessed lighting, and each table was appointed with a linen tablecloth, gleaming silverware, napkins folded in the shape of a bishop's mitre and a crystal vase that contained a single rose. Other accents included wrought-iron chandeliers, flocked wallpaper and carpeting with intricate arabesque patterns.

Victor Kosa's most memorable touch, however, was an artificial tree that stood at the center of the main dining area. Kosa's nephew, Dr. George D. Beelen, recalled that the tree was "fashioned out of…springs and the interior and underside of an automobile," and he added that the staff "hung new apples on it every day."

In the evening hours, Cicero's engaged in informal "catering" whenever patrons of the neighboring Chez Paris, a cozy piano bar, requested appetizers to go with their drinks. "The Chez Paris didn't have food," recalled Patti Ferraro Druzisky. "But on occasion, depending on the crowd, the guys would send somebody next door to Cicero's to order appetizers and hors d'oeuvres, and they would bring over trays of food for us."

The development of the Uptown District continued into the early 1960s, when a third fine-dining establishment opened in the neighborhood. The Mansion, an upscale restaurant owned by Lee and Lou Tiberio, was based in a three-story structure on the corner of Princeton Avenue and Market

The stylish main dining room of Cicero's featured an artificial tree that was strung daily with fresh apples. Local artist and designer Victor Kosa reportedly fashioned the tree from salvaged materials, including the main spring of an old automobile. *Courtesy of Mahoning Valley Historical Society.*

The Mansion was a venue for celebrations ranging from anniversaries to after-prom dinners. Elegant private dining rooms were available for organizational events. *Courtesy of Mahoning Valley Historical Society.*

Street. First known as the Rigney Mansion, the building later hosted the Yahrling-Rayner Music Co., a firm that sold musical instruments and provided lessons.

After purchasing the old estate, the Tiberio brothers remodeled the space, basing their designs on the interior of Ernie's Restaurant, a landmark in San Francisco.[52] "I seem to remember that it had velvet wallpaper, and the lighting was kind of subdued," said Father John C. Harris, who dined there on special occasions. "Overall, it had an extravagant Victorian feel, and I remember there were oil paintings in gilded frames hanging on the walls."

The atmosphere of casual elegance was underscored by the presence of upholstered chairs, plush couches, wall sconce lighting and an antique fireplace. Patrons who were content to order a cocktail or two had the option of gathering at the restaurant's stylish bar. "The bar was rectangular, so you had a 360-degree view of the customers," recalled Joseph Planey. "The Mansion was the kind of place you might take a date, but I would also occasionally stop there for a drink after work."

Jim Graycar, who worked as the Mansion's second bartender in the mid-1960s, recalled that he was constantly moving. "We really hustled, and…on a good weekend, it wasn't uncommon for me and the head bartender to split the tips, at $90 apiece—a lot of money back then," he recalled. Regular patron Patti Ferraro Druzisky noted that the restaurant also had a piano bar located in a smaller lounge area. "They drew a wonderful bar crowd," she added.

Patrons who came to dine, however, encountered a level of service and professionalism that was unforgettable. "When you went to the Mansion, you experienced upscale dining," noted Attorney Robert E. Casey, a regular customer. "People would greet you as you walked in, there were linen cloths and napkins on the table and they had a full menu. The name itself offered a promise of elegance, and they certainly delivered on that promise."

Fine Dining Elsewhere on the South Side

Although many of the South Side's fine-dining establishments were concentrated in Market Street's Uptown District, several upscale restaurants could be found elsewhere. In 1961, Antone's Restaurant made its debut on the corner of Market Street and East Chalmers Avenue, less than ten blocks south of the Market Street Bridge. The restaurant had been established by Anthony Gianfrancesco, previous owner of the Manila Grill.

"Originally, my grandfather owned a shot-and-beer place," explained Chad Scianna, the founder's stepgrandson and COO of CAS Wholesale Distributors, a firm that operates Antone's restaurants throughout the area. "At the time, he was dating my grandmother, Helen Scianna, and it turned out she had learned how to cook during a prior marriage, [from which] she had my father [Ross Scianna]."

Chad Scianna noted that his grandmother's former husband, an outstanding chef, taught Helen Scianna everything he knew. "So my grandmother started making daily specials at the Manila Grill…soups and sandwiches and pastas and things of that nature," he added. "After a year or so, the menu really took off, and people began to crave her food."

As the Manila Grill developed its reputation for fine food, a large house on Market Street became available, and Anthony Gianfrancesco seized the opportunity. "I believe my grandparents were married at that time," Scianna said. "They purchased the house, remodeled it and turned it into Antone's Restaurant & Confetti Lounge."

The restaurant's name was the product of a compromise. While the couple considered naming the new restaurant "Anthony's" or "Tony's," they "met in the middle" and called it Antone's, Scianna explained. Inspired by the restaurant's popularity, the Gianfrancescos expanded its range of entrées. "The menu had everything from steaks to seafood, and it also featured a few Italian dishes, obviously," he said. "It was around this time that the Antone's salad was created."

Antone's signature salad was a product of the large crowds the restaurant attracted soon after it opened. "My grandmother never wanted anyone to wait or to be hungry," Scianna noted. "So as soon as you sat down at your table, you received what was called a 'monkey dish' of Antone's salad—I mean, as soon as you sat down at your table."

Given its location near downtown Youngstown, the restaurant became a destination for professionals and business executives with offices at the city's core. "From hearing the stories, Youngstown Sheet & Tube was booming then," Chad Scianna said. "The downtown was incredibly vibrant, and businesspeople that stopped in often had a two- or three-cocktail lunch."

By the late 1960s, Anthony Gianfrancesco's stepson, Ross Scianna, had become actively involved in the restaurant, and within a few years, he assumed a leading role in its operation. In time, Scianna initiated construction of a state-of-the-art banquet facility that complemented Antone's popular restaurant service.

On January 22, 1961, the arrival of yet another fine-dining establishment on the city's South Side was announced in a full-page photo spread that

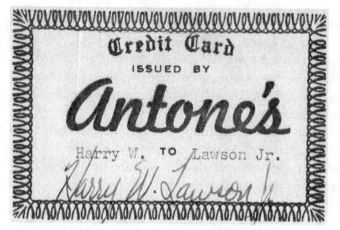

Local restaurants like Antone's began to issue credit cards in the 1950s and 1960s. Antone's Restaurant earned a reputation for high-quality Italian fare, and branches continue to operate throughout the Youngstown area. *Courtesy of Mahoning Valley Historical Society.*

appeared in the *Vindicator's* rotogravure section. Within weeks of its official opening, the Chateaubriand Restaurant & Cocktail Lounge at the corner of South and East Dewey Avenues became a destination for diners seeking a formal and romantic environment.

A low-slung brick building with a quadrilateral sign fashioned of cedar, the Chateaubriand had a roomy midcentury modern interior. The restaurant's main dining area, known as the Champagne Room, featured panel lighting, molded upholstered chairs, linen tablecloths and a view of the establishment's other dining areas, which were set off with glass partitions.

The most stylish of these was the Executive Lounge, furnished with a piano bar, lounge seating, glass-globe table lamps and a raised brick hearth that dominated one corner of the room. Banquets and business meetings were held in a third dining area known as the Char-Sherry Room, which was named for owner Sam DeMar's two daughters, Charlene and Sherry.

For Sam DeMar, the Chateaubriand was the latest in a series of projects. An energetic entrepreneur, DeMar was a local pioneer in the postwar pizza craze, and his first business was a pizzeria in Geneva-on-the-Lake, Ohio. Later, he showcased this novelty at a tavern he operated on Youngstown's North Side.

Interestingly, even the Chateaubriand was developed on the site of a former pizzeria, which DeMar had opened seven years earlier, in 1954. "Sammy DeMar started it out as a pizza parlor, and they did a good trade there in carryout," recalled Joseph Planey. "Then, he fixed the place up and made it classier, so you could sit down and have a meal."

This process of refinement concluded with the opening of the Chateaubriand, which was far removed from its origins as a pizzeria. "From what I've heard, it was a very expensive restaurant, with prices comparable to what you would find in restaurants today," said Sherry DeMar, who acknowledged she has no personal memories of her father's restaurant.

When the restaurant closed in the late 1960s, the building served as the site of a popular Brown Derby restaurant. "From what I understand, it was like white tablecloths," said Jamie Szmara, who managed the Brown Derby Roadhouse decades later, in the 1990s. "That's where you got dressed up to go [for] anniversaries, special events, when it first opened."

Predictably, within a few years of the Chateaubriand's grand opening, another high-end restaurant opened on the South Side not far from Youngstown's Idora Amusement Park. Less elegant than the Chateaubriand, Courtney's Steakhouse enjoyed a popularity that depended largely on the quality of its food.

Located in the South Side's Fosterville district, near the corner of Glenwood and Indianola Avenues, Courtney's was based in a large house with numerous additions. "If you looked at it from the outside, you might not even know it was a restaurant," recalled Dennis Alexander, who bused tables there in the 1960s and also worked in the kitchen. "It was nice inside, but it wasn't fancy…It was the food and the people that made it famous."

Patrons who entered the restaurant encountered a rectangular wooden bar that abutted the kitchen, and those seated near the bar could look on as their meal was prepared by the restaurant's chef, Jesse Hudson. "The owners had the good sense to put in a glass window, so you could watch the chef cook your steak," explained Dennis Alexander's sister-in-law, Florence, a member of the restaurant's waitstaff.

Cofounded by Boardman natives Don and Bob Courtney, the restaurant emerged as a major destination for local diners, and it was best known for its "Courtney's Special," a ten-ounce steak prepared with fresh mushrooms. To ensure high quality, steaks were freshly cut and marinated in oil. "They used to buy sides of beef, and then they had their own butchers," recalled Florence Alexander. "They would come in…and cut all the steaks for the weekend."

Almost as popular as the steak dinners were the restaurant's signature fries, called "Courtney Fries," said Dennis Alexander, who often prepared the fries. "You'd slice the potatoes, pour oil on the iron skillet, put all these sliced potatoes in and mash them down," he explained, noting that he then covered the potatoes and cooked them at a high temperature. "People just loved them, and it was like their trademark potato," he said.

Other house specialties included veal scallopini, shrimp cocktail and blue point clams smothered in hot sauce. Some customers, however, settled for the house salad, which was a meal in itself. A rich blend of lettuce, carrots, celery, olives and tomatoes, the salad was topped off with Courtney's signature dressing. "Our big seller was the Roquefort dressing, because we made the… dressing fresh," recalled Florence Alexander. "We cleaned off the wheels of cheese and picked them into little pieces and added the mayonnaise and the Worcestershire [sauce]."

Courtney's Steakhouse flourished until the late 1970s, when an arson fire nearly destroyed the restaurant.[53] "We never knew how that fire started," recalled Florence Alexander. "It was unfortunate. They were very good to us." While Bob Courtney struggled to rebuild the business, the restaurant eventually closed. Not long afterward, a blaze destroyed Idora Park's famous roller coaster, the Wildcat, which contributed to the demise of another South Side landmark.

In the mid-1960s, however, such developments seemed unimaginable. Even a spike in violent crime failed to diminish the South Side's vitality, and many residents treated Idora Park as their personal playground. Over the next decade, the district served as a destination for those seeking recreation, and its restaurants continued to thrive.

However, a high-profile murder that occurred on the city's South Side in the early 1960s could easily have dampened the popularity of the district's businesses. While the bombing death of a local restaurateur did not have the negative impact some South Side businesspeople had feared, the incident helped undermine Youngstown's national reputation.

"Murder Town, USA"

Shortly after midnight on July 17, 1961, Vince DeNiro, co-owner of the Cicero's restaurant, started up a late model convertible on Market Street, between Princeton and Indianola Avenues. As the *Vindicator* later reported, DeNiro unknowingly triggered a powerful charge "that rocked and shattered Youngstown's Uptown District…hurtling lethal pieces of metal and flesh as much as 200 feet across the street and over buildings."

The bomb, which was the equivalent of ten sticks of dynamite, obliterated the front end of the vehicle, hurling one fender into a nearby candy store and sending the car's left front tire across Market Street, where it smashed into a furniture store's display window. "Large plate glass windows on virtually every store in the Uptown between Indianola and Princeton…were shattered by the concussion," the *Vindicator* reported. "The blast was felt for miles and rocked homes for blocks."[54]

The grisly murder shocked the public for reasons including the identity of the victim. While it was known that DeNiro had competed with other racketeers for control of the area's underground gambling industry, he enjoyed wide popularity, and unlike most local gangsters, he lacked a reputation for personal violence.

Regional newspapers offered few tributes to the fallen racketeer. "He will be missed by his Mafia cronies, we suppose," commented an Akron editorial that was reprinted in the *Vindicator*, "but the reaction of respectable citizens to DeNiro's demise is 'good riddance.'" The editorial went on to suggest that the chief reason for "civic indignation" over the murder was the reckless manner in which it had been carried out.[55]

This observation rang true. Since 1960, Youngstown had witnessed three gangland slayings, including the shooting deaths of racketeers Sandy Naples and Joseph Romano. The two previous murders,

This photograph of Cicero's canopy affords a view of Market Street's busy entertainment district. Cicero's popularity declined only slightly after July 1961, when owner Vince DeNiro was killed by a car bomb near the restaurant's main entrance. *Courtesy of Mahoning Valley Historical Society.*

however, did not pose an obvious threat to innocent bystanders.

Less than a year later, on July 1, 1962, another bomb claimed the life of racketeer Bill Naples, whose body was found in a garage that had collapsed on his incinerated vehicle. Like DeNiro, Naples's legitimate activities included the operation of a restaurant. Two years earlier, in 1960, he had taken over the Center sandwich shop, established on the East Side by his late brother, Sandy.[56] Like DeNiro's bombing death, Billy Naples's murder would go unsolved.

Worse yet, these murders were followed by another fatal bombing—one that claimed the life of a child. The target of the third car bomb was sixty-year-old Charles "Cadillac Charlie" Cavallaro, a grape salesman with a stake in the underground gambling industry.

On Friday, November 23, 1962, at 11:30 a.m., Cavallaro stepped into the family's two-car garage with his two youngest children, Charlie Jr. and

Tommy, who expected a ride to football practice. When Cavallaro turned the sedan's ignition key, a bomb ripped through the vehicle, instantly killing him and eleven-year-old Tommy.[57]

The tragedy caught the attention of U.S. attorney general Robert F. Kennedy, who urged federal law enforcement agents to solve the crime. The investigation was headed by federal agent Edward A. Hargett, who was in charge of the FBI's Cleveland office, and "20 agents reinforced the five regularly assigned to the Youngstown area."

Less than four months later, in March 1963, an exposé on the community appeared in the *Saturday Evening Post*, and almost overnight, Youngstown acquired a new nickname: "Murder Town, USA." Journalist John Kobler, who visited the city while researching the article for the *Saturday Evening Post*, devoted considerable space to Joseph "Fats" Aiello, the well-coiffed racketeer who greeted guests at downtown's A Lounge (formerly the Colonial Bar), an upscale establishment at the corner of South Hazel and West Boardman Streets.[58]

Despite their embarrassment, many Youngstowners were forced to concede that mobsters were a ubiquitous presence in their community. More than a few local racketeers—including Aiello, DeNiro and the Naples brothers—had turned to the restaurant industry because it provided them with a visible means of income while also enabling them to mingle with (and charm) members of the general public.

Interestingly, Cicero's, which played a role in the drama that enveloped Youngstown in the early 1960s, survived the murder of its cofounder Vince DeNiro. While questions swirled around the slain racketeer's $500,000 estate, Cicero's remained a popular destination well into the 1960s.

The end came in the early morning hours of July 24, 1969, when a fire swept through the restaurant's plush interior. Before firefighters were able to control the blaze, the roof had collapsed, and the building's steel support beams "crumpled from the intense heat." The structure, then valued at $60,000, was treated as a complete loss.[59] To this day, the site of what many regarded as Youngstown's most glamorous restaurant remains a vacant lot.

Novelty Restaurants in the Uptown District

Not all restaurants in the Uptown District were geared to formal dining. The district hosted at least two Isaly's outlets, a Toddle House diner and drive-in restaurants such as Humble's and Handy Andy's. Casual diners could also choose from a range of taverns including the Emerald Inn, Mickey's Bar, the Alcove Lounge, Lee 'n Eddie's Lounge and the Jambar Lounge. While Ohio law required that taverns provide food, relatively few offered a wide menu, and several in the Uptown District focused on entertainment for young adults.

A growing attentiveness to the youth market was also reflected in the rise of mini-chains and novelty restaurants that often featured takeout services. As early as 1948, California-based entrepreneurs Richard and Maurice McDonald developed a prototype for "a radically new method of preparing food" that "was designed to increase the speed, lower prices, and raise the volume of sales."[60] While an "assembly-line" approach to food preparation did not immediately take hold in Youngstown's restaurant industry, a growing number of establishments promoted novelty foods, including hamburgers, pizza and fried chicken.

In the Uptown District, the most enduring of these was the Pizza Oven, which opened in 1960 on the spot where Southern Boulevard veers off from Market Street. From the outset, customers were struck by the restaurant's distinctive appearance. "The Pizza Oven's design was based on a Colorado eatery," explained public historian Richard S. Scarsella. "It featured a soaring wood-planked ceiling, arches and tinted windows."

Few Youngstown residents knew that the Pizza Oven was part of a Colorado-based chain that had been cofounded by Youngstown natives Rudy and Robert Parella. "My one uncle, Robert Parella, established the first one out West," noted James Esposito, a nephew of the cofounders and, later, a manager of the restaurant on Southern Boulevard. "He was in the U.S. Air Force out there in Colorado, and he settled there as a young man."

James Esposito, along with his mother, Rose Parella Esposito, played a key role in the family business. Before Esposito joined the U.S. Navy in the late 1950s, Robert Parella invited him to Colorado to "learn the business," and he opened restaurants around the country. "When I came back, I was part of the crew that opened the Pizza Oven here in Youngstown," Esposito recalled.

Managing the weekend crowds at the Pizza Oven proved a challenge, given that a large percentage of its patrons were high school students. "It was a lot of hard work, putting up with the mass of kids that would come in after the football games," Esposito recalled. "We would have to hold them back at the doors and get them to sit down and stay in one place, and then try to wait on them."

Over time, the Pizza Oven—later known as "the Oven"—became increasingly family-oriented. Yet the restaurant's continuing popularity with high school and university students helped to ensure its longevity. For Esposito, however, the restaurant's endurance had more to do with

The Oven Restaurant is family owned and has operated at the same location for the past 32 years.

Their delicious sauce is made from an old family recipe, using only the finest ingredients.

In the sixties, they introduced their famous SPS sandwich, consisting of a medium-hot sausage pattie, topped with melted provolone cheese and sauce on our delicious homemade roll. Other homemade items from the kitchen are lasagna, spaghetti and pizzas made to order.

On Friday, the fresh fish dinners (fried or broiled) are the best in the area. Daily luncheon and dinner specials are also offered, with a variety of selections.

New menus with reduced prices are available. Private security is provided for the customer's convenience.

THE OVEN RESTAURANT
2841 SOUTHERN BLVD.
YOUNGSTOWN, OH 44507

The Oven Restaurant, a South Side institution for more than four decades, was well known for its pizza and pasta dishes. A popular destination for high school and college students, the restaurant also drew families and moviegoers from the neighboring Uptown Theater. *Courtesy of James Esposito.*

the quality of its food. "It was probably the first restaurant of its type at that particular time with pizza and spaghetti and sandwiches and chicken," he said. "Everything was made from scratch, all handmade."

Unlike the Oven, the Dog House chain focused on a food product that was commonplace. Hot dogs, after all, were available in taverns, diners and ballparks around the city. Local entrepreneur Rocky Marino, however, found a new way to make them fun and appealing.

Patrons of the Dog House were given the choice of ordering their food at a takeout window or competing for one of six stools that lined the counter inside. The chain's convenience was enhanced by its twenty-four-hour schedule, which enabled it to accommodate industrial workers and others who kept late or irregular hours.

In 1953, the Dog House's premier restaurant opened on the corner of Market Street and Midlothian Boulevard, and it turned out to be the first of 221 outlets in thirty-three states. The chain's explosive success was driven, in part, by the eye-catching design of its buildings. Each diner was equipped with a porcelain façade resembling an oversized dog house, and this façade was flanked by freestanding cartoon images of howling canines.

The Dog House was the latest in a string of successes for Rocky Marino, who, at various times, operated two popular downtown businesses, Rocky's and Moore's taverns. Both establishments showcased his wife's zesty chili dogs. "He got the great idea of broadening that business, and the Dog House was born out of that idea," explained his grandson, Mark Marino.

Rocky Marino's creativity didn't end with the Dog House's concept. The restaurant's theme was reflected in a whimsical menu that included the following varieties of hot dogs: Mexican, with chili sauce; German, with sauerkraut; Boston, with baked beans; Western, with barbecue sauce; Irish, with green relish; Swiss, with cheese; American, with relish and mustard; Poodle, with onions; and Scotch, with nothing.

In 1954, Rocky Marino's son, Ross Marino, left his insurance business to join the franchise and eventually became president of the Dog House Inc. Ross Marino presided over the chain's expansion into Pennsylvania, Florida and other states, and in time, he oversaw a dramatic revision of the firm's business model. "We wanted to build on a solid foundation," Marino stated in a 1966 interview, "so in 1960 we stopped all expansion, updated and upgraded our package, redesigned our building and expanded our menu."

The restaurant's design became more elaborate, and it soon resembled other chain restaurants of the period. The diner with the porcelain façade gave way to a cleanly designed glass building that could accommodate almost thirty customers, while offering more than seventy food items.

Initially, Ross Marino's innovations paid off. In 1966, at its zenith, the Dog House Inc., was worth $23 million.[61] By the end of the 1960s, however, the chain had imploded. "At one point, the chain was growing faster than McDonald's, but there were locations out West, especially in Arizona, where the business model didn't work as well," explained Mark Marino. "The Dog House was a twenty-four-hour operation, and the towns out there rolled up at nine o'clock, so there was a lot of nonprofitability there, you might say."

In 1953, the same year the first Dog House restaurant appeared on Market Street, another high-volume takeout restaurant was introduced into the area—one that specialized in fried chicken. The Golden Drumstick was the latest project of Harry and Faye Malkoff, who established several restaurants in the Youngstown area, the most famous of which was the 20th Century.

The Golden Drumstick was established on the former site of the El Morocco, an upscale restaurant known for its gourmet fare and rarefied atmosphere. "Even though it was incredibly elegant, they didn't make any money on it," explained their son, Dr. Kurt Malkoff. "And subsequently, they

The Dog House, a Youngstown-based chain, once boasted franchises in thirty-three states. Local businessman Ross A. Marino opened the first Dog House diner on the corner of Market Street and Midlothian Boulevard in the early 1950s. This franchise was located in neighboring Austintown Township. *Courtesy of Mark Marino.*

At the peak of the Dog House chain's popularity, president Ross Marino maintained a corporate plane and sponsored a national race car. The chain's rapid expansion contributed to its implosion in the late 1960s. *Courtesy of Mark Marino.*

took another trip out to [Arizona]—they would do that regularly—and they saw a high-volume fast-food restaurant called the Golden Drumstick."

Harry Malkoff was so impressed with the restaurant's design that he "flew out with his architect, rented a car, sat in the parking lot of that building [for five hours], and the architect [copied] the structure." Those plans were used to renovate the site of the El Morocco, transforming it into the Golden Drumstick.

The next step was to secure the finest recipe for fried chicken available. "The special recipe for the chicken actually came from an operation called Gaylord's, in Texas," Dr. Malkoff explained. "And Gaylord's subsequently, I think, was bought by several other corporations, but probably the most recent was Church's."

Despite his confidence in the project, Harry Malkoff understood the challenges involved in turning a fine-dining establishment into a fried chicken restaurant. Given the need to promote an entirely new kind of business, he made an uncharacteristic move and initiated a full-scale advertising campaign.

On the day of the Golden Drumstick's grand opening, Harry and Faye Malkoff drove from the North Side, "just to see how things were going," and found that "the restaurant was wrapped with people." To meet demand, Faye Malkoff helped bake five thousand biscuits, while Harry staffed the fryers. "When I...tell this story, I tear up, because I know their work ethic," Dr. Malkoff said. "They served 2,200 people on that Sunday...and then, it was like the rest is history."

While technically located in Boardman Township, the Golden Drumstick was a South Side destination, and many former residents of the district look back fondly on the restaurant. "You would always see a lot of families eating there," Patti Ferraro Druzisky noted. "The breaded and fried chicken was delicious, and they served honey with their biscuits, which was the first time I was introduced to that."

In the end, the Golden Drumstick proved so popular that the Malkoffs faced pressure from customers to introduce its fried chicken at the 20th Century restaurant—pressure they prudently resisted. The Golden Drumstick continued to thrive, even under new owners, who rented from the Malkoffs, and the couple collected ten years of rent on the property before selling it to the First Federal Bank.

The Rise of Arby's

The most successful and enduring restaurant franchise to come out of Youngstown was launched in neighboring Boardman Township on July 23, 1964. The now famous Arby's brand was developed by Forrest and Leroy

Raffel, who previously operated a restaurant equipment and commercial interior business in downtown Youngstown.

The Raffel brothers' restaurant equipment business, which offered turnkey solutions to local restaurateurs, gained recognition for its design work on the Mural Room's "Tiki Lounge," an elegant bar with a Polynesian theme.[62] Trends in the restaurant industry, however, led the Raffels to reconsider their options.

"In the early '60s, two things adversely affected our equipment business," Leroy Raffel noted. "First, the school kitchen business was drying up, because the postwar building program was completed; and second, our customer base of [local] independent restaurants was being threatened by the coming on of chains and franchises." Given that chains and franchises failed to patronize local supply houses, the brothers could see the writing on the wall.

While Forrest and Leroy Raffel had cut their teeth as entrepreneurs in the Youngstown-Warren area, they were raised in neighboring New Castle, Pennsylvania, where they spent their youth at the Leslie Hotel, an establishment managed by their father, Jacob. An enterprising man, Jacob Raffel also operated a chain of taverns for workingmen that was popular in the 1930s and '40s. During this period, the brothers worked at several of their father's businesses, and this real world experience was eventually supplemented with degrees from Ivy League institutions.

Their decision to establish a restaurant chain was not fueled entirely by their grasp of industry trends. The brothers were also inspired by information they received from one of Forrest's friends, Mike Davis, who invited them to tour his chain of sub shops in Albany, New York. On their way to a convention in New York City during the early 1960s, the Raffel brothers decided to make a side trip to Albany, where Davis showed them his operation and described his next venture: a roast beef sandwich shop.

Davis referred them to a particularly successful operation of this kind known as Kelly's, which operated in Revere Beach, Massachusetts, near Boston. As the brothers left Albany, they were curious to see Kelly's in operation, and they drove on to Boston.

Nine months later, they perfected their concept, and the pilot unit for their franchise opened in Boardman. It was unique in a landscape already dotted with fast-food eateries. "The building looked something like a Conestoga wagon, with a yellow curved roof," Leroy Raffel explained. "It had sandstone walls, ceramic tile floors, recessed lights in a curved ceiling, which was covered in orange and tan striped vinyl. There was a stone patio with colorful umbrella tables."

While the Raffels counted on their distinctive building and product to draw customers, they were also determined to provide a unique dining

Youngstown-area entrepreneurs Forrest and Leroy Raffel gained national recognition through the success of their Arby's franchise. The corporation's first restaurant, shown here, was opened in nearby Boardman Township. *Courtesy of Mahoning Valley Historical Society.*

environment. "It was our philosophy that dining out was a total experience, using all the senses," Leroy Raffel explained. "As you entered Arby's you were surrounded by sound and desert colors. The music played. A huge slicer pounded back and forth. A succulent beef roast revolved in a glass enclosed rotisserie on the front counter."[63]

The first Arby's was an instant success, and the franchise grew quickly. By 1970, the Raffels had opened 350 units, while 50 more were under construction. However, since they had started out with little capital and were reinvesting profits into the business, they felt vulnerable to any downturn in the economy. Therefore, they agreed to have Goldman Sachs and Bear Stearns guide them through a public offering on Wall Street, in the hope that they would have more working capital, even during an economic slump.

Sadly, their initial public offering was preceded by a downturn in the market, which was exacerbated by the bankruptcy of Penn Central, a development that dried up the market for credit and effectively doomed their IPO. In the wake of these developments, the Raffels were unable to seek new financing without declaring bankruptcy, which they did in 1971.

They quickly turned the company profitable, though, and by 1974, it had emerged from bankruptcy. Chastened by their experience with Wall Street, they decided that financial stability lay in merging with a larger company. In 1976, they sold the company to RC Cola, and Leroy Raffel remained as president and CEO. At the time, their company had four hundred units. When Leroy Raffel retired three years later, however, there were eight hundred stores in the chain. Along with the Good Humor Bar, which also originated in Youngstown, Arby's roast beef sandwich remains one of the U.S. food industry's most iconic and enduring products. In 1989, Arby's marked its twenty-fifth anniversary with a special tribute to Boardman High School's graduating class of 1964, in recognition of the fact that class members had staffed the first Arby's restaurant on U.S. Route 224. "We had the twenty-fifth reunion all planned out, and Arby's came in and paid for everything, from the programs to the entertainment," noted Boardman High School alumnus B.J. Thompson.

Casual and Family Dining on the South Side

For those who wanted something beyond the convenience of fast food, though without the formality of a fine-dining experience, the South Side hosted a number of restaurants that provided a pleasant, comfortable environment. Among them was Palazzo's Restaurant, located on Midlothian Boulevard, which marked Youngstown's southern border.

The restaurant's establishment in 1955 was the realization of a long-held dream for proprietor James Palazzo. After securing a site on Midlothian Boulevard, Palazzo and his wife, Mary, upgraded the facility, tapping the skills of designer Victor Kosa, who helped create an atmosphere that reflected their Italian roots. The artist even designed a family coat of arms, working from a Palazzo family crest featured in a book on Italian heraldry.

For the restaurant's lounge, Kosa designed a latticed ceiling draped with grapevines. "Our bar ceiling was a scalloped wood covered with bead-embedded carpet," recalled Chris Palazzo Febinger, one of the owner's two daughters. "The space was enhanced with beautiful lighting techniques." Meanwhile, the restaurant's heavily upholstered—and remarkably comfortable—chairs were supplied by Gasser Chair, which is still located on Logan Avenue in Youngstown.

The striking interior of Palazzo's Restaurant, located on the South Side's Midlothian Boulevard, reflected the pervasive influence of designer Victor Kosa. *Courtesy of Laurie Palazzo Sunyog.*

Mary Palazzo played a crucial role in the restaurant's success. A talented cook, she was also a "workhorse" when it came to the restaurant's daily operation. Identified as "Mama Palazzo" in the restaurant's promotional material, she presided over the kitchen. Her daughter Laurie Palazzo Sunyog recalled that all of the restaurant's entrées were "made from scratch," and several specialties—including Palazzo's cavetelli, ravioli and zabaglione—were prepared in accordance with family recipes. This was also true of the restaurant's signature red sauce, based on a recipe from the family's ancestral town in the Abruzzo region.

Palazzo's neighbors included Berndt's Restaurant & Cocktail Lounge, which sat on the corner of Midlothian Boulevard and Shirley Road. Berndt's was owned and operated by Pearl Furbee Berndt, a talented cook and entrepreneur who drew her entire family into the enterprise. "Grandma was a tough German American woman who didn't take much flack," her granddaughter, Paula Berndt, recalled. "She ran a really tight ship, but she was fair, and people really loved her. For that time, she was an extremely ambitious and resourceful woman."

Despite the presence of a cocktail lounge, Berndt's was known as a family restaurant. Bob Casey recalled that his mother, Winifred Kelley Casey, belonged

Berndt's Restaurant, located on the city's South Side, was popular with local families and known for its home-style baked goods. *Courtesy of Paula Berndt.*

to a women's organization whose members met for dinner twice a year, around Christmas and Easter. "They met at Berndt's quite a bit," he said. "I remember that they had great homemade pies, and it was just a nice, pleasant restaurant."

For members of the Berndt family, the restaurant wasn't merely a business; it served as the site of numerous dinners and get-togethers. "Some of my earliest memories involve hanging out at the restaurant," Paula Berndt noted. "I remember sitting in the kitchen with the pastry chef while she was making my grandmother's chocolate Bavarian pies or strawberry Bavarian pies, which we were always known for."

Over the decades, Pearl Berndt's descendants derived more than memories from their involvement in the family business. Pearl's son, the late Thomas Berndt, eventually opened the Hasti House Restaurant in downtown Youngstown, and he went on to establish the Village Bakery & Deli in nearby Columbiana, Ohio. Meanwhile, Paula Berndt and her brother, John, served for a time as proprietors of JP's Downtown Grill in Youngstown. More recently, John Berndt, one of the area's notable chefs, established his own restaurant, Johnny's, which operates in Boardman.

Farther to the west, and just south of Midlothian Boulevard, on Hillman Way, sat the Newport Deli. Like its neighbor, the Golden Drumstick, the Newport Deli was technically in Boardman, but its proximity to the city ensured that it would be popular among South Side residents. Established by Stella and Alan Ziegler, the business had the distinction of being the only Jewish delicatessen to serve the South Side in the 1960s.

The Newport Deli's location was a natural choice for Alan Ziegler, whose family had owned and operated Boardman's first grocery store. Alan Ziegler entered the business with skills including a knack for dealing with the public. His stepdaughter, Wendy Aron, said that he reminded her of Fred MacMurray's character in the 1960s television sitcom *My Three Sons*. "I can't remember that he ever raised his voice or swore," she said.

Stella Ziegler, a former medical worker, brought other gifts to the partnership, including excellent cooking skills and a knack for developing recipes. "My mother was very artistic," Mrs. Aron observed. "So when they catered an event, everything was beautifully presented."

Wendy Aron, daughter of Stella and Alan Ziegler, poses in the main dining area of the Newport Delicatessen, a traditional Jewish deli that catered to residents of Youngstown's South Side and Boardman Township. *Courtesy of Wendy Aron.*

During its years of operation, the Newport Deli was known for its corned beef (prepared in-house), homemade potato salad, rich soups and New York cheesecake. "I remember that, when they made the corned beef, they boiled it on the stove, and then they cooled it slowly by running cold water over it," Mrs. Aron recalled. "They always had three or four briskets cooking on the stove, in large pots with lids."

Before his death in the 1970s, Alan Ziegler made monthly trips to Cleveland to secure baked goods that were difficult to find in Youngstown. "There was a pleasant odor of food whenever I walked in, and my mother always had the radio playing," Mrs. Aron recalled. "My mother liked country and western music, so you had country and western music playing in the Jewish deli."

The South Side also hosted scores of taverns and lounges that provided tasty food at a modest price. "The taverns around the South Side were neat," recalled Loretta Ekoniak, who grew up in the neighborhood. "There was the Wonder Inn, the Drift Inn and the Cactus Bar…They had these neat names, and I have vivid memories of going into them with my dad, usually for fish

An advertisement for the Newport Delicatessen promotes the Zieglers' home-style corned beef during the period leading up to Passover. *Courtesy of Wendy Aron.*

on Fridays." She noted that it wasn't unusual for her entire family to go to a tavern for dinner.

Less than a mile to the northwest of the Newport Deli stood the Crystal Tavern & Spaghetti House, located near the corner of Sherwood and Glenwood Avenues, not far from Courtney's Steakhouse. "We used to go there every Friday," recalled Joseph Planey. "I liked the way they divided the place into two sections, so you wouldn't feel bad bringing children into the restaurant because you weren't in the same space as potentially heavy drinkers."

Many of the most popular taverns, however, were located east of Market Street on South Avenue. Among them, the Coconut Grove, in particular, earned a reputation for quality food and generous portions. "You'd get an antipasto there, and it was a platter that would serve four to six people, and it was supposed to be a one-person serving," Bob Casey recalled.

Meanwhile, fans of Eastern European food gravitated to Pauline Bakalik's Ramp Tavern, which introduced homemade pierogi in the 1960s. The proprietor's son, Bob Bakalik, recalled that his mother and her longtime friend Ann Dubiel made several hundred of the stuffed dumplings one evening and decided to sell them at the bar. "She told me that she was amazed she managed to sell those pierogi," he said. "Up to that time, no one was selling pierogi commercially."

A few years later, when the business was forced to close due to highway construction, the Bakalik family purchased a vacant club near the corner of East Ravenwood and South Avenues, where they established Boomba's

The South Side's Boulevard Tavern, in operation since the 1930s, retains the atmosphere of a neighborhood restaurant-bar. *Courtesy of Thomas G. Welsh Jr.*

Lounge. "From those two hundred to three hundred pierogi my mother made that first day, it eventually ended up that we were selling thousands every Friday," Bob Bakalik recalled. "On the bigger holidays, Christmas and Easter, our production would go up to ten thousand or twelve thousand per week."

Another typical family-owned tavern of the era was Nudo's, which operated on South Avenue between 1934 and 1951, when proprietor Theresa Nudo retired due to illness. "On Friday evenings, it was standing room only when they served their fish dinners," recalled Joseph Nudo, the proprietor's son. "On Saturdays, people came in droves for my mother's homemade spaghetti with chicken sauce, which was our signature dish."

Undoubtedly, the most popular tavern-restaurant of the South Side was the Boulevard, which continues to operate under new management on the corner of Southern Boulevard and East Ravenwood Avenue. Located in the vicinity of St. Dominic Church, the Boulevard had its origins in a neighborhood grocery store that had been established by Italian immigrant Martin Petrella, who reopened it as a spaghetti house in 1937.

Ten years later, in 1947, Petrella's sons, Ange and Joe, took over the business and introduced the Boulevard's popular Friday fish dinners. The business continued to grow, and in 1961, the Petrella brothers added a back room to the building in order to accommodate the Boulevard's growing base of customers.

As the years passed, the owners offered patrons more than homemade Italian-style food; they also provided a feeling of continuity in a changing community. Indeed, a 1970s newspaper description of the restaurant's clientele could have been written three decades earlier. "In the queue are children in parents' or grandparents' arms, toddlers, pre-teens, teens and inbetweens," the *Vindicator* reported. "There are minks and jeans, safety shoes and tennis shoes, clerical collars, white collars, blue collars."[64]

Some patrons indicated that they practically grew up in the restaurant. "As an infant I was here, and I remember eating spaghetti at the Boulevard," observed longtime customer Dr. Fred Kurz. "Later, I remember bringing my boys, Fred and Jeff, here to eat."

Meanwhile, some part-time staff members have worked at the restaurant, on and off, for decades. Retired restaurateur Douglas M. Bouslough attended St. Dominic Elementary School with Ange Petrella's son, Nick, and gained his first exposure to the restaurant industry at the Boulevard. "I met Nicky in the summer of fifth grade, going into sixth," Bouslough recalled. "He took me over to the Boulevard Tavern, and we had a spaghetti dinner and a Coke, sitting in those big wooden booths…It was fabulous."

When he was old enough, Bouslough secured a coveted position on the restaurant's all-male waitstaff. "The whole Petrella family—the uncles, the fathers, the grandfathers—took a turn working there," he recalled. Nick's uncle, Joe Petrella, worked in the kitchen, while his father, Ange, handled the front end.

On Friday evening, Jimmy "Skip" DeMichael, Martin's brother-in-law, ran the floor. "That guy never used a writing pad to take an order," Bouslough noted. "He kept in his mind what you ordered, went in and wrote it down; and then, when it came time for you to leave, he wrote everything up for you and gave you the bill."

Dining on the East Side

Despite postwar zoning trends that sharpened distinctions between commercial and residential districts, many restaurants and eateries continued to serve as neighborhood gathering places. Family-owned restaurants and hamburger joints alike played a role in drawing people together. Youngstown's East Side, traditionally separated from the rest of the city by the Crab Creek Valley, fostered its share of distinctive restaurants and eateries.

Vic & Syl's Curb Service, established in the late 1940s on the corner of McCartney and Jacobs Roads, was among the district's most popular youth hangouts. Teenagers and young adults from the East Side and neighboring

Campbell, Ohio, appreciated the friendliness of proprietors Sylvester and Victoria Frazzini, and they were also drawn by the novelty of curb service.

"It was a '50s-style restaurant with a jukebox," recalled Rose Makosky, whose parents owned and operated Vic & Syl's. "When the teenagers wanted you to wait on them, they would flash their headlights, and we'd go out and take their orders. Then we'd come out with the trays that you could hang on the car windows."

Mrs. Makosky was ten years old when her parents opened the business as a frozen custard stand. "One day, a truck was delivering the milk to make the custard," she recalled. "He got too close to the building, and as he was leaving, he pulled the top of the building with him." Her father, Sylvester Frazzini, used compensation from the accident to build a new family home, with an addition including a restaurant and a new custard stand.

The proprietor's son, Sylvester Frazzini Jr., recalled that his father held two jobs while running the restaurant. "He would get up in the morning and open the restaurant, and then he would go and drive a school bus for the City of Youngstown," he explained. "Then, he'd leave there, and he'd go to J.W. McCauley Co., which installed awnings and did porch enclosures; and around 2:30 p.m., he'd pick up the bus and drive the kids home from school, go back to finish his second job and come back to the restaurant and work till closing time."

Meanwhile, his mother, Victoria Frazzini, managed the kitchen, greeted customers and engaged in crowd control. "What I enjoyed most was watching my mother interact with people," Sylvester Jr. said. "You'd have kids hanging out in the parking lot of the restaurant, and they were hoodlums; some people would be afraid to go out and break them up. Well, she'd go right out there in the middle of them—and they listened to my mother."

Before it closed in 1958, Vic & Syl's became known for its hot sausage sandwiches, foot-long hotdogs and banana splits, although the restaurant also served full meals. "Our dinners were cheap," Rose Makosky noted. "They had a steak dinner for a dollar, and you would get your French fries and rolls and coffee. We would get families to come in, because the dinners were so economical."

Vic & Syl's was a close neighbor of another East Side landmark, Gaetano's Airport Tavern, also located on McCartney Road, across from what had been the largest airport between Cleveland and Pittsburgh until 1951. (The twenty-two-acre plot of ground eventually became the site of a flea market.) "The Airport Tavern was directly across the street from us," recalled Sylvester Frazzini Jr. "It was a nice sit-down restaurant with a great atmosphere." Like many customers, Frazzini enjoyed the restaurant's spare ribs. "I've never had better spare ribs in my whole life, to this day," he said.

Frazzini noted that his uncle, Joseph Frazzini, often took advantage of the restaurant's takeout service, and the tavern's ribs became the centerpiece of family gatherings. "I don't know how he had the money, but my uncle would buy four or five racks of ribs and bring them back to his house," Frazzini recalled. "All the nephews would go over there, and we'd eat ribs all night long."

Other customers were drawn by the Airport Tavern's Italian cuisine. Fred Ross recalled that he and his wife, Josephine, dined at the restaurant on Friday evenings. "They had ribs that were great, which my wife enjoyed, because she didn't eat calamari," Ross said. "They served a calamari sauce over *capellini* that was almost second to none." Ross added that a portion of the restaurant's menu was printed in Italian.

Diners seeking a more rarefied atmosphere frequented Chicone's Restaurant on the corner of Albert Street and McGuffey Road. Former customer Richard S. Scarsella described a "warm and intimate" environment supplemented with good service. "It was a very nice, semiformal—not casual—restaurant, and popular with East Side, North Side and downtown business leaders," he said. "Members of the Cafaro family were regulars, because the McGuffey Plaza was nearby." Chicone's specialties, he added, included an "excellent" hot turkey sandwich served with homemade mashed potatoes.

A more typical East Side eatery was the Castle, housed in a white stucco building on the corner of Poland Avenue and Center Street, not far from the Center Street Bridge. With its tile roofing and mock turret, the eatery was a welcome sight to generations of steelworkers who labored in the mills that stretched along Poland Avenue.

Built in the early 1920s, the Castle had been owned and operated by Edward and Nancy (DeGise) Nappy since 1947.[65] The couple was known for serving good food at a reasonable price. "They specialized in breakfast and lunch," recalled George Pavlich, whose family operated the nearby Flat Iron Café. "I remember that for $1.02, or something like that, you could get bacon and eggs and toast and coffee—unbelievable prices."

Fred Ross often stopped at the Castle for breakfast. "They specialized in a superb old-fashioned breakfast—fried potatoes with eggs and ham and bacon and homemade bread," he said. "When you left there, you were full." Ross noted that while Nancy Nappy staffed the counter—chatting with customers and refilling cups of coffee—Ed "would be back in the kitchen, peeking out that little window once in awhile."

Good food wasn't the Castle's only attraction. The restaurant's regular customers appreciated the Nappys' kindness and consideration. "They knew

The Castle, located at the intersection of Poland Avenue and Center Street, offered hearty food at a reasonable price for workers at surrounding industrial plants. *Courtesy of the Mahoning Valley Historical Society.*

everything that was going on in the area of the mills," Fred Ross recalled. "They were open for the people that were going to work at 7:00 a.m. at Republic Steel and those that were coming off the midnight turn...The prices were great, and there was never a problem of money—if you didn't have it, they fed you."

The Castle's closest neighbor was the Flat Iron Café, on the corner of Poland Avenue and Shirley Road. The structure was built in the 1920s by Croatian immigrant George Pavlich, who arrived in Youngstown with his wife and four children via McKeesport, Pennsylvania. "The building was called a 'flatiron' because it looked like a piece of iron when you ran it through a press," explained the founder's grandson, George, who was named in his honor.

Pavlich originally opened a confectionary on the spot, but after securing a liquor license in 1934, he closed the business and opened a bar. "My father, Anthony, and his brother, Joseph, both worked for my grandfather at the time," George Pavlich said. "They continued to work there when the new addition to the Flat Iron Café was built in 1946."

Following the deaths of his brother and father—in 1953 and 1954, respectively—Anthony Pavlich took over the business and operated it for the next twenty years. "There were three major shifts at the mills—the 11:00

p.m. to 7:00 a.m. shift, the 7:00 a.m. to 3:00 p.m. shift and the 3:00 p.m. to 11:00 p.m. shift," George Pavlich recalled. "We were continually in the flow of those shifts."

While the Flat Iron Café offered little in the way of food, besides pickled eggs and potato chips, Anthony Pavlich often treated customers to a traditional Balkan feast. "At one point, my father and some of the guys formed a club they called the Flat Iron Club, and he built a shack out back where they would barbecue lamb," George Pavlich explained. "On those occasions, the lamb was served on the house, no charge."

Other neighborhood eateries included the Ritz, the Center and the Workingman's Tavern. Those with a craving for ribs patronized Foy's Bar-B-Que on Wilson Avenue in the East Side's Haselton District. "When I would go, about 2:30 in the morning, everything else was closed," recalled Tom Price. "They had this huge grill, and the ribs were stacked up maybe a foot high...Their ribs were absolutely the best, and the people there always treated you like a million dollars."

Farther to the northeast, on the main thoroughfare of McCartney Road, stood the popular Beacon Restaurant, which (like Vic & Syl's) offered curb service and drew a younger crowd. Travelers moving west, past the point where McCartney Road merged into Oak Street, eventually encountered Orlando Nolfi's and Dave Mazzaca's Lincoln Park Tavern. "It was always crowded during the weekends," area resident Richard Koker recalled. "They were really known for their hot sausage sandwiches."

As Oak Street wound to the northwest, it cut through the center of an Italian American neighborhood whose landmarks included Immaculate Conception Church. In the shadow of the nineteenth-century edifice stood another neighborhood fixture, the Royal Oaks Tavern, whose specialties included chili dogs, sausage sandwiches and pasta fagioli. "They had a hot dog machine where I have my Jagermeister machine today," explained Lou Kennedy, the tavern's current co-owner. "It was always steamed hot dogs and steamed buns and chili."

Dining on the North Side

Travelers moving west along Oak Street eventually found themselves on East Rayen Avenue, where the North Side enclave of Smoky Hollow came into view. Those approaching the neighborhood just south of Smoky Hollow could make out the dome and spire of Our Lady of Mount Carmel and Sts.

Cyril & Methodius Catholic Churches, testaments to the area's large Italian and Slovak American populations.

Less visible, though equally vibrant, was the district's Spanish American population, which expanded slightly in the late 1930s, when the Spanish Civil War drove some refugees into the area. Most onlookers, however, failed to distinguish these residents from the neighborhood's larger Italian American population, given that many of them belonged to the Italian national parish of Our Lady of Mount Carmel.

The community's leaders included Francisco Roca, who operated a small restaurant on Wood Street that sat across from Sts. Cyril & Methodius Church. "He established the restaurant some time before World War II, and it continued to operate into the '50s," recalled Pearl Berezo Sinistro, a member of the local Spanish American community. "At that time, there were still a lot of young, single Spaniards living in and around the Smoky Hollow district and the East Side. They would congregate at Casa Sevilla, where Señor Roca would make sure they had a good home-cooked dinner."

Among Casa Sevilla's specialties was *sopa cocida*, a soup consisting of ham, rice, garbanzo beans and a traditional sausage known as chorizo. "After the soup was cooked, Señor Roca would remove the beans, ham and sausage, which would be served separately," Mrs. Sinistro explained. "The broth was very smooth and very rich."

The most well-known business in the Smoky Hollow district was Casa Sevilla's northern neighbor, the Mahoning Valley Restaurant, or MVR, located on the other side of Oak Street, at the point where rolling Walnut Street flattened out into the basin of the hollow that gave the neighborhood its name.

Established by Carmine Cassese, a youthful immigrant from Naples, Italy, the business had its origins in a pool hall that operated on the site in the 1920s. "My father's original house was right where you're sitting—at the bar, here," explained Carmine Cassese's son, eighty-two-year-old Joseph Cassese, as he gestured toward the restaurant's hand-carved bar. "They moved the whole house back, put it on logs and rolled it back, with horses."

With the repeal of Prohibition in December 1933, Carmine Cassese, along with scores of other small business owners, rushed to secure a liquor license. "In 1934, this was the first issuance of a liquor license in Youngstown, Ohio," Joseph Cassese claimed. "We were registered as the MVR—the Mahoning Valley Restaurant—but a lot of people just called it 'Cassese's bar.'"

In those days, he noted, the business offered modest fare. "Most of our customers were the shot-and-beer guys from the neighborhood," he said. "My grandmother Cathy set up a small kitchen in a little cubby hole that

The Mahoning Valley Restaurant (MVR), located in the North Side's Smoky Hollow neighborhood, slowly evolved from a neighborhood bar into one of the city's most enduring Italian American restaurants. *Courtesy of Carmine Cassese.*

was just beyond the bar—and that was the first kitchen." While the MVR occasionally served breakfast, the tavern's menu developed slowly over time.

By the early 1960s, Joseph Cassese had taken over the business from his father, Carmine, who had passed away during the previous decade. "I suppose the food trade started to develop when I took over, and a lot of the credit goes to my wife, Carmella—a great cook," he said. "We still use her recipe for meatballs, and we roll them fresh, about six hundred or seven hundred a week."

Meanwhile, Joseph Cassese's son, Carmine (named in honor of his grandfather), was already helping out. "I always loved coming down here," Carmine Cassese recalled in a December 2012 interview. "I don't want to say I was tending bar illegally, but I was working behind the bar when I was ten years old…because I loved it…I poured pop. I grabbed beers. I did whatever."

The tavern's clientele, he said, was like an extended family. "It was family and old-timers and shot-and-beer [customers]," Carmine Cassese recalled. "It was an era where that was fine…and my dad was always there. And we had great relationships with our customers."

A Moveable Feast

The surrounding neighborhood, while still populous, showed signs of decline. "The Hollow had fifty or sixty businesses at one time," Carmine Cassese noted. "You had everything within walking distance...I got my hair cut right across the street until I started high school, which was 1969." He added, however, that the neighborhood featured a growing number of vacant lots. "There [were] mostly remnants of...where the tailor shop was, where the funeral [home] was, where the body shop was," he explained.

Yet in what proved to be an extraordinary case of adaptability, Joseph and Carmine Cassese managed to turn the MVR into a major destination for local diners, even as the surrounding neighborhood practically disappeared. This occurred later, however.

The district to the west of Smoky Hollow was also changing, mainly due to the growth of Youngstown College (later Youngstown State University). In the 1950s and early '60s, the leafy district that abutted campus was still dotted with mansions dating back to Youngstown's industrial heyday. Some of these stately edifices were acquired by the college for reuse as classrooms and offices, but scores of others were pulled down to make way for new construction.

While most students and faculty members patronized restaurants in nearby downtown, the campus area hosted a number of eateries that drew a segment of the college crowd. A convenient destination for many was the restaurant at the Lincoln Hotel, a drab brick building that stood at the corner of Lincoln Avenue and Phelps Street until the early 1960s. "It was reasonably priced, and it was right across the street from campus," recalled Nick Pacalo, who attended Youngstown College in the 1950s. "You could order a sandwich and maybe soup and stay within your budget." Josephine Houser, also a student at the time, recalled the restaurant's chocolate and peanut butter sundaes and sticky rolls, which she described as "delicious."

No less popular was the Wickwood restaurant, located on Wick Avenue between East Rayen and Wood Street. The restaurant was often crowded, but its dependence on students and Sunday worshippers limited it to serving breakfasts and other light fare—a situation that contributed to the Wickwood's closing in the late 1960s. "You had the Sunday crowd and the college students," recalled Gregory Speero Jr., whose family operated the restaurant. "They got volume but not too much profit."

Students and professionals alike stopped in for breakfast and a cup of coffee at the Toddle House, less than a half mile north of the Wickwood. Like its southern neighbor, the Toddle House offered cheap fare and depended on high-volume sales. Open twenty-four hours a day, the diner became a preferred destination for local fraternity brothers, recalled James D. Bennett, who made late-night "runs" for the Toddle House's homemade-style chili but also enjoyed one of its signature desserts. "They had a specialty called an icebox pie, which was like a pudding with whipped cream," Bennett said.

He and his fraternity brothers also frequented a campus-area sandwich shop known as Cioffi's. "It was just north of the downtown," Bennett recalled. "It was a carryout place, and they had great Philly sandwiches. We'd order our food and take it straight back to the fraternity house."

Meanwhile, scores of students and faculty members journeyed a mile north of campus to stop for burgers, beer and conversation at the Golden Dawn Restaurant. "A good friend of mine, Jack Pearson, and I used to walk up from our zoology class at night and stop in for a beer," recalled Nick Pacalo. "It was a nice quiet place...not like some college hangouts, where a lot of students would be in there revving it up."

From its inception, the Golden Dawn Restaurant was noted for its friendly, orderly environment. Founded by Andrew and Marycarmen Naples in 1934, the restaurant initially occupied a building on the corner of Elm Street and Madison Avenue, just north of present-day Youngstown State University.

Andrew Naples, a man of quiet authority, showed no tolerance for the habits of America's pre-Prohibition saloon culture. "You had to behave yourself," explained Andrew Naples's son Carmen. "When they first opened, some of the guys...were used to spitting on the floor. So, my dad said, 'Could you do that out in the hall?'"

The proprietor also insisted that workers at the restaurant maintain a respectable appearance. Male staff members were required to be clean-shaven and to wear a fresh shirt and tie during business hours, and Andrew Naples himself was often resplendently attired in a shirt, tie and pressed bar jacket. The Italian immigrant's insistence on decorum and civility helped turn the restaurant into a popular destination for professionals, business leaders, politicians, unionists and steelworkers. Over the years, the Golden Dawn's clientele would continue to reflect a broad cross-section of the community.

In 1937, the business made the first of several relocations, when the district surrounding the Elm Street restaurant was abruptly declared "dry." Therefore, the Golden Dawn relocated to a spot on Phelps Street, just north of downtown Youngstown. Within a year, the restaurant relocated a third time, to the first of two locations on Logan Avenue. In 1946, the business moved to its current address, 1245 Logan Avenue.

In the face of multiple relocations, one thing remained constant—the Golden Dawn's homemade Italian fare. "My grandmother's recipes were in everything," recalled Marycarmen Naples's grandson, Tim Curtin. "Originally,

This May 1942 photograph was taken at the Golden Dawn Restaurant's third location, at 1219 Logan Avenue, a block from its current site. Pictured are some of the restaurant's regulars, including (left to right) longtime waitress Emma, local physician "Doc" Nutt, Carmel Naples, Kester Jenkins, owner Andrew Naples, "Bud" Montana, Jack Sweeney and Al Lindsey. *Courtesy of Marycarmen Curtis Kelly.*

it was my grandmother's spaghetti sauce." Curtin's sister, Marycarmen Curtin Kelly, described her grandmother's commitment to quality when she prepared the restaurant's signature red sauce. Mrs. Kelly explained that her grandmother and mother, Carmel Naples Curtin, regularly purchased bushels of tomatoes from a farm in Hubbard, Ohio, and boiled them down in the restaurant's basement to make the base for their sauce.

Likewise, members of the Naples family prepared the restaurant's pizza dough from scratch, while grinding fresh pork for Italian sausage. The restaurant's popularity was enhanced by the fact that its food was reasonably priced. "I didn't discover it until the '60s," recalled Dr. George D. Beelen. "And even in the '60s, you'd get a very, very nice luncheon for two dollars and thirty-five cents."

By the outset of the 1960s, the Golden Dawn was owned and managed by Andrew Naples's sons, Ralph and Carmen, who attracted other graduates of Rayen High School, better known as the "Rayen School." Notable alumni who visited the restaurant included Hollywood actor Joe Flynn, who had a history with the establishment. "Ed O'Neill's cousin, Joey Flynn, who was in *McHale's Navy*, would come in here when he was a little boy," explained Tim Curtin, "and my mother used to give him candy at the end of the bar."

Elm Street Attractions

Residents traveling west of the Golden Dawn eventually encountered the Elm Street Delicatessen. Since 1946, the business had occupied a spot at the edge of the Elm Street Bridge, a closed-spandrel arch bridge between Tod Lane and Saranac Avenue. The delicatessen, however, had been established seven years earlier, in 1939, at a site located a half mile to the south, near the corner of Elm Street and Thornton Avenue.

In the late 1930s, the restaurant's founders, Herb and Rose Kravitz, were still in their twenties, and they were mired in the challenges of the Depression. Despite their youth, the pair had acquired some professional experience. Rose Kravitz worked in the gourmet food department at downtown's McKelvey's Department Store, while her husband, Herb, was employed as an insurance agent, although health issues forced him to consider another career.

As Rose and Herb Kravitz considered their next move, they learned that Rose's mother, Sidonia Hirschl, had rented a vacant space on Elm Street, with plans to turn it into a knitting shop. Aware of the couple's desire to become self-employed, Mrs. Hirschl approached her daughter and asked if she were interested in renting the space instead. "We didn't have any money, but that didn't hold us back," Rose Kravitz recalled in 2010. "We didn't even know that you had to have money to open a business."

Strapped for cash but brimming with ideas, the couple secured credit from suppliers, while bartering with local handymen to bring the facility up to code. "So we went ahead and decided to open this food business," Rose Kravitz recalled. "And we got credit from our meat company. We got credit from the fixture people—and then, we had to borrow money for change."

During its first decade of operation, the Elm Street Delicatessen shared a crowded row building with Sturgeon's Market, a Maytag appliance store and a doctor's office. Ultimately, the restaurant was profitable, and despite challenges that included the onset of wartime food rationing, the Kravitzes were in a position to purchase a building that would accommodate their expanding business and growing family.

With two daughters in tow, the Kravitzes selected the new site on Elm Street because its assets included a seven-room apartment. "You had the

The Elm Street Delicatessen, founded by Rose and Herbert Kravitz, became a popular North Side gathering spot after World War II. The business reemerged as Kravitz's Delicatessen after its relocation to Liberty Township in 1970. *Courtesy of Solomon "Jack" Kravitz.*

apartment upstairs, over the store, and it was beautiful—overlooked Crandall Park," Mrs. Kravitz recalled. "It was real, real nice, and we stayed there about twenty years."

The proximity of the family's living quarters made it possible for Rose and Herb Kravitz to play the role of attentive parents while running a full-time business. At the same time, the boundary separating the family's public and private lives grew more tenuous.

"When my parents were running the delicatessen on Elm Street, there was definitely a lack of privacy," recalled Linda Kravitz Kantor, the couple's oldest daughter. "There was a buzzer system in place. My mother would buzz once for Donia, and she would buzz twice for me; and at that point, we were expected to run downstairs, no matter what we happened to be doing at the time."

Despite such disruptions, the Kravitz children enjoyed quality time with their parents. "The deli business, back then, was a very demanding business, time-wise," noted Donia Kravitz Foster, Linda's younger sister. "But my family always did get together for dinner…and every Friday night, the family would go out together."

The delicatessen was known mainly for its corned beef, which was cooked on site. By the 1950s and early '60s, however, customers also appreciated the establishment's baked goods. The couple's son, Jack, who currently operates Kravitz's Delicatessen in Liberty, explained that his parents "bought out a bakery" in the 1940s and began to produce pastries and other goods that they had previously purchased in Cleveland.

Surprisingly, one of the last items to be produced in-house was the delicatessen's signature bagel. When Rose Kravitz decided to carry bagels, she contacted her friend Dora Schwebel, proprietor of Youngstown's Schwebel's Bakery, and asked her to make them for the delicatessen. While Mrs. Schwebel had no interest in manufacturing bagels, she agreed to show Rose how to make them herself. "My mom tweaked the recipe to what she liked, and the original Kravitz bagel was started," Jack Kravitz explained.

The bagels were a hit, and when Sunday school let out at nearby Temple Emanuel, scores of customers crowded into the delicatessen. "We would go through a hundred dozen bagels on a Sunday morning, and they were handmade," Jack Kravitz recalled. "One of my memories from childhood is going downstairs, and all the bakers would be rolling the bagels out by hand on the table."

While the Elm Street Delicatessen was popular among members of the local Jewish community, it also attracted residents of the immediate neighborhood, who reflected a broad spectrum of the North Side's population. "We had St. Edward's [Church] around the corner, so we had lots of Irish Catholics," recalled Donia Kravitz Foster. "We had people from Eastern Europe...And we also had...the Scandinavian community."

The Kravitzes accommodated the neighborhood's Swedish American population by stocking items such as *lutefisk* and lingonberries. These Swedish delicacies became such fixtures at the delicatessen that Ms. Foster grew up thinking they were traditional Jewish foods. "The line was very blurred for what was traditionally Jewish and what was from the other backgrounds, because it was involved in the same way—and with the same respect—as if it [were] mine," she noted.

Farther north, on the corner of Elm Street and Dennick Avenue, stood Nudel's Delicatessen, which was established in 1962 by Ben and Minerva Nudel. Over the years, Ben Nudell had held positions at Youngstown Sheet & Tube and other industrial companies, but he decided to take a gamble when a building at the end of his street was put up for sale.

"We had no background in the restaurant business up to that point," recalled ninety-year-old Minerva Nudel. "We carried a lot of the kosher

This undated photograph shows Minerva Nudel at the counter of Nudel's Deli, which she operated with her husband, Ben, on the city's North Side. *Courtesy of Carole Nudel Sherman.*

foods. We used to go to Cleveland on Saturday mornings and bring back bagels and coffee cakes—a whole carful of stuff from Cleveland."

Most items, however, were produced on site, recalled Mrs. Nudel's daughter, Carole Nudel Sherman. "At that time, everything was homemade and brought in fresh," she explained. "The corned beef was raw and uncooked, and you had to boil the potatoes to make the potato salad. There was no such thing as jarred potato salad."

Mrs. Sherman added that her mother grated fresh cabbage for the coleslaw, while her father sheared razor-thin slices from a smoked fish to produce lox. "Nowadays, you can get lox that's already sliced in a tray," she said. "My father would cut it by hand with a sharp knife, and people would come in and watch him slice it…It wasn't pre-sliced, so it wouldn't dry out."

During religious holidays, Minerva Nudel's mother, Sarah Chazonoff, baked traditional pastries, which were sold at the delicatessen. "She made the best sponge cake and honey cake in all of Youngstown," Mrs. Sherman recalled. "She made air *kitchels*, which were a kind of light-as-air cookie. She made *tegalach*, a dough ball containing honey and nuts, which we sold during Rosh Hashanah."

While Minerva Nudel gained a reputation for her homemade stuffed cabbages and tastefully arranged trays, her husband, Ben, was known for his kindness and consideration. "My dad was a people pleaser," explained Mrs.

Sherman. "If it was pouring down rain, and a customer was parked along Elm Street, he would go out in the rain and get their car and pull it up to the door so that they could get in their car."

Sadly, the family business did not survive Ben Nudel's untimely death at the age of fifty-one. More than four decades later, his children continue to look back fondly on the family business. "We were very close," recalled Stan Nudell, Mrs. Sherman's brother. "Being involved in the delicatessen heightened our awareness of the importance of family life."

Approaching the Northern Limits

A few blocks to the west of Elm Street ran the main artery of Belmont Avenue, which stretched north from the downtown area into the expanding suburb of Liberty Township. By the 1960s, the portion of Belmont Avenue located to the north of Gypsy Lane—the traditional dividing line between Youngstown and Liberty—was the site of a glittering commercial strip that challenged the supremacy of downtown Youngstown.

The segment of Belmont Avenue located south of Gypsy Lane, however, still hosted a cluster of businesses that included some of the area's popular dining spots. These ranged from barbecue joints and family-friendly taverns to full-fledged restaurants.

In the 1960s, the neighborhood between Wood Street and Madison Avenue was a bustling African American business district that featured several notable barbecue restaurants. None was more established than Bill Robinson's Bar-B-Que, located in a converted house that stood at the intersection of West Rayen and Belmont Avenues.

Founder Bill Robinson established the business in the late 1930s, drawing on a barbecue recipe secured from an elderly widow who relocated to Youngstown from the Deep South. Local restaurateur Charlie Staples, who purchased Robinson's business in the 1970s, noted that Robinson had been in the furniture repair business and got the barbecue recipe as part of a bartering arrangement. "She told him that [she] and her husband had made a lot of money in the barbecue business," Staples explained. "And she said, 'You give me this particular price on this furniture, and I'll sell you this sauce.'"

By the 1960s, Bill Robinson's business had a rival in Garland's Bar-B-Que, established by a former employee of Robinson's and later taken over by Arthur "Sonnyman" Hopson. Garland's continues to operate in a brick building between Grant and West Scott Streets, and its customers include actor Ed O'Neill, who stops in during visits to the Youngstown area. "It wasn't the most attractive place in the world, but they had just about the best ribs in town," recalled Elder Rosetta Carter, who grew up on the North Side.

Bill Robinson's and Garland's were subsequently joined by Young's Cop-n-Shop and, later on, the Pit. Then, in the early 1970s, Bill Robinson's Bar-B-Que was officially replaced by C. Staples' Bar-B-Que. "He'd been right there on that corner for thirty-five years before I took over," Charlie Staples recalled. "In 1974, the Bill Robinson sign came down, and the C. Staples sign went up."

Decades later, barbecue continues to hold a special place in the local restaurant industry. "Youngstown has world-class barbecue," contended Charlie Staples. "You start from scratch, from tomatoes, vinegar, and work your way on through…The other thing is, it's still cooked on…charcoals… the way barbecue was one hundred years ago."

Farther up on Belmont Avenue, in a district just beyond St. Elizabeth's Hospital, stood Avalon Gardens, a North Side landmark since the late 1930s. The tavern was owned and operated by Gennaro Massullo, a native of Bagnolese, Italy, who arrived in the area as a teenager. After operating a barbershop from 1920 to 1938, Massulo decided to open a neighborhood bar.[66]

"They had apartments on top of the building; and my father, Edmund, and his brother, Mario, and his mom and dad lived up there," explained Anne Massullo Sabella, the proprietor's granddaughter and current owner of Avalon Downtown, an eatery in downtown Youngstown. "The business was always known as Avalon Gardens, and I…think the name goes back to the stories of King Arthur's Court," she added.

Avalon Gardens was known for its tasty Italian food, which was prepared by Gennaro Massullo's wife, Lena. The menu, combined with the tavern's convivial atmosphere, ensured its rise as one of the city's most celebrated gathering spots. "It's amazing to me the number of people who talk so fondly about it," Mrs. Sabella said. "I suppose the Avalon was to the North Side what the Boulevard was to the South Side. It was a neighborhood place where everyone knew each other."

By the mid-1960s, Gennaro Massullo was nearing his seventieth birthday. Yet he continued to operate the tavern until 1971. At that point, he sold the business to Michael Sabella Sr., who, years later, became his granddaughter's father-in-law. "Obviously, I was very young, and I was never planning to marry the son of the man who bought the family business," Mrs. Sabella explained. "It was kind of weird, to say the least."

Fans of Italian food were also drawn to the Bell-Fair restaurant, located three blocks south of Avalon Gardens in a neighborhood that bordered Belmont Avenue. "The Bell-Fair restaurant was connected to a bar, but their menu was very good—strictly Italian," Fred Ross recalled. "They served good pizza, and their antipasto salads were very famous at that time."

Since the early 1950s, the restaurant had been owned and operated by Orlando Thomas and his brother-in-law, Frank Julian, whose entrées were prepared with fresh ingredients. "Our red sauce was fantastic," recalled Orlando Thomas's son, John, adding that the sauce contributed to the popularity of the Bell-Fair's pizza.

The neighborhood hosted several other Italian restaurants, including the Victoria Café, the Venetian, Ambrosio's and Lavanty's—all known for their pizza. The first of these operations to appear on Belmont Avenue was the Victoria Café, established in the late 1930s by Louis Montane, a native of Buffalo, New York, who claimed to be the first entrepreneur to produce and sell pizza in Youngstown.

Originally located just north of St. Elizabeth's Hospital, the Victoria Café moved farther up Belmont Avenue, on a spot between Broadway Street and Oxford Avenue. The restaurant was named in honor of Montane's wife, Victoria, who prepared the dough for its New York–style pizza.[67] The restaurant's other specialties included spaghetti, ravioli and wine steaks.

JoAnn Blunt described the restaurant as clean and attractive, with a pleasant atmosphere and outstanding food. "When we were growing up, our mother only took us to nice restaurants," she added, "and we all had a positive impression of the Victoria Café." Former customer Bert Lockshin, however, discerned an undercurrent of tension between the proprietor and his wife. "Louie was a big fat guy, and he used to sit on his tail at one of the tables all day long," he said. "His wife was the cook, and when it was busy, she did the serving, and she was the cashier…And they used to fight like cats and dogs."

In the early 1960s, the Victoria Café closed after Louis Montane shot his wife in a fit of jealous rage. The former restaurateur was briefly imprisoned "and then paroled to go east under the care of relatives because of his mental condition."[68]

In the wake of the Victoria Café's closing, North Siders in search of good pizza had a range of options. By the late 1960s, entrepreneur Nick Lavanty had turned a former gas station near the corner of Belmont and Alameda Avenues into Lavanty's Pizza, which developed into a restaurant-lounge that could seat up to fifty people. Within less than a decade, Lavanty purchased a neighboring property and established the first of the area's Nicolinni's restaurants.[69]

The 20th Century's Art Deco design was inspired by the owners' frequent visits to tourist-friendly restaurants in Miami, Florida. The 20th Century's eclectic menu offered everything from snacks to full-course dinners. *Courtesy of Morris Levy.*

The most widely known restaurant in the commercial corridor between Fairgreen and Redondo Avenues was the 20th Century, a streamlined structure located on the "Belmont point," the spot where the avenue merged with Wirt Street. Established in 1941, by Harry and Faye Malkoff, the restaurant had flourished, earning a faithful following among professionals, businesspeople, political leaders, students and many others.

The restaurant's attractions included a full menu that featured dishes ranging from broiled T-bone steak and Polynesian baby ribs to deli sandwiches and spaghetti. "They had great spare ribs, wonderful chocolate cream pie, a blue burger that was made from bleu cheese and good juicy hamburger [meat] and their great Spinning Bowl Salad, which was their trademark," Attorney Robert S. Fulton recalled. "It had a great deli-type atmosphere—very lively, a little noisy. You could hardly go in there without running into someone you knew."

The 20th Century was best known for its signature Spinning Bowl Salad, versions of which can still be found in restaurants throughout the area. Dr. Malkoff noted that the salad made his parents "very famous from a legacy standpoint," while also boosting the restaurant's profits. "In 1966, that salad was sixty-five cents, and they still made a lot of money at sixty-five cents," he recalled.

While Faye Malkoff's version of the Spinning Bowl Salad had its own unique qualities, her son acknowledged that it was based on a salad introduced earlier at Lawry's Steakhouse in Los Angeles. One of Faye Malkoff's greatest gifts, he added, was her capacity to re-create dishes she discovered during her frequent trips around the country—and to improve upon them.

By the close of the 1960s, the 20th Century was under the management of Joseph and Morris Levy, who purchased the restaurant, along with their brothers, Marvin and Jacob Newman. The new owners prudently retained staff members who had worked with Faye Malkoff, and over the next decade and a half, the 20th Century remained a beloved fixture of the North Side.

To the north of the 20th Century, and also occupying a spot on the "Belmont point," was Don White's Moo Shop, a cleanly designed structure of glass and steel. "At that time, it was the most modern-looking building on that part of the North Side," recalled Mary Ann Dudzik, who worked at a nearby store and often dined at the restaurant.

The Moo Shop's light menu included deli-style sandwiches and ice cream products. "They were known for their banana splits, which were just huge— and not very expensive," Mrs. Dudzik noted. "When you went there, you got your money's worth."

At the edge of Youngstown's border with Liberty Township, on the south side of Gypsy Lane, stood Spiegle's Delicatessen. Limited to carryout service and lacking space for in-house dining, the delicatessen was nevertheless a major destination for Jewish shoppers, who were drawn by Spiegle's specialty items.

"The interior was extremely clean and well organized," recalled Judith Lukin, who often drove from Canfield, Ohio, to the North Side to shop at the delicatessen. "You were able to purchase traditional delicacies that weren't available elsewhere. Their corned beef and tongue were high quality, and they carried baked goods that were difficult to find here in this area."

Mrs. Lukin indicated she had fond memories of the delicatessen's proprietor, Walter Spiegle, whom she remembered as friendly, courteous and articulate. "He was a very, very educated man," she said. "He not only waited on you with a smile, but he was also able to talk knowledgeably on international affairs. So not only did you have a pleasant shopping experience, but you also learned something."

Conventions gave restaurateurs and food manufacturers/distributors a chance to bond with colleagues. This undated photo includes Thomas Berndt (standing, far left), owner of Berndt's Restaurant, and Don White (standing, sixth from left), manager of the Moo Shop. Standing to the right of Mr. White are Pearl Berndt (Thomas's mother) and James Palazzo, co-owner of Palazzo's Restaurant, whose wife, Mary, sits to his left. The second figure to the right of Mr. Palazzo is Dora Schwebel, owner of the Schwebel Baking Company. *Courtesy of Paula Berndt.*

In the late 1960s, North Side businesses like Spiegle's Delicatessen, the 20th Century and the Moo Shop were still holding their own. Yet few observers could overlook the fact that the bulk of the commercial growth along Belmont Avenue was occurring north of Gypsy Lane.

As early as the 1940s, retail outlets had appeared in Liberty Township. Two decades later, they were joined by national and regional chain restaurants like Morgan's Wonder Boy, Howard Johnson's and the Red Barn. The community's economic center of gravity was shifting away from downtown and its environs, and the implications of this trend would become more apparent over time.

Dining on the West Side

Like the East Side, Youngstown's West Side developed its own distinct character. The portion of the West Side that bordered the city's sprawling industrial plants was the home of a large Italian American population with connections to the North Side's Brier Hill district. On the whole, however, the atmosphere of the West Side was shaped by a heavy concentration of Eastern European immigrants.

Soaring steeples and onion-shaped domes dotted the landscape, and many of the churches connected to them served the needs of specific ethnic groups. West Side landmarks included Sts. Peter & Paul Ukrainian Orthodox Church, Holy Name Slovak Catholic Church, Holy Trinity Serbian Orthodox Church, Our Lady of Hungary Catholic Church, St. Michael's Carpatho-Russian Orthodox Church and St. Mary's Byzantine Catholic Church, which also catered to the area's Carpatho-Russian community.

While the West Side boasted its share of ethnic food, most of it was served in homes, church social halls and private clubs. There were few sit-down restaurants, and most diners gravitated to family-friendly taverns. Many were located on Mahoning Avenue or Steel Street, which ran north of Mahoning and merged with Salt Springs Road. They had names like the Polar Bear Lounge, the Open Hearth, the New Deal Café, Stanley's Tavern, the Palm Café, Tiny's Tavern and Molly O'Dea's.

The Polar Bear Lounge exemplified the sort of family-run tavern that characterized the West Side. Established in 1957 by Jerome "Mike" Kennedy, the tavern initially operated on a shoestring. "Back in those days, the banks required you to put down a third of the money on a loan, so we had practically no money left for repairs and upgrading," recalled Julie Kennedy, wife of the late proprietor.

Over the years, however, the Polar Bear Lounge emerged as a West Side landmark, an outcome assisted by the tavern's location in a bustling business district. "At that time, there were plenty of businesses along Mahoning Avenue, so we pulled in folks from Passarelli Brothers' garage, Wonder Bakery, Moss Plumbing and Ward Bakery, to name just a few," Mrs. Kennedy recalled.

The tavern's success owed to other factors, including the Kennedys' social network. "We benefited from the fact that my husband and I were both Chaney High School alumni, and my husband had been a football player there," Mrs. Kennedy explained.

In the early 1960s, former area resident Dr. Paul McBride lived on nearby Lakeview Avenue, and he frequently dined at the tavern with his wife and parents. "The proprietors were exceptionally friendly," he recalled, noting

These charming mermaids graced the former site of the Club Merry-Go-Round until their partial destruction in a recent renovation. The bas-reliefs along the nightclub's walls were the work of Victor Kosa, one of the community's most prolific interior designers. *Courtesy of Joseph Cherol.*

that the Kennedys occasionally sat down and had a cup of tea or coffee with regular customers. "The restaurant was modest in its furnishings and décor, but the food was fine and the atmosphere so welcoming," he added.

Many customers were drawn by the tavern's food, which was prepared by Lucille Walsh, who ran the kitchen she leased from the Kennedys. "Lucille's burgers were among the most popular on the West Side—one-fourth of a pound of juicy Angus beef for just twenty-five cents," Mrs. Kennedy recalled. "Lucille was also famous for her macaroni and cheese, which had this incredible sauce that included five different types of cheese."

The Polar Bear Lounge was located near the intersection of Mahoning Avenue and Steel Street, a gritty artery studded with workingmen's taverns. These establishments included Charles Serednesky's Open Hearth Grille, whose menu featured an engaging mix of American favorites and traditional Ukrainian dishes, including cabbage rolls, smoked sausage, stew and potato pancakes. Serednesky and his wife, Chris, continued to operate the tavern until his death in 1990.[70]

Those traveling farther north on Steel Street, beyond the point where it merged with Salt Springs Road, encountered Cherol's Bar, sandwiched between a neighborhood market and a banquet hall, which occupied the former site of the Club Merry-Go-Round. While the tavern offered barroom favorites like chili dogs and hamburgers, it also sold traditional Italian food, which Joseph and Laura Cherol prepared.

Steve Moritz, the current chef at Molly's Restaurant & Lounge, became an unofficial "helper" at Cherol's as a young boy. "I begged Joe for a job for over a year, and finally, he let me help out," Moritz recalled. "I would go out with Laura when she picked the tomatoes, and I learned how to make tomato sauce from scratch." He recalled that the building's cavernous basement contained a wine press, which the couple used to make barrels of wine.

One of Cherol's closest neighbors on Salt Springs Road was Molly O'Dea's, established in the early 1950s by entrepreneur Nick Conti. While the tavern's name left some passersby with the impression that the business specialized in corned beef and cabbage, its menu was strictly Italian. "It was named after Nick's sister, Madeleine O'Dea, the head cook in the kitchen," explained Jim Precurato, who bought the business from Conti two decades later. "I secured the recipes for the pizza and hot sausage from Nick, and they're still used today."

Hearty Italian cuisine was also featured at Tiny's Tavern, where owner Sam Krish created a welcoming environment for customers who wanted to compete at *morra*, an Italian hand game, or to play traditional Italian card games. "All the Italian food they served was homemade," noted former patron John Thomas, "and we used to spend hours back there playing *scopa*, *briscola* and *tressette*." Thomas added that the tavern's near neighbor, Blake's Bar, under owner Pat Malandra, offered a similar Italian American menu.

By and large, however, the taverns in the vicinity of Steel Street and Salt Springs Road specialized in modest fare, and hot dogs were a perennial favorite. Many area residents fondly recall the kraut dogs served at Stanley's Tavern, located just south of Cherol's. Former patron James McNicholas recalled that the hot dogs were dressed with lightly cooked, crunchy sauerkraut that was drenched in Stanley's secret hot sauce.

Likewise, the majority of the taverns along Mahoning Avenue offered little food, with a few notable exceptions. James "Red" Ventresco's Il Sole Mio Tavern, for instance, provided a range of Italian dishes. "Everything they served was good," recalled John Thomas. "But they were really known for their hot sausage, which is what we usually ordered."

Another exception was the Town Tavern, which sat on the corner of Mahoning and Bon Air Avenues. This upscale bar not only offered a full menu—ranging from sandwiches to full-course dinners—but also provided customers with a stylish environment enhanced by mahogany paneling and decorative mirrors.

"I used to work the night turn at the Youngstown Police Department," recalled area resident Tom Anderson. "We always ordered takeout from the Town Tavern, and their homemade sausage sandwiches were just delicious." Another favorite item, Anderson noted, was the tavern's rib-eye steak sandwich.

In the late 1950s and early '60s, a number of West Side taverns began to feature a style of pizza that entrepreneur Nick Lavanty promoted as "Brier Hill Pizza." "My uncle, Jimmy D'Amato, was the one that said: 'Your mother made the best pizza in Brier Hill, and you should use that recipe and make pizza,'" Lavanty recalled.

Early customers of the novelty included "Tootsie" Marinelli's Tokay Tavern, Henry Spencer's Thirteenth Frame, Bobby Clemens's Bob's Tavern and Marty Timlin's Shaker Lounge. "At one time, Marty Timlin said, 'Nick, why don't you take the kitchen?'" Lavanty explained. "Then, I turned around and I found a place on Belmont Avenue."

Despite the prevalence of family-friendly taverns, diners who wished to celebrate special occasions often drove across the municipal border into Austintown Township, where their options included the Mark, a steakhouse on the corner of Mahoning Avenue and Meridian Road; El Rancho, a casual restaurant located on Mahoning Avenue; and Michelangelo's, a family-owned Italian restaurant known for its pizza and pasta dishes.

Oddly, the only conventional sit-down restaurant on the city's West Side at the time was a small establishment called Libby's, on the east side of Meridian Road, a few blocks south of Industrial Road. Owned and operated by the Vechiarella family, the restaurant focused on breakfast and lunch and rarely kept late hours. "Mrs. Vechiarella would catch some of the workers in the morning, coming in off the midnight turn," recalled Fred Ross. "She had an extensive breakfast menu that featured a lot of homemade-style foods."

Later, the restaurant was purchased by Irma DeLuca, a native of Germany who had married a Youngstown resident. Mrs. DeLuca reopened the business as a German-themed restaurant called Irma's. "She still spoke with a strong accent," Fred Ross recalled, "and I remember that the restaurant was immaculate." Although Irma's menu featured German favorites like *Wiener schnitzel*, *sauerbraten* and *spätzle*, it also served mainstream American dishes. "She really crammed them in there, especially on Friday nights with her fish special," Ross said. "She had all these young waitresses in there that were speedy and efficient."

Urban Exodus

During the late 1950s and early '60s, Youngstown's restaurant industry seemed to hold its own amid the rapid expansion of suburban communities and the rise of national chain restaurants. With that said, the cumulative effect of the population shift to outlying areas became more apparent over time, given that it was no longer masked by the postwar baby boom.

In 1965, the Ohio Department of Development (ODD) reported that the city's population had slipped from 166,689 in 1960 to 164,242 in 1964—a loss of 2,447 residents.[71] This figure, however, should not be interpreted as evidence that residents were leaving the Mahoning Valley in general. The following year, in 1966, the ODD indicated that the population of the Youngstown metropolitan area, on the whole, had jumped from 509,006 in 1960 to 548,303 in 1965—an increase of 8 percent.[72] This pattern remained consistent over the next decade, as suburban communities continued to grow at the expense of the city.

The impact of Youngstown's declining population was compounded by a simultaneous loss of important businesses. As early as 1958, Youngstown Sheet & Tube Corporation, which traditionally occupied the top five floors of the Stambaugh Building (now the Realty Building), relocated its corporate offices to Boardman, a move that adversely affected high-end restaurants in the downtown area. Two years later, in 1960, the downtown lost one of its most visible landmarks when Westminster Presbyterian Church, on the corner of Market and Front Streets, moved to a new site in Boardman—a development that reflected the growing pace of suburbanization.

Urban depopulation and suburbanization were accelerated by a series of ill-fated efforts to revitalize the city. "During the 1950s and early 1960s, Youngstown demolished whole neighborhoods as part of a citywide 'urban renewal' campaign," wrote historian Sean Posey. "The total destruction of the north side neighborhood of Caldwell—known as the 'Monkey's Nest'—drove large numbers of displaced African Americans into the lower south side." This situation was compounded in the 1960s by the construction of an arterial expressway, which led to the destruction of more urban neighborhoods.[73]

Nevertheless, Youngstown's decline proceeded at a relatively slow pace throughout the 1960s, enabling some urban restaurateurs to entertain the possibility that the city would stabilize. By the close of the 1970s, however, the hollowing out of Youngstown's center would be accelerated by a crisis of unprecedented dimensions.

Chapter 3
"TIMES THEY ARE A-CHANGIN'"

By the late 1960s, a host of destabilizing trends had driven thousands of residents into suburban communities, while also dampening the vitality of urban neighborhoods. Challenges arising from trends like demographic change, deindustrialization and suburbanization were compounded by urban construction projects that transformed whole sections of the city.

In Youngstown, as elsewhere in the United States, entire neighborhoods were swept away to accommodate highway construction projects. Worse yet, few urban dwellers experienced the benefits of highway construction projects, given that these roads facilitated the flow of suburban commuters to and from the city, even as they "sliced through urban neighborhoods, thereby eliminating housing and disrupting communities."

Meanwhile, the highways encouraged the flow of capital out of the city and into the suburbs. As Robert A. Beauregard noted, interstate highways "gave impetus to the trucking industry and improved its competitiveness relative to railroads and international shipping." As ports and railway yards became less important, highways "enabled businesses...that relied on trucking to relocate outside the city, where they would have better access to the metropolitan market via the new regional highway network."[74]

The negative impact of highway construction on downtown Youngstown was especially dramatic. As Sherry Linkon and John Russo observed, the community's Interstate 680 beltway "effectively cut downtown Youngstown off from much day-to-day traffic, directing drivers and, more importantly, shoppers" to newly built suburban shopping plazas and malls.[75]

Those who built suburban plazas and malls contended that they were merely responding to the dominant trends of the period. "Now, we're in the shopping mall business, and people will say, 'You guys destroyed downtowns,'" Anthony Cafaro Sr. stated. "No, we didn't destroy downtowns. What happened was, in the years after World War II, a lot of returning veterans wanted to move to the suburbs—and they moved to the suburbs."

Cafaro added that the movement of returning veterans to outlying communities was accelerated by subsequent trends. "People who started building shopping plazas… were following the population shift to the suburbs," he explained. "The next thing that happened was that President Eisenhower initiated the building of the interstate highway

The McKelvey's Grille, located on the corner of North Hazel and Commerce Streets, was a popular dining spot for professionals and shoppers alike. Many former patrons recall the eatery's incomparable milkshakes. *Courtesy of Mahoning Valley Historical Society.*

system in the 1950s because of his experience with the autobahn in Germany and its capacity to move people and equipment quickly on four-lane highways."

Before long, he continued, miles of four-lane highways "looped" around the nation's cities. "So we built those malls right on those looping interstates, along the suburbs," Cafaro observed. "People were going out there, and the road patterns were concentrated out there. And that's why the malls were built out there."

A Changing Downtown

As late as the 1950s, however, few observers could have imagined the dramatic decline of Youngstown's downtown. Family-oriented businesses—including movie theaters, restaurants and shoe stores—were found on nearly every

AIR-CONDITIONED
for your Comfort

Hollander's Grill

In the Center of Convenience

131 WEST FEDERAL STREET - YOUNGSTOWN, OHIO

The menu for Hollander's Grill featured a $1.19 steak special, a signature cubed-steak sandwich, fried chicken and a wide variety of soda, seltzer and ice cream products. *Courtesy of Mahoning Valley Historical Society.*

corner of the downtown area, and on the surface, the city's core appeared vibrant. When restaurants closed, their sites were usually leased to other businesses.

This was true of the Petrakos Grill, which closed in the mid-1950s, only to be replaced by Hollander's Grill. The new restaurant, operated by meat purveyor Louis Hollander, established a reputation for serving some of the finest steaks and burgers in town. "Our signature dishes included a steak special for $1.19," recalled Louis Hollander's son, Mervyn. "This was a shell steak, which was a short loin with no tenderloin." He added, "We offered a cubed-steak sandwich, fried chicken and a whole range of soda, seltzer and ice cream products."

Upon entering the restaurant, patrons could choose from a series of wooden booths that held two, four or six people. Each booth was equipped with a miniature jukebox, enabling diners to select their own "atmosphere" music. Yet while Hollander's Grill offered customers a cozy, intimate atmosphere, the business's operations were actually spread over all four floors of the building it occupied.

The restaurant maintained two kitchens: a small grill located on an upper floor and a much larger kitchen in the building's basement. Meals prepared in the basement were delivered to the main dining area through a dumbwaiter. "Besides that, we had a candy kitchen on the fourth floor, where we produced hand-dipped chocolates," Hollander recalled. "We called them Marsha Joy candies—that was my sister's name—and sold them at the restaurant."

Marsha Joy candies were among the items advertised in the restaurant's two large display windows, which were decorated by window trimmer "Obie" Oblonsky, who also worked for neighboring Lustig's Shoes. "We would have seasonal displays of candy and other products, around the holidays or St. Patrick's Day, or whatever," Hollander recalled. "You'd see kids pressing their noses against the windows. They were totally awestruck."

For many of those who grew up in Youngstown during the 1950s, the downtown entertainment district was a smorgasbord of sights, sounds, smells and flavors. Connie Kushma recalled that each restaurant had its own specialties. "When my mom took me to Hollander's...she'd say, 'You have to have...the cubed-steak sandwich,'" Ms. Kushma explained. "And my grandmother would take me to Woolworth's, and we'd get a BLT...So, every restaurant had its little favorite that we would go for, and I think that is what [made] it unique."

Within a few years, however, evidence of decline became obvious. "Hollander's Grill was closed in the early 1960s...and it was really a sign of the times," Mervyn Hollander observed. "You started to see the development of the suburban strip plazas; and we were located between Hartzell's Men's Wear and Lustig's Shoes, so we could see the writing on the wall."

By that time, Raver's Restaurant had been closed for several years. In 1958, Jack Raver—in the wake of his mother's and brother's departures from the family business—elected to move on to a second career as a supervisor of food services for local public schools, first in Youngstown and then in neighboring Warren.

Another casualty of urban decline was the Star Oyster House, a restaurant that had catered to local seafood lovers since the 1920s. The restaurant's offerings included broiled whole Maine lobster, broiled South African lobster tail, fresh crab meat á la Newburg (a dish prepared with dry sherry and sour cream), fried frog legs on toast, milk oyster stew, clam cocktail and broiled black sea bass.[76]

Since the early 1950s, the restaurant had been operated by Greek immigrant John Combis, who arrived in the United States via Canada. Combis, after purchasing the business from longtime owner Harry Magulas, maintained the high standards that customers appreciated. "He did very well—that is, until the suburban plazas started drawing business away from the downtown," recalled Combis's youngest child, Faith Hodnick.

Meanwhile, other downtown restaurants were engaged in a battle for survival, including the Palace Grill, which had depended on the business of Youngstown Sheet & Tube's executives and therefore suffered when the firm relocated to Boardman in the late 1950s. "That was the end of it," recalled James Vallos's daughter, Deanna. "In the good old days, they would sell a prime rib every day; and by the end, they couldn't sell half of a prime rib."

While the Standard Slag Corporation took over Youngstown Sheet & Tube's former offices in the Realty Building, it lacked its predecessor's huge staff, and the Palace Grill's business continued to slide. "At one time, everything was downtown, so people would stop by after catching a show at the Palace Theatre," noted James Vallos's son, William. "That began to change in the late '50s."

In October 1962, another well-known downtown eatery prepared to close its doors as Trevett A. Wilson Jr., manager of the Hotel Pick-Ohio, announced that the Purple Cow Coffee Shop would shut down after more than two decades of operation. The manager attributed this development to a "business decline" but also made reference to "the undesirable element that loitered in and around" the eatery.[77]

Over the years, the Purple Cow had figured in a number of front-page stories and editorials regarding a series of disturbances that included one shooting and several "brawls." A 1960 *Vindicator* editorial offered faint praise to the eatery when it observed, "Perhaps conditions are not quite as bad as they were prior to the fifties when the man sitting next to you probably was carrying a gun."[78]

While some downtown landmarks were holding on, many of them seemed the worse for wear. James D. Bennett recalled that, one afternoon in the 1960s, he was invited to lunch by Attorney William Houser (later Judge Houser), who served as his company's corporate attorney. When Judge Houser gestured in the direction of Moore's Tavern, a fixture on Central Square, Bennett was surprised, given that the building "looked as though it should be condemned."

"I said, 'You've got to be kidding,'" Bennett recalled, noting that he was overwhelmed by the smell of beer upon entering the tavern. "It was dark and dingy, and I can remember they had this poor old soul that looked like she was about ninety years old," he recalled. "The woman came up—and I swear she had three mugs on her fingers—and she was dragging one leg behind her."

Bennett compared the experience to a scene from an old western film, adding, "She threw the mugs on the table and said, 'What do you guys want?'" When Judge Houser ordered what he described as the tavern's

Moore's Tavern, as it appeared shortly before an October 1960 campaign speech by then presidential candidate John F. Kennedy. The downtown landmark was known for offering the tastiest roast beef sandwiches in town. *Courtesy of Mahoning Valley Historical Society.*

"great" roast beef sandwich, Bennett followed suit but watched nervously as the server retreated into the cellar. "This place was in an old building, so you can imagine the cellar had to be damp," he recalled.

"Well, she came up with a roast beef sandwich, and it was the best roast beef sandwich I'd ever had," Bennett added. "I ended up going back there and eating, seeing at the time that there were a lot of professionals that ate there—judges, attorneys and some doctors."

Yet by the end of the decade, Moore's Tavern had given way to an urban renewal project that claimed much of the downtown's eastern district. In the spring of 1969, the *Vindicator* reported that the tavern's last day of business would be May 29, "when some friends may be expected to hoist a last stein." To underscore its longevity, the paper noted that the tavern "in its early days often played host to groups of the Blue Army, which made up the Tod Post of the Grand Army of the Republic and which had its headquarters in the courthouse."[79]

"Times They Are A-Changin'"

A Promise of Renewal

Several years before the razing of Moore's Tavern, the eastern rim of Central Square had witnessed dramatic changes. In December 1963, a firm called the Legal Arts Corporation spent a reported $150,000 to purchase the former site of a Sears, Roebuck & Company store on the corner of Market and East Boardman Streets. The group failed to publicize its plans for the building, which stretched 75 feet along Market Street and 150 feet along East Boardman Street.[80]

Less than a year later, in April 1964, the building firm of Stephen C. Baytos & Associates announced that it would raze the structure to pave the way for a $2 million five-floor edifice called the Legal Arts Building. The firm also publicized plans to raze the Palace Theatre complex (former site of the Palace Grill, Rodney Ann's and Sweetland) to make way for a $3 million eight-floor shopping mall to be called Plaza One.

The firm was no stranger to major projects. In 1963, Baytos & Associates built the $1.5 million Voyager Motor Inn on the former site of Westminster Presbyterian Church, located at the corner of Market and Front Streets. Moreover, Stephen Baytos, as president of Bonovest Development Corporation, had overseen construction of fifty-two shopping centers across the country.

As though to ease the concerns of residents who opposed demolition of the Palace Theatre complex, the firm announced that Plaza One would feature a 1,200-seat Cinerama theater to be called "the New Palace Theater." The firm also indicated the mall building would contain a ground-floor parking area capable of accommodating several hundred vehicles, "including those of tenants in the 45 apartments on the upper five floors."

Dazzled by the Baytos & Associates plan, Mayor Anthony B. Flask described it to members of city council as "the most startling development of the city in 50 years."[81] This might have been the case were it not for the fact that large portions of the plan failed to materialize.

On the positive side, the envisioned Legal Arts Building was completed. In line with publicized plans, the building featured "an exterior of dark gray brick facing, set off by large brass vertical mouldings and large panels of contemporary design in various colored mosaic tile." The structure's Market Street entrance, which was "glass-enclosed with a saw-toothed overhang," hosted a ground-floor coffee shop.[82]

For the next few decades, the Hub coffee shop served as a popular gathering spot for those who frequented downtown. "The Hub was a really fun spot for breakfast, and it had a very urban atmosphere," recalled Father John C. Harris, a regular patron. "You had your attorneys, your judges; and you had street people go in there, too. Everybody was just elbow to elbow,

Housed in downtown Youngstown's Legal Arts Building on Central Square, the Hub proved a popular dining spot for professionals and others who frequented the district. The restaurant opened in the mid-1960s. *Courtesy of Mahoning Valley Historical Society.*

and it reminded me of one of the coffee shops that I would stop at when I was in Manhattan."

As noted, the Voyager Motor Inn was also completed. Designed to impress, the building's main entrance led into a sunken lobby that hosted a large dining area, while the hotel's mezzanine basement featured a series of shops and offices. The Voyager's center floors hosted the facility's one hundred guest rooms, and the fifth floor featured a ballroom known as the Cloud Room.[83]

The timing of the hotel's grand opening, however, proved unfortunate. On the morning of Friday, November 22, 1963, local dignitaries, including Youngstown mayor Harry N. Savesten, gathered outside the hotel for a ribbon-cutting ceremony. Standing next to the mayor were local developer Stephen Baytos; the hotel's comanagers, James Tassone and J. Kenneth Gran; and Akron native Margaret A. Emerson, who had been selected as "Miss Ohio."[84]

Earlier, attendants had gathered in the Cloud Room for a breakfast prepared under the supervision of the hotel's German-born chef, Karl Weirich. Guests were probably encouraged by the opening of a luxury hotel in the old Central Square, and the theme of the event was the "Beginning of Progress in Downtown Youngstown."[85] "This was a big event, and the food they prepared was out of this world," recalled Jim Graycar, who served as second bartender at the hotel. "They had three suckling pigs, at least two steamship rounds of steak and trays of whole salmon…The hotel was filled to capacity with salesmen who were in for the weekend."

By the afternoon, however, the festive mood at the Voyager had evaporated, as news spread of President John F. Kennedy's assassination in Dallas, Texas. "After that, they cancelled the grand opening, and they put all the food in the freezer," he recalled. "There weren't any television sets in the bar or restaurant portion of the hotel, so they pulled a couple of TVs out of the rooms…We couldn't take our eyes off the TV, and we couldn't eat—and everybody was devastated."

Despite this inauspicious beginning, the Voyager Motor Inn was relatively popular during its eleven-year run. "It was reminiscent of what you would have seen at Miami Beach," recalled James D. Bennett, a patron of the hotel's restaurant. "The interior had a kind of late '50s or early '60s aesthetic, and I enjoyed attending events at the banquet room on the top floor." He added, "It was especially nice to be up there at night and to look out on downtown Youngstown."

Sadly, Stephen Baytos's vision of a revitalized downtown was never realized, given that his plans to build an eight-story shopping mall on the site of the Palace Theatre fell through—an outcome that led many to criticize the apparently pointless destruction of a cherished landmark.

Mixed Signals

By the close of the 1960s, one of downtown's most beloved dining spots was in deep trouble. Located near Vindicator Square, an area on the western fringe of downtown that hosted the offices of Youngstown's newspaper, the Mural Room was threatened with the loss of critical parking space. In early 1970, the *Vindicator* followed through on its announced plan to build a large production plant on a parcel of land that once served as the Mural Room's parking lot. The prospect of limited parking wasn't the restaurant's only challenge, however. Business had been falling off steadily for some time.

The situation couldn't have been more different in the late 1940s, when the restaurant opened its doors to the public. Many had viewed the restaurant as an ideal venue for special occasions. "For years parents and grandparents have treated their young ones to birthday dinners and holiday banquets, chuckling as the children chose a gift from the treasure chest near the organ," the *Vindicator* stated.

Milt Simon, sole owner of the restaurant since 1962, said he found it difficult to break up the Mural Room's fifty-five-person staff, whose members had "worked so well together for so long." Staff members included the restaurant's "gracious hostess," Helen Clarkson; its "inimitable organist-pianist," Joe Baumgartner; and Simon's longtime assistant, Tom McQuade, who went on to serve as catering manager at the Voyager Motor Inn.[86]

Amid largely discouraging trends, however, local diners witnessed a few hopeful signs in the downtown area. In December 1969, for instance, fans of Asian food were excited about the opening of Dan Hom's Hong Kong Restaurant on South Phelps Street, near the corner of West Federal Street.

An area native born to Chinese immigrants, Hom prided himself on his restaurant's eclectic menu, which included specialties such as Shanghai Threads, a dish that combined pork, bamboo shoots, noodles and eggs; and Four Seasons, "a combination of lobster, chicken, pork, duck, mushrooms, chestnuts, along with a variety of Chinese vegetables."

Given "the large exodus in recent years," Hom was questioned on his decision to open a business in the downtown area. The restaurateur insisted that he would overcome any challenges related to his location. "When the customer is looking for an excellent product at a bargain price, it makes no difference where you are located," he said.[87]

Over the years, the restaurant won loyal customers, including South Side native Loretta Ekoniak, who enjoyed the restaurant's barbecued ribs and sweet and sour pork. "The Hong Kong Restaurant gave me my first experience of Chinese food," she recalled. "I remember being excited that there was a Chinese restaurant in Youngstown, Ohio, because the pizza and pierogi featured at many local restaurants was also available at most of the churches."

Despite a dominant pattern of decline, a handful of other restaurants opened downtown in the late '60s and early '70s. In 1969, Strouss' Department Store announced plans to build a $150,000 restaurant on the fourth floor of the adjacent Wick Building. Fred Gronvall, president and general manager of Strouss', and Earl Brauninger, president of the neighboring Union National Bank, revealed that the colonial-themed restaurant would be called the Western Reserve Room.[88]

For many area residents, the Western Reserve Room helped fill the vacuum created by the closing of formal restaurants at the city's center. Betty Swanson, an employee at Union National Bank, often dined at the restaurant with close relatives. "My mother would bring my children downtown, and that was a big treat, because I would take them around and show them off at the bank," she recalled. "Then, I would always take them up to the Western Reserve Room for lunch."

Dr. Regina Rees, a professor at Youngstown State University, also shared fond memories of the Western Reserve Room. In the 1970s, Dr. Rees was a young employee at Strouss' Department Store, and on payday, she and her colleagues occasionally "splurged" by getting manicures at the nearby Victor George Beauty Academy and then stopping for lunch at the Western Reserve Room. "It was a real treat," she recalled. "It was an elegant restaurant with cloth tablecloths, and everything was beautifully presented."

Another new attraction was Lum's, a sandwich shop on the north side of West Federal Street, just east of the former Warner Theater, which reopened as Powers Auditorium. Former patron James D. Bennett recalled that Lum's specialty was a hot dog boiled in beer. "It was entirely different than Jay's," he said. "Jay's had slender hot dogs. These were thick hot dogs, and you put anything you wanted on them."

Then, in 1976, local real-estate speculator Andrew Marino promoted the idea of turning a former nineteenth-century bank building into a two-leveled business called the Sidewalk Café. Located across from Strouss' Department Store on West Federal Street, the building had seen better days, and its renovation was estimated to cost between $100,000 and $150,000.

Marino explained that the upper floor would host an upscale restaurant, while the ground level would be the site of a food court with international dining options. "Downstairs here we'll have, for example, Chinese food at one counter...Italian at another counter...maybe a Jewish deli in the back," he told the *Vindicator*.[89] As he predicted, the Sidewalk Café became a major destination for downtown-based workers and professionals, who appreciated its blend of variety and convenience.

Meanwhile, private institutions like the Youngstown Club continued to draw business leaders and professionals. Over the years, the club proved remarkably durable. In February 1963, an arson fire resulted in more than $1 million in damage to the club's dining room and lounge, while also ravaging the top three floors of the Union National Bank Building.[90] Despite extensive damage, combined with a scandal involving allegations of an "inside job," the Youngstown Club remained a fixture on Central Square.

Graphic designer and advertising consultant Sandra Cika enjoyed a taste of the Youngstown Club's atmosphere while still in elementary school. During the 1970s, she visited the club every holiday season as a guest of her godmother, Carolyn Maresky, an executive at a local insurance company.

"When Carolyn came to the house to pick me up for my annual dinner, my mother would joke, 'Look, my seven-year-old daughter is going to the Youngstown Club, and I've never even been there.'"

Ms. Cika didn't take these occasions for granted. She was attired in a fur coat, gloves and red patent-leather go-go boots, which were fashionable at the time. "As the elevator doors opened, we walked directly into the club, and I was always struck by the elegant ambience of the place," she recalled. "It was ultra-formal, with plush furnishings and beautiful paintings; the elegant servers were dressed in outfits that resembled tuxedoes."

When the pair exchanged gifts over dinner, Ms. Cika invariably received a jar of the Youngstown Club's well-known cheese spread, which she shared with her family. "I recall that we always sat at a table near a window overlooking Central Square," she said. "The huge tree and brightly lit decorations added to my impression that I was getting a taste of life in New York City, right here in Youngstown, Ohio."

In subsequent decades, downtown Youngstown remained a center of activity for municipal employees, along with many lawyers, judges and bank employees. Therefore, restaurants and eateries never completely disappeared. At the same time, downtown's role as a metropolitan entertainment district was waning, and the days when area residents gathered in the district for "a night on the town" appeared to be coming to an end.

Notably, efforts to boost downtown didn't end with the Baytos & Associates truncated plan. On October 31, 1973, Youngstown's municipal government held a groundbreaking ceremony for the so-called Federal Street Mall. The $1.7 million project, which paralleled similar efforts across the country, was designed to create a "pedestrian mall" that would enhance "shopper enjoyment and convenience."[91]

According to the plan, Federal Street, which ran east and west, would be closed to vehicle traffic, with Walnut and Phelps Streets, running north and south, serving respectively as the western and eastern borders. (Walnut and Phelps Streets would be open to emergency and service vehicles only.)

At the same time, Market Street, a north–south running thoroughfare that bisected the Federal Mall and ran through Central Square, would remain open to vehicle traffic, although crossing points for pedestrians would be located at quarter points on the square, with traffic signals coordinated to ensure safety. The goal of what came to be known as "Federal Plaza" was to create "an overall feeling…of informality and casual flowing space, emphasized by brick walkways and pavements."[92]

Despite such efforts, however, the district's decline continued, and the failure of projects like the Federal Plaza was replicated across the country, as municipal governments struggled to implement strategies to preserve beleaguered city centers.

Restaurant Redux

As Youngstown moved into the 1970s, scores of urban restaurants closed in the wake of suburbanization, while others secured new leases on life. Those in the latter category included the Elm Street Delicatessen, a North Side landmark since 1939. Thirty-one years later, in 1970, owners Rose and Herb Kravitz decided to relocate their business to Liberty Township—a move that reflected their awareness of troubling developments in the city.

This decision did not come easily, given that the Elm Street Delicatessen had been an integral part of the neighborhood. The Kravitzes' second daughter, Donia Kravitz Foster, noted that she was raised to appreciate the ethnic and religious diversity of the North Side. "My mother and father believed that they needed to serve…anybody that was in the community," Ms. Foster said

Dramatic changes were overtaking the North Side, however, and the Kravitzes couldn't help but notice. "People were leaving the neighborhood," Ms. Foster recalled. "My friends left the area. A lot of their parents were getting older, and they moved out to the suburbs." The Jewish community was also migrating north to Liberty.

Numerous factors contributed to the Kravitzes' decision to move the delicatessen to Belmont Avenue, a main artery in Liberty. Jack Kravitz, the youngest of the Kravitzes' three children, recalled that his mother often discussed the business's location in relation to Youngstown State University, whose expansion disrupted traffic. "They blocked off Elm Street," Kravitz explained, "so Elm Street was no longer a major corridor from downtown into the North Side suburb."

Reinvented as Kravitz's Delicatessen, the business thrived in its new location amid a suburban retail and entertainment district. It was then that Jack Kravitz began to assume a larger role in the business. "When we moved here, Liberty Plaza was the shopping area of Youngstown," Kravitz recalled. The delicatessen benefited from the presence of popular stores like Strouss', JCPenney, Kresge's and Stambaugh-Thompson's.

Other established restaurants were also in transition. The 20th Century restaurant, a North Side dining destination since the early 1940s, faced an uncertain future due to the declining health of proprietor Harry Malkoff. "When my father wanted to retire…he looked at me and said, 'Do you want to go into the restaurant business?'" recalled the restaurateur's son, Dr. Kurt Malkoff. "I just saw the hours he worked and…I wanted to go to graduate school."

While Dr. Malkoff pursued his education, eventually earning a doctorate in clinical psychology, a longtime customer took an interest in the family's restaurant. "Harry was either traveling or he was sick," recalled Joseph Levy, the restaurant's accountant in the 1960s. "So I would go up there, and I would do payroll for him; and by doing that, I got to meet all the employees."

Levy's interest in the restaurant traced back decades. "When I was in high school, I really liked the restaurant," he recalled. "And I always said to people that, 'Someday I'm going to buy this place.'" This predication, which he made at the age of sixteen, came to fruition fourteen years later. As a thirty-year-old accountant, Joseph Levy seriously considered purchasing the business he had admired for so long. "The more I worked there, the more interested I got," he explained. "I knew that Harry…wanted to sell it, so I convinced my father that we should buy it."

In 1970, after securing his father's permission and support, Joseph Levy purchased the restaurant and formed a partnership with three of his brothers, Morris, Marvin and Jacob Newman. Although Joseph Levy served as the principal partner, his brother Morris ("Blondie") agreed to work alongside him in the restaurant.

The Levy brothers readily understood that their decision to purchase the 20th Century made them stewards of a local institution. "It…had so many specialties…and just numerous ones of a kind," explained Joseph Levy's brother Morris. "You could only get a Spinning Bowl Salad in Youngstown at the 20th Century." He added, "The Malkoffs were so unique and clever in the creation of a restaurant that it went from snacks and specialty foods all the way up to full-course dinners, and as far as prime rib and chicken in a pot."

An important factor in the restaurant's continuing popularity was the Levy brothers' prudent decision to retain original staff members, including Mary McMillen, who had been trained by Faye Malkoff. Joseph Levy recalled that her specialties included an "outstanding" New York cheesecake—the recipe for which she carefully concealed. Other signature desserts included a whipped cream torte, German chocolate pie, German chocolate cake, chocolate pecan pie, ice cream sundaes and a "Banana Royale," which was described as "almost a meal in itself."

Meanwhile, the 20th Century's numerous entrées included grilled chopped sirloin beef, an open-faced rib-eye sandwich, Polynesian baby ribs, grilled baby beef livers, roasted Ohio farm turkey, sautéed chicken livers, filet of sole, filet of haddock, spaghetti and meatballs, ravioli and meatball parmigiana. Those seeking lighter fare sampled the restaurant's unique deli-style sandwiches.[93]

Yet despite its assets and legendary reputation, the 20th Century failed to secure the longevity of some other North Side restaurants, including the Golden Dawn, the MVR, Avalon Gardens and Kravitz's Delicatessen. "The worst problem I ever had was the neighborhood," Joseph Levy recalled, adding that customers began to complain that visiting the restaurant was "too dangerous."

Levy's effort to establish a branch of the restaurant on Midlothian Boulevard proved ill fated. The suburban branch, called 20th Century South, opened on the site of the Golden Drumstick, which the Malkoffs had sold separately in the early 1970s. "What I tried to do [was] re-create the Golden Drumstick and the 20th Century together as one," Levy explained. "What I should have done was just made it the 20th Century, because that's what I knew."

The demise of the 20th Century's Boardman branch wasn't the only challenge Levy faced. By the early 1980s, urban trends and increased competition from suburban-based chains combined to undercut the restaurant's profitability, and Levy indicated that he lacked the capital to relocate the business.

South Side Developments

By the close of the 1960s, another popular restaurant had relocated in order to expand its business. Scarsella's had operated in the vicinity of the Pyatt Street Market since 1957. Over the years, however, Mary Grace Scarsella grew frustrated with the tiny building. In September 1969, when Gluck Insurance moved out of a building on the corner of Market Street and West Florida Avenue, Mrs. Scarsella "made the deal and moved in," recalled granddaughter Connie Kushma.

Turning the former offices of an insurance company into an Italian American restaurant was no small feat, and the job required the assistance of the entire family. When the task was completed, Scarsella's interior featured a dozen Formica-topped tables, and its modest décor included an old-fashioned cash register, framed prints of Italian scenes and a smattering of family photographs. The new location could seat about forty guests.

Beyond the restaurant's authentic Italian dishes, its attractions included a "homey" atmosphere. Youngstown native Dr. Daniel Greenfield recalled that when he was growing up, his parents often took him to Scarsella's, where he routinely ordered cavatelli and a cup of wedding soup. "When we finished our meal, old Mr. Scarsella would always give me a candy bar," he said. "It was a warm, welcoming environment, and they treated us almost as though we were members of the family."

While the new site was an improvement over the original location, it had limitations. "Parking was a problem, because you had to either park on the street or…go to the [city hall] annex and park your cars." Over

Connie Kushma and her mother, Theresa Kozar, pose in the dining room of Scarsella's, on the city's South Side. The family business was established in 1957 by Mrs. Kushma's grandparents Mary Grace and Luigi Scarsella. *Courtesy of Thomas G. Welsh Jr.*

time, other problems arose, including a rise in crime in the neighborhood. Nevertheless, the building on the corner of Market Street and West Florida Avenue served as the site of Scarsella's restaurant until 1996, when it moved to its current location, a few blocks south of Midlothian Boulevard.

Farther south on Market Street, another landmark restaurant was operating under new management by the early 1970s. The Colonial House had been established in 1949 by partners Carl Rango, Frank Fetchet and Vince DeNiro. In the mid-1950s, DeNiro quit the partnership, and then, in the early 1970s, Rango suddenly passed away.

While Fetchet retained the property, he showed little interest in operating a restaurant. "That's when the Colonial House fell into our hands," recalled Patricia Lyden Yank, daughter of Bertram Lyden, who ran the restaurant with brother Paul between 1971 and 1982. She noted that her uncle, Paul Lyden, had previously owned several local businesses, including the South Side's Jambar Tavern, which he ran with Marcus "Corky" Kilch.

The Lyden brothers' purchase of the Colonial House in 1971 was facilitated by their cousin Bill Lyden, president of the Lyden Oil Company. "He got my uncle down at the Colonial House, and they struck a deal," Mrs. Yank recalled. "The idea was that my uncle, Paul Lyden, would run the Colonial House, and my dad, Bert Lyden, would run the Jambar, along with Corky's widow, Rosemary." Within two years, however, this arrangement proved unworkable. Therefore, Paul Lyden sold the Jambar, which enabled the two brothers to devote their time and energy to the Colonial House.

One of the Lyden brothers' most powerful assets was their social network. "If you were to look in my dad's yearbook from the Rayen School, you would see all the major businessmen and professionals in Youngstown," Mrs. Yank explained. This close-knit North Side crowd gravitated to the Colonial House, along with other local luminaries.

Some high-profile customers came to view the Colonial House as a welcome refuge from the glare of the media. Yank recalled that during a trial that pitted Mahoning County prosecutor Vince Gilmartin against Attorney Don Hanni, the media framed the contest as a personal feud. "People thought there was a big war going on between them, but they were meeting at lunch every day at the Colonial House," Mrs. Yank noted. "They were good friends, and that was their hangout—and it was considered private."

While the Lydens introduced a few changes and remodeled the interior, much remained the same. The menu continued to feature a range of classic Italian American entrées. "One of my favorite meals was the Colonial Veal Special," Mrs. Yank recalled. "It was sautéed veal in a wine sauce, with peppers and onions, and it was covered with provolone cheese and placed under the broiler."

Meanwhile, other South Side eateries were revamped, as their owners set out to upgrade facilities and widen menus to attract high-end clients. A dramatic case involved the transformation of the Cave Lounge, established on Market Street in the early 1960s by Leander "Lee" Quaranta and his brothers, Edward and Ron.

Overall, the Cave Lounge offered a limited menu. Designed to attract younger singles, the nightclub capitalized on the popularity of Stone Age imagery in films like *One Million Years B.C.* and television cartoons like *The Flintstones*. "My father knew a gentleman named Bill Johnson, who created cave-like interiors using a papier-mâché process, and he applied it to the ceilings and walls of the restaurant," recalled Lee Quaranta's son, Jerry. "I remember there was lighting worked into the crevices to create a glowing effect, and there were stalactites hanging from the ceiling."

In the mid-1970s, Lewardo's Restaurant took the place of a popular singles bar called the Cave. While owners Leander and Edward Quaranta introduced a gourmet menu, they chose to retain the previous business's papier-mâché stalactites. *Courtesy of Anna M. Quaranta.*

Early on, Ron Quaranta left the partnership to open Ronnie's Tavern on South Avenue. (He later opened the Isle of Capri in Struthers and Caffe Capri in Boardman.) The remaining partners, Lee and Edward Quaranta, went on to make a surprising business decision. In 1975, they refurbished the Cave and reopened it as an upscale Italian restaurant called Lewardo's, a moniker that combined their given names.

Nineteen-year-old Jerry Quaranta wasted no time joining the staff as a full-time chef. "We kept the cave-like interior, and musicians with violins would stroll from table to table, playing music on request," he recalled. Lewardo's attracted discriminating diners, and in March 1975, its recipe for mozzarella marinara was requested by *Gourmet* magazine. "We had a gourmet menu, and…we introduced specialties like veal rollatini, beef fettuccine Alfredo, veal saltimbocca, stuffed chicken fraçaise and filet pizzaiola," Jerry Quaranta recalled.

Saturday evenings drew the biggest crowds, and patrons without reservations could not get tables. As the evening progressed, however, scores of "regulars" drifted in, and they asked the chefs, Joe Rotundo and Jerry Quaranta, to "get creative" in the kitchen. "So we'd have a chance to use our skills and imagination to put together something that wasn't on the menu," Jerry Quaranta recalled.

This flexibility reflected the kind of atmosphere Leander Quaranta encouraged, said his daughter, Anna M. Quaranta. "We used to get together every Sunday for a meal with my entire family, and I think my father wanted to create that kind of family-like atmosphere at Lewardo's," she said.

Despite its solid reputation, Lewardo's had a brief run, closing its doors in 1980. Afterward, Jerry Quaranta served as a chef at Sandalini's Top of the Mall in Niles, Ohio, where he worked with notable chefs like Jimmy Chieffo, Mario Puccetti and Mark Pearce.

Amid the sobering developments of the 1970s, a surprising number of local entrepreneurs tried their hands at the restaurant business. Some were experienced businesspeople who understood the risks involved. Others appeared to enter the restaurant industry on a whim. All found themselves in a smaller, increasingly competitive market.

The early 1970s witnessed the opening of the Fireplace Restaurant & Lounge, which became a major South Side destination. The business was the product of a partnership involving Thomas Campana Sr. and his brother-in-law, Fred Spotleson. "Freddy...was always interested in getting into business," recalled Carmen Vecchione, a longtime friend of both men. "Tom was a barber, and at that time, things were getting a little slow, because everyone wanted a special haircut—so Tom was primed."

In 1972, Campana and Spotleson saw an opportunity to go into business together when the former Hurricane Lounge, near the corner of South Avenue and Midlothian Boulevard, was put up for sale at $60,000. "You got the license; you got the place; you got the land—and everything inside of it," recalled Campana's son, Thomas Jr., current owner of the Fireplace Restaurant & Lounge in Poland, Ohio. "So, they took a chance with it."

The partners' first challenge was to refurbish the interior, which reflected the previous business's Polynesian theme. In the end, the tavern's most salient feature was a fireplace. "When they were working on that fireplace, they couldn't decide on a name," Vecchione recalled, "and Mrs. Spotleson—that's Freddy's mom—she's sitting there, and she says, 'Why don't you just call it the Fireplace?'"

Early on, food became one of the Fireplace's chief attractions, and many entrées were based on family recipes. The restaurant's three main cooks—Anna LaSalle, Emma Badaline and Louisa Rubino—were so experienced that they routinely watched soap operas while preparing food. "These ladies would be rolling dough, and all I had to have for them was the TV up there," he said. "They didn't even have to look down."

During the restaurant's Friday fish specials, Thomas Campana Sr. distributed numbered chips to customers, which enlivened the tedious process of waiting for a table. "What he'd do was give you a number, but these numbers were random," his son explained. "People will always come up to me and say, 'I remember when your father would call those numbers—and never in order.'"

Given the Fireplace's proximity to WKBN television station, the tavern's "regulars" included newscaster Tom Holden and sportscaster Don Gardner. Vecchione noted that former WKBN cameraman Jack Hamilton is still a patron at the restaurant's new location. "He was the first original customer," Vecchione added. "They have the first dollar he spent there."

Meanwhile, the tavern emerged as a hangout for teachers from Boardman and Mooney High Schools, and Campana recalled that he occasionally served his own instructors. Former high school teacher James G. Doran, then part of the "Mooney crowd," noted that many regular patrons formed lifelong friendships. "It sounds like a cliché, but I always think of the line from the old *Cheers* theme song," Doran said. "This really is a place where everybody knows your name."

The Fireplace remained a South Side landmark until the 1990s, when rising crime and other factors led Thomas Campana Sr. to sell the building. Still in his thirties when the sale was completed, Thomas Campana Jr. eventually secured a new site on East Western Reserve Road in Poland's Five Points District. "It's amazing how many people who have moved away stop in here when they're back in town," he said.

Ethnic Cuisine Takes Center Stage

By the mid-1970s, Boomba's Lounge, on South Avenue, had won a regional reputation for its unique, home-style pierogi. "The dough is one of the most important things when you're making pierogi, and our dough was of such a texture that we couldn't use a dough sheeting machine," explained Bob Bakalik, who co-owned the restaurant with his mother, Pauline. "Everything had to be rolled out by hand, and each one of our cooks took turns rolling." He added that, when his cooks crimped the edges of the dough by hand, it was rare that a pierogi actually fell apart.

While some customers pressured Bakalik to reveal his trade secrets, many others questioned him about the origins of the restaurant's unusual name. "They assumed it was something in Polish or Slovak, like *babcia*," he said. In

Lois Bakalik, co-owner of Boomba's Lounge, enhanced her mother-in-law's pierogi recipe by introducing flavors such as spinach, prune, sweet potato, apple cinnamon, peach, apricot and kielbasa with sauerkraut. *Courtesy of Bob Bakalik.*

truth, he added, the name came about when his daughter, Brenda, was playing with her grandmother. "My mother was trying to get her to say, 'Grandma,'" he explained. "All she could come up with in baby talk was 'Boomba.'"

Before it closed in 1998, Boomba's was an established South Side landmark. "There was no decline," insisted Bakalik. "But when I reached sixty-five, I just wanted to retire." At its peak, the restaurant maintained fourteen full-time workers who produced about four thousand pierogis each week.[94] Boomba's offered fifteen varieties of pierogi. "The traditional pierogi were stuffed with mashed potatoes and sauerkraut and cabbage and cottage cheese," Bakalik noted. "But my wife, Lois, really was the one that developed all these other varieties with apple, cinnamon, peach and apricot filling."

In many ways, the popularity of Boomba's Lounge reflected the growing visibility of Eastern European food. Unlike Italian food, which was commonly served in local restaurants and taverns, Eastern European cuisine was rarely available outside private homes until the 1960s. "My mother was an excellent cook, and so we didn't eat out several times a week like people do now," explained Joseph Planey, who grew up in a Slovak American household. Exceptions, he added, were neighborhood church social halls and ethnic clubs as well as the South Side's Shady Run Picnic Grove, located on Shady Run Road.

By the later 1970s, another South Side business had gained recognition for its Eastern European specialties. Teenie's Tavern, also on South Avenue, became a major destination for fans of traditional entrées like *halupki,* pierogi, *halushki* and kielbasa with sauerkraut. For customers like Michael and Loretta Ekoniak, however, Teenie's main attraction was its pierogis, which they regard as the best in town. "A lot of times you get pierogi, and the dough is kind of thick," Loretta Ekoniak explained. "Here, they use exceptionally thin dough, so the filling stands out."

Mrs. Ekoniak noted that her oldest son, now thirty-two years old, stops at Teenie's whenever he returns to the area from his current home in Virginia. "Whenever he's home, he makes sure we're here on a Friday for dinner," she said. "He's traveled all over the world, but this is still his favorite pierogi." At one point, she added, her son asked Teenie's owner John Gordulic for the recipe. "You see, living in Virginia, he can't get pierogi at the churches, like you can here," she explained. "So he makes his own pierogi down in Virginia."

For public historian Richard S. Scarsella, the area's ethnic diversity was a key element in the development of its restaurant industry. He noted that visitors periodically commented on the "novelty" of finding the following items on the menus of local restaurants: "ravioli, lasagna, cavatelli, pierogi, *halushka*, corned-beef hash, blintzes, *Wiener schnitzel*, 'pan pizzas' from various Italian regions, escarole and endive wedding soups, *pasta fagiola*, fried pepper and onions in olive oil, macaroni and cheese, kielbasa, eel, octopus, squid and specialty desserts ranging from *pizzelles* to angel wings."

Despite the overwhelming economic difficulties that affected the community later on, a surprising number of these food traditions survived. "Even people who haven't lived here for years will talk about Brier Hill Pizza, or they'll go to St. Stanislaus Church for pierogi or, like my son, to Teenie's Tavern," Loretta Ekoniak observed. "I think the persistence of these traditions has a lot to do with the fact that it was such an ethnically diverse area to begin with—and I guess we've done a pretty decent job of passing that down to our kids."

"Bad Moon Rising"

Perceptive residents of the Mahoning Valley probably understood that Youngstown, by the mid-1970s, was economically stagnant. Few, however, could have predicted the scope of the tragedy that unfolded at the end of the decade. In 1977, Youngstown gained national attention for losing tens of thousands of manufacturing jobs overnight, while also securing an unsavory reputation for crime and corruption.

Worse yet, the disappearance of traditional industrial elites left behind a yawning "power vacuum," and some observers contend this vacuum was filled by interest groups that set out to develop "their own plan of action in the wake of the city's decline and competed with each other to achieve their own narrow goals." As Sean Safford observed in his comparative study of Youngstown and Allentown, Pennsylvania (two communities deeply affected by deindustrialization), "The result has been nothing short of catastrophic decline and hollowing out."[95]

As local businesspeople, including restaurateurs, struggled with challenges arising from suburbanization, the city's position as a major manufacturing center was eroded by factors including the unchecked deterioration of its industrial infrastructure. Worse yet, the industrial sector's collapse in the late 1970s and early 1980s occurred against a backdrop of perceived economic stability—a circumstance that amplified its impact.

In the wake of subsequent steel plant closures, the community was stripped not only of a viable future but also of a meaningful past. Sherry Linkon and John Russo noted that the community's loss of industry precipitated "the fragmentation of Youngstown's constitutive narrative as locals began to argue about how to think about their shared history."[96] The question on everyone's mind was articulated in a *Vindicator* article published five years after the initial plant closures: "How could an industry so much a part of the history of the community, and so vital to its economic life, simply cease to be or move away?"[97]

Chapter 4
FEAST TO FAMINE

By the late 1970s, local restaurateurs faced an unprecedented challenge in the collapse of the community's industrial infrastructure. The beginning of the end came in January 1969, when the New Orleans–based Lykes Corp. engaged in a hostile takeover of Youngstown Sheet & Tube, borrowing $150 million in bank loans and issuing about $191 million in debentures to finance the move.[98] Therefore, the newly merged company "assumed a debt liability of nearly $350 million."[99]

Not surprisingly, Lykes Corp. failed to invest in upgrading Youngstown Sheet & Tube's facilities, plundered its resources and sent the steel company into a downward spiral. Then, on Monday, September 17, 1977, representatives of Lykes Corp. announced the closing of the firm's large facility in nearby Campbell, along with huge plants in neighboring Struthers. The Campbell shutdown alone resulted in the loss of five thousand jobs in the Youngstown area, and it would be the first in a series of crippling blows.[100]

In the wake of Black Monday, representatives of the national media descended on Youngstown, which had emerged overnight as a symbol of deindustrialization. Carmen Naples, co-owner of the Golden Dawn Restaurant, recalled that award-winning NBC news correspondent Tom Petit was among the first to arrive. "They taped here because they wanted a cross-section of the people," Naples explained, "and somebody was in New York at the time, at NBC, and told them: 'Go to the Golden Dawn in Youngstown. You'll meet the president of the company and the guy that sweeps the floor at the same place.'"

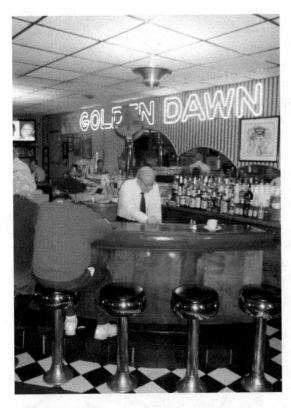

The Golden Dawn, a fixture on the city's North Side, retains much of its Old World atmosphere. Ninety-three-year-old Ralph Naples, who continues to tend bar in a shirt and tie, produces the restaurant's homemade pizza dough. *Courtesy of Thomas G. Welsh Jr.*

Petit and his crew were overwhelmed by the scene at the Golden Dawn. They found themselves in a traditional urban tavern "jammed" with customers, and they were disarmed by the generosity of the people they encountered. "They would tell us that in all the countries they went to…they'd have [to give] $100 bills, $500 bills, and how much these guys all had their hands out," Carmen Naples recalled. At the Golden Dawn, however, the television crew was invited to store its bulky equipment in the building's upstairs apartment free of charge.

The nationally telecast interviews at the Golden Dawn caught one of Carmen Naples's nephews by surprise when he glimpsed the coverage at his home in Atlanta, Georgia. "Ralph's son…always watches the morning show on NBC…and he's watching this show when Ralph is on," Carmen Naples explained. "He was drinking coffee—he dropped the cup of coffee."

The Decline of Urban Fine Dining

The plant shutdowns in Campbell and Struthers, Ohio, were followed by the staged withdrawal of U.S. Steel in 1979 and 1980, which culminated with the closing of its facilities in neighboring McDonald, Ohio.[101] More closings came with the bankruptcy of Republic Steel in the 1980s, ensuring that within a few years, the "Steel Valley" (which comprised Mahoning and Trumbull Counties in Ohio and portions of western Pennsylvania) would lose about forty thousand manufacturing jobs.[102] As the effects of deindustrialization and unemployment bore down on the community, the population fell dramatically—a trend that continued over the next several decades.

Significantly, the population had been slipping even before Black Monday. Preliminary census records released in 1980 indicated that between 1970 and 1980, Youngstown's population had fallen from 140,509 to 112,146, a drop of more than 20 percent.[103] This pattern became more pronounced over time, and twenty years later, in 2000, the city's population was recorded at just 82,026.[104]

In the decades after the first plant closings, deindustrialization intersected with the ongoing trends of suburbanization and demographic change, creating conditions that led to the virtual disappearance of high-end restaurants within the city limits. This process, however, unfolded in a manner that was neither consistent nor entirely predictable—and postindustrial Youngstown managed to sustain scores of modest independent restaurants.

One of the first of the city's fine-dining establishments to close was Antone's Restaurant & Confetti Lounge, which had been in a state of transition before the steel crisis. By the early 1970s, Anthony Gianfrancesco, the restaurant's founder, relied increasingly on his stepson, Ross Anthony Scianna. "My dad really started taking things over around '73, '74," explained Ross Scianna's son, Chad. "At that point, he decided to add what we would call a banquet facility—and that really took off, for weddings and proms and all kinds of events."

Ross Scianna wasn't content to upgrade the restaurant on Market Street, however. He was also developing strategies that would enable his family to exploit the growing suburban market. In the mid-1970s, he established Antone's II on U.S. Route 224 in Boardman, at the former site of the nation's first Arby's restaurant. The suburban branch eschewed a fine-dining atmosphere in favor of "pasta and sandwiches—more like what Antone's is today," Chad Scianna explained. Like many restaurateurs, Ross Scianna understood that "family dining" establishments were overtaking independent upscale restaurants.

In December 1980, when a $100,000 fire swept Antone's Restaurant & Confetti Lounge, the owners found themselves at a crossroads. "I remember…my grandfather and father took me there afterward, and it was a mess," Chad Scianna recalled. "They decided at that time that they weren't going to rebuild there." Later, in the mid-1980s, Ross Scianna built a $1.5 million facility on Boardman-Poland Road and South Avenue, which featured seating for 250 people and hosted a banquet center that could accommodate 380 guests.[105] Ultimately, however, he returned to the business model exemplified by Antone's II.

In 1984, just four years after Antone's departure from Market Street, another neighborhood landmark exited the scene. On the evening of March 4, the Mansion Restaurant & Cocktail Lounge was damaged in an arson fire. In October, the ruined structure, then owned by businessman John J. Perry, was pulled down, leaving behind the restaurant's signage and several concrete steps that were still covered with green carpeting. For those who remembered the heyday of the Uptown District, these remnants were a depressing reminder of how much the neighborhood had changed over time.

The Mansion's chief rival, the Colonial House, also began to lose customers in the 1980s, but it proved more resilient. When proprietor Paul Lyden died in 1982, ownership of the restaurant was transferred to his brother, Bertram. The following year, in 1983, Bertram died, and the restaurant was passed on to his wife, Alice, who ran it with her daughter, Patricia, until Christmas 1989. "It was too much," Patricia Lyden Yank recalled. "There was also a big decline in the Uptown District…and to be honest, a lot of the old-time North Siders who had supported the business were starting to die off."

In December 1989, the Colonial House was purchased by Robert H. Van Sickle and John Ridel, who hired local chef Jeff Chrystal as general manager. Van Sickle predicted the Colonial House would remain a gathering spot for local powerbrokers. "I've made more deals there than I ever did in my office," he said.[106] By January 1995, however, the business had closed its doors, a development attributed to a "deterioration of an established customer base."[107]

Another casualty of postindustrial trends was La Fontanella, an upscale Italian restaurant located on Midlothian Boulevard, just within the city limits. During its final years, the restaurant was co-owned by Dominic DeMart and Thomas Lyden, who had previously operated the Centennial Room, based at the Holiday Inn in Liberty, Ohio.

Within a couple years, however, the partnership ended; and when Lyden opened the Moonraker Restaurant in Boardman, Ohio, he drew away a percentage of La Fontanella's patrons. Plagued by competition from chains, the growth of suburban independent restaurants and the decline of the surrounding neighborhood, La Fontanella closed its doors in 1985.

Within a few months of La Fontanella's closing, the building was refurbished to make way for the 680 Seafood & Steak Restaurant, a business established by then mayoral candidate Ronald Schroeder and his Korean-born wife,

Ok-Soon. The couple had previously operated Ok-Soon's Oriental Food & Restaurant, located a few blocks down the street.[108] The new business, however, was relatively short-lived, and the Schroeders eventually reopened an Asian grocery store elsewhere on Midlothian Boulevard.

High-end restaurants weren't the only victims of urban change. Eating establishments that offered a semiformal, family-oriented atmosphere also began to suffer in the wake of the economic downturn. In 1989, for instance, the owners of Palazzo's Restaurant on Midlothian Boulevard announced the imminent closing of the business.

Thirty-four years earlier, in 1955, Palazzo's was the first restaurant north of Boardman Township to serve alcoholic beverages, and its warm atmosphere and zesty Italian food appeared to guarantee its success. Owner James Palazzo emerged as a community leader, assisting in the development of a hospitality program at Youngstown's Choffin Career Center, while also participating in a visionary (if unsuccessful) effort to establish a common supply center for local independent restaurants. By the late 1970s and early '80s, however, the restaurant was struggling with challenges that included James Palazzo's deteriorating health.

Bucking the Trend

While the decline of formal restaurants was a dominant trend by the late 1970s and '80s, a small number of entrepreneurs and investors took steps that must have struck many as counterintuitive. In the late 1970s, for example, pizzeria owner Nick Lavanty, driven by a desire to open a full-fledged restaurant, purchased a burned-out building next to Lavanty's Pizza and turned it into an establishment he called Nicolinni's. With the assistance of two friends, Lavanty transformed the wreckage of the Bel Mar Bar into a plush restaurant that could seat up to 220 diners.

The interior featured a sunken main dining area that resembled a Mediterranean courtyard, while the building's second floor hosted banquet facilities for private parties. Lavanty wanted to give customers the impression they were visiting an exotic Latin country, and the main dining area was flanked with twenty-foot-high columns and iron arches. Robert "Smitty" Smith, a Brier Hill native and employee at Lavanty's Pizza, recalled that the owner imported wrought-iron light fixtures from Mexico, while investing in slate walls, tile flooring and light shades composed of stained glass.

Lavanty's flair for innovation was reflected in Nicolinni's menu, which included specialties like veal française, chicken marsala and steak Messina—the last of which the owner invented. Lavanty's steak Messina consisted of two pieces of lightly sautéed filet that were covered in crab meat and topped with a layer of gruyère cheese. This was then placed in the broiler and, when finished, covered with sauce and mushrooms.

While he continued to operate the pizzeria at one end of the complex, Lavanty kept the businesses separate. "We didn't offer pizza in Nicolinni's, because our goal was to operate a gourmet restaurant," he said. "If five guys came in after a golf game and ordered a pizza, they'd take up a whole table and pay five bucks…You wanted people to buy fifteen-dollar meals."

Despite Nicolinni's popularity, Lavanty encountered financial problems and was forced to sell the property. Later on, he opened another Nicolinni's restaurant in Austintown, Ohio. (Two restaurants currently operate in the metropolitan area, but Lavanty is no longer involved in the family business.)

Meanwhile, within a year of the original site's closing, the building reopened under new management as Stewart's Copper Fox, a popular venue for events in the local African American community. "Sadly, there was trouble with the license," Robert Smith recalled. "So it was limited to pop and food—and it didn't make a go of it."

About a decade after Nicolinni's opened its doors, another unexpected development occurred on the North Side when the Wick Pollock Inn opened for business. Housed in a late nineteenth-century mansion designed by local architect Charles Owsley, the five-story hotel featured a forty-seven-thousand-square-foot addition that included a banquet hall and ballroom.

The hotel initially thrived, but events such as the 1992 bankruptcy of the Youngstown-based Phar-Mor discount drugstore chain deprived the Wick Pollock of important clients. The business closed in 1998, and full ownership of the property reverted back to YSU. The mansion, which has been restored to its original state, currently serves as the residence of YSU president Randy Dunn and his wife, Ronda.

Campus-Area Highlights

The Wick Pollock Inn wasn't the only food-oriented business to sprout up in the vicinity of Youngstown State University. As the steel industry and its satellite businesses disappeared, YSU's visibility grew, given that it was now one of the community's major employers and most valuable assets.

By the 1980s, its campus was dotted with independent and chain restaurants, and relatively few students bothered to travel downtown or to other parts of the North Side. Indeed, the construction of Kilcawley Student Center in the 1970s prompted even more students to dine and socialize on campus, and before long, chain restaurants opened branches in the student center itself.

Students, of course, were always in the market for cheap, convenient food, and restaurants of one kind or another had operated along the periphery of campus for decades. The number of campus-area restaurants, however, began to expand dramatically in the 1970s. In 1972, the first of the area's Inner Circle Restaurants opened on Lincoln Avenue, just south of campus. Cofounded by Don Larcinese and John Anthony Conti, the restaurant was a perfect fit for college students, given that its specialties included pizza, deli sandwiches, pasta and Italian salads. Furthermore, the restaurant served alcoholic beverages, and on weekends, it was a popular venue for local bands.

At the same time, students and others who enjoyed live music gathered at campus-area bars like Pogo's Pub and Tony's Hideaway. The development of a campus-area restaurant and entertainment district continued as the decade progressed. In 1976, a branch of the Cincinnati Chili Parlor opened at the corner of Elm Street and Lincoln Avenue, one of many businesses to occupy this coveted spot.

By the late 1970s, the only downtown-area business that drew large numbers of teenagers and young adults was the Tomorrow Club, a nightclub based in the old State Theater on West Federal Street. This situation would not change until the early 1980s, when the Cedars Lounge & Restaurant, located on nearby Hazel Street, emerged as the community's main center of youth culture and underground music.

Many restaurants that opened in the vicinity of campus were short-lived. At one time or another, campus-area thoroughfares like Lincoln and Fifth Avenues hosted businesses including the Fortune Garden Express, an Asian restaurant specializing in stir-fry dishes; the Point Café, an eatery featuring Middle Eastern cuisine and gourmet coffee; Coyoacan Mexican Grill; and University Pizzeria & Italian Restaurant, which continues to operate. Some establishments, like the Brass Lion, a pub with a Celtic theme, fizzled out despite high levels of investment and attractive furnishings.

One of the more enduring campus-area eateries, the Beat Coffeehouse, appeared on Lincoln Avenue in the early 1990s. Despite changes in

The Beat Coffeehouse has been a popular venue for students and faculty at Youngstown State University since the early 1990s. *Courtesy of the Mahoning Valley Historical Society.*

ownership, the coffeehouse remains a popular site of poetry readings, musical performances and art exhibitions. Local entrepreneur Jacob Harver was among scores of area residents who patronized the coffeehouse as a high school student. "It was then that I discovered the downtown," Harver recalled. "I started to go to the Cedar's Café and the Beat Coffeehouse, and I became plugged into the cultural scene."

Out of Nowhere

Despite the fact that the 1980s were characterized by serial closings of restaurants, the decade saw the rise of two of Youngstown's most memorable eating establishments—the Park Inn and the Pyatt Street Diner. The first to appear on the scene was the Park Inn, located on Glenwood Avenue, in the midst of the city's beleaguered South Side. Owned and operated by brothers and business partners Kim and James Westerfield, the Park Inn was known for its wet burrito, a tortilla filled with ground beef and refried beans and topped with sauce and cheese.

The Park Inn's wide menu also featured regional favorites like Cajun-style blackened chicken, recalled Patti Ferraro Druzisky, who dined there with co-workers. "It was a fun, casual place to meet," she said. "In the evening, they started to bring in bands and feature other kinds of live music, but we were there basically to eat and have margaritas." Whatever the time of day, the Park Inn hosted an eclectic crowd. "I used to tell people that the Park Inn had a…very unique draw," Father Edward P. Noga noted. "I remember saying once, 'You could be in a booth at the Park Inn, where on one side of you would be the ladies of the B'nai B'rith and, on the other side, a motorcycle gang.' And it was like they all fit."

Throughout the 1980s and early '90s, the restaurant was a hot spot in an otherwise declining neighborhood. Its tenure, however, was marked by difficulties, including repeated violations of state building codes.[109] A more serious threat to the Park Inn's restaurant trade, however, was the growing perception that the nightclub portion of the business had taken priority. Toward the end, many patrons saw the business mainly as a venue for local bands. In November 1988, the Park Inn's manager, Chris Sotkovsky, promised to strike a balance between the two halves of the business—a project that involved reintroducing Mexican food nights. "I'm going to try to get back to that original ID," he said.[110]

Ultimately, however, the Park Inn failed to overcome challenges connected to the rapid decline of the South Side. By the early 1990s, fewer suburbanites were willing to travel into the city, which they regarded as dangerous. On February 1, 1994, Kim Westerfield closed the business and announced it was for sale. Several days later, the *Vindicator* reported that the Park Inn, "which once drew huge crowds for live rock entertainment," had "failed to maintain the strong attendance it once enjoyed."[111]

In the late 1980s, as the Park Inn struggled to restore its restaurant business, an enterprising couple pooled their resources to preserve an imperiled South Side landmark, the Pyatt Street Market. Since the 1920s, the facility had operated just east of Market Street, but rising crime and a decline of independent grocery stores had taken their toll on the market. In 1987, one year after they purchased the Pyatt Street Market, Bill and Janet Umbel decided to expand a lunch and breakfast diner they established on the premises. At first, the diner was a "greasy spoon" that offered hamburgers

The Pyatt Street Diner, located on the city's South Side, developed a regional reputation for its gourmet entrées, which were prepared by chef Andy Witt. *Courtesy of Janet Umbel.*

and French fries, Bill Umbel recalled. "Eventually, we started getting more of the downtown trade and decided to expand our menu," he added.

The couple's next step was to hire local chef Andy Witt, who had attended the Culinary Institute of America in Hyde Park, New York. "Both Umbel and Witt understood Youngstown's ethnicity—particularly its appetite for exotic meats and breads, freshwater fish and fruits and vegetables in season," *Ohio Magazine* reported a couple years later. "Chef Witt's first experiment was to roast whole pigs and lambs in a barbecue pit that Bill Umbel constructed along the edge of the parking lot." As a further draw, Witt offered fresh, whole lobsters "at cost," and patrons who lined up sampled other specials, including "blackened red snapper, orange roughy and a bowl of Cajun shrimp served with linguini oglio," the magazine stated.[112]

While the surrounding market continued to deteriorate, the Pyatt Street Diner thrived. In the 1980s and early '90s, the restaurant drew a new crowd when it became a venue for music and poetry readings. "We noticed that they couldn't seat everybody during the weekends," Janet Umbel recalled. "So we started the Creole Café for those customers."

In time, the café was supplemented with a third business, a basement jazz club called Pyatt Street Down Under, and the Umbels eventually added a bocce court. Finally, in 2000, the couple established a suburban branch of the Pyatt Street Diner in Boardman, but the enterprise was short-lived. Three years later, in 2003, Bill Umbel, overextended and facing legal problems, was forced to close the restaurants.

Now divorced, the Umbels remain friends, and they look back fondly on their years in the restaurant business. "Our children were raised in the restaurants," Janet Umbel observed. "They started out skateboarding in the Down Under, and they became busboys as teenagers...They are very personable, and it's probably because they were around so many different types of people when they were growing up."

"The Beat Goes On"

As new restaurants came and went, owners of more established businesses struggled to meet the demands of a tightening market. Avalon Gardens on Belmont Avenue was one of many landmarks that witnessed dramatic changes in the 1980s. "At the Avalon, you had your old-timers, your shot-and-beer guys, who were drinking there when the steel mills were going full blast," Robert Smith recalled. "Slowly but surely, they died off."

Faced with this reality, proprietor Michael Sabella Jr., son of the tavern's second owner, Michael Sr., altered the format. "Michael plugged into the night life," Smith explained. "He brought in bands, and they would move the booths and tables to give people room to dance."

Over time, Avalon Gardens emerged as a meeting place for professionals, politicians, college students, faculty members and alumni of neighboring Rayen and Ursuline High Schools. Former Youngstown resident Bill Eberhart, who currently lives in Hawaii, described Avalon Gardens as the site of countless reunions. "It was the first place I went to when I came back to town to visit family and friends," he recalled. "I would have dinner with my mom and dad and then call my friends and tell them to meet me at the Avalon to catch a band or play bocce."

As Avalon Gardens became more family oriented, Friday fish dinners and bocce tournaments surfaced as major attractions. While the growing popularity of bocce (an Italian form of lawn bowling) was reflected at other local taverns, the game was played in earnest at the Avalon. "The men's league was more serious, and they played in Las Vegas and also Rome, New York, where the national championships were played," Smith recalled.

Meanwhile, the tavern won recognition for its Brier Hill Pizza, given that Robert Smith, its cook, had learned his craft at Lavanty's Pizza.

Farther south, in the shadow of expanding Youngstown State University, another North Side landmark was shaped by a flurry of urban trends. For decades, the MVR (Mahoning Valley Restaurant) was at the center of a largely Italian American neighborhood called Smoky Hollow, located in a gulley just east of YSU.

By the late 1960s and early '70s, however, Smoky Hollow was dying. "The houses that were originally [owned by] Italians, Slovaks and Jewish people turned into rental properties and then low-end rental properties," explained the MVR's then proprietor, Carmine Cassese. "And they never were big, because the old homes…weren't designed to rent."

At one point, this atmosphere of decline was supplemented by racial tension. While Youngstown was spared the devastating riots that erupted in other U.S. cities after Dr. Martin Luther King Jr.'s assassination on April 4, 1968, a number of businesses were vandalized, including the MVR. "Some people came down here and knocked out the front windows," recalled Carmine Cassese's father, Joseph. "Instead of putting the windows back, we just bricked it all up."

These negative trends, however, were overshadowed by developments that enabled the MVR's owners to reinvent the business. While other neighborhoods became textbook examples of urban blight, the aging houses in Smoky Hollow were razed by YSU to make way for student parking. "The growth of the university always helped," Carmine Cassese noted. "They… tore out a whole bunch of scrappy homes, and they built that [parking deck]."

In some cases, the university bought properties owners couldn't sell. "If you were the third generation in your grandparents' [house], and your house was worth $3,000, and you went to YSU…they'd pay your taxes—or give you $3,000 or something—and tear it down," Cassese added. "And that was the only way they did things…So it was a very, very slow process."

Meanwhile, Joseph and Carmine Cassese developed a social network that helped them draw patrons to the restaurant. One of the MVR's most prominent boosters was late YSU coach Bill Narduzzi, who promoted the restaurant among the campus crowd. "Years and years ago, he became great friends with my dad because YSU practiced across the street," Carmine Cassese recalled. "And then, the next thing you know, he brought YSU people down here—and that helped."

The late Carmine Cassese was especially adept at forging durable relationships. After teaching for five years at Youngstown's Cardinal Mooney

The patio and bocce courts of the MVR teem with activity during the warmer months of spring and summer. *Courtesy of Carmine Cassese.*

Joseph and Carmine Cassese (left to right) led the MVR through dramatic changes, and the restaurant remains an important local symbol of continuity. Carmine Cassese's untimely death in June 2013 elicited an overwhelming community response. *Courtesy of Thomas G. Welsh Jr.*

High School, he moved on to an administrative position at YSU's athletic department, where he worked for more than three decades. "So through teaching, through the university, through interaction with all the different people, I promoted [the restaurant]," he explained. "So we were starting to bring an influx from the suburbs...because about that time, we were losing everyone around here."

Over time, the business evolved into a full-fledged restaurant, and the MVR became known for its Italian American entrées and Friday fish dinners. "When we started doing fish...I can tell you, the piece was big," Carmine Cassese recalled. "Well, there was a reason because I had to get you out of your comfort zone." He added, "Once I got you here, I felt OK, that I'd be able to blend and mix and you'd like the place...because I had a lot of family...friends, and it was sincere."

During the late 1980s, another local landmark with roots on the North Side struggled to reinvent itself. In May 1988, Kravitz's Delicatessen in Liberty Township held a "grand reopening" to call attention to its refurbished interior. The delicatessen, after expanding into commercial space next store, occupied 4,200 square feet, and its two dining rooms could accommodate 110 patrons. During the event, Rose Kravitz's son, Jack (along with his wife, Cindy), launched a marketing campaign to promote the business's line of bagels, described as "the only bagel to be baked fresh locally."[113]

Kravitz's shift into wholesale bagel production was a natural development, Jack Kravitz explained. "[W]e found out we had excess production time that we could utilize and started to sell bagels to other restaurants and other businesses," he recalled. "And it grew till we were doing 500 to 1,000 dozen bagels a day in our postage-stamp of a back room." The couple opened a five-thousand-square-foot bakery in neighboring North Jackson, Ohio, and by January 1993, the Youngstown-based *Business Journal* reported that Kravitz Bagels Inc. was "capable of producing 8,000 bagels per day."[114]

At its peak, Kravitz's Bagels boasted production of 120,000 bagels per day, and its clients included deep-discount stores like Phar-Mor and Sam's Club. The firm's main distributor was Youngstown-based Schwebel's Bakery, and its products were sold to major bakeries such as Stroehmann, Entenmann, Brownberry and Lewis Bros. "We had a good twelve-year run in the wholesale bagel business, and then we had three years that weren't so good," Kravitz recalled. Toward the end, the firm was hampered by the loss of a major client, growing competition and trends in the food industry. "You could definitely see the decline when the 'low-carb' craze hit," Kravitz recalled.

Kravitz's Delicatessen, a descendant of Youngstown's Elm Street Delicatessen, continues to operate in Liberty Township. Jack Kravitz, son of the restaurant's founders, recently established a second branch of the deli at the Poland Public Library in Poland, Ohio. *Courtesy of Thomas G. Welsh Jr.*

Eight years before Kravitz's moved into wholesale bagel production, Jay's Famous Hot Dogs (originally Jay's Lunch) closed its facility in downtown Youngstown and relocated to U.S. Route 224 in Boardman. Established in 1980, at the former site of a Der Wienerschnitzel hot dog franchise, the new restaurant thrived under the management of Sam Petrakos's brother, Frank, who continued the tradition of dressing an "arm-full" of hot dogs. "I make the best hot dogs in the world," Frank Petrakos stated in a 1995 interview with the *Business Journal*. "It's hard work and long hours but I've been very successful," he added.

Like any landmark business, Jay's saw its share of celebrity customers, and the restaurant's interior featured signed photographs of sports figures like Bernie Kosar, Ray "Boom Boom" Mancini, Jeff Lampkin and Ernie Shavers. Also on display was an autographed picture of former U.S. president Ronald Reagan.[115] A special place of pride, however, was reserved for a 1940 photograph of President Franklin D. Roosevelt's motorcade passing through downtown Youngstown. At one corner of the image was a clear shot of the signage and exterior of Jay's Lunch.

The Petrakos family's awareness of Jay's roots in downtown Youngstown may have influenced their decision to establish a presence at the Phar-Mor

In the early 1990s, Frank Petrakos continued to impress customers with his dexterity at the Jay's Hot Dogs branch in neighboring Boardman. *Courtesy of Greg Petrakos.*

President Franklin D. Roosevelt's limousine cruises along Youngstown's West Federal Street during a campaign stop on October 11, 1940. Signage for Jay's Hot Dogs, an iconic downtown eatery, can be seen in the upper right-hand corner. *Courtesy of Greg Petrakos.*

Centre in 1988. In general, however, the business's expansion occurred elsewhere. In 1984, four years after the Boardman restaurant opened, the family established a presence on the city's West Side. Two years later, in 1986, a branch opened in Austintown, and over the next decade, stores appeared in Niles, Campbell and North Lima.

While some of these facilities have closed, Jay's remains a local icon. "This area has a great history that involves lots of hardworking families who opened restaurants, and people still have fond memories of them," said Greg Petrakos, manager of the Boardman location. "In the case of Jay's, we have the great-grandchildren of original patrons who come in and share stories that have been passed down to them."

New Kids on the Block

As the hollowing out of Youngstown's center city continued, three new restaurants managed to secure the status of "modern classics." Incredibly, all three of these businesses were located within—or on the periphery of—the declining South Side. The first appeared in 1988, when Douglas and Cecelia "Cece" Bouslough purchased the Newport Deli on Hillman Way and reopened it as the Newport Café.

The couple brought decades of experience to the project. Doug Bouslough, a native of the South Side, had worked at the Boulevard Tavern and Italian Baking Company. During a stint in the U.S. Army, he gained additional experience as a mess sergeant, and following his discharge, he found work as a baker for the Sparkle Market grocery chain. Then, in the 1980s, Bouslough served as chef and part owner of the Boathouse Restaurant in Boardman while working at the Boatyard Restaurant in Liberty. It was then that he met his wife, Cece, who had been involved in the food service industry since 1975.

Determined to put their own stamp on the business, the Bousloughs also tried to create a feeling of continuity. Along with the business, they purchased scores of Stella Ziegler's recipes—including those for cheesecake and mushroom barley soup—and they initially retained many of the Newport Deli's suppliers. "Before anyone was really selling bagels, we were getting bagels prepared under rabbinical supervision from Cleveland," Doug Bouslough explained. "And I tried to carry a lot of the things that were offered by the Newport Deli—the gefilte fish, the black trout, chicken liver, lox and bagels—and they were so expensive."

Former world boxing champion and actor/producer Ray "Boom Boom" Mancini (center) on the set of the 2001 film *Turn of Faith*. Filmed on location at the Newport Café, the movie starred Mancini, Mia Sara, Costas Mandylor, Tony Sirico and Academy Award–winning actor Charles Durning. *Courtesy of Cecelia Bouslough.*

Over time, however, certain items disappeared. "We tried to keep the customers from the Newport Deli, but they didn't sustain our business," Cece Bouslough explained. "So we had to move over and add things that would keep the people coming." New customers were drawn by the restaurant's hearty breakfasts and lunches, which featured deli-style sandwiches, salads and veggie plates, along with Doug Bouslough's inimitable corned beef hash. Meanwhile, Cece Bouslough prepared homemade desserts, including bread pudding, chocolate cake and apple cobbler.

Between 1988 and the restaurant's closing in 2006, the Newport Café drew a remarkably varied crowd. "We had kings and princesses and the people that were under the bridge," Doug Bouslough observed. "Judges, lawyers, all of them—they would do business up there. We would have parties for elected officials." He added that, at one point, he introduced Youngstown's future mayor, Jay Williams, to prominent local business leader Bruce Zoldan.

Other well-known patrons included late WKBN owner J.D. Williams, philanthropist Denise DeBartolo York, realtor and ex–professional baseball player Jack Mayo, hairstylist Joe Dohar and former boxing champion Ray "Boom Boom" Mancini. Interestingly, Mancini, in his capacity as a producer and actor, arranged for scenes from the 2002 movie *Turn of Faith* to be filmed at the Newport Café. "They borrowed our restaurant for two days, and it was a big production," Doug Bouslough recalled. "They got everyone in the neighborhood to be in the movie."

Doug Bouslough described the Newport Café as "a rocket shooting straight up," but success offered no guarantee of longevity. In the spring of 2006, Cece Bouslough was diagnosed with breast cancer, and the couple took what they thought would be a temporary break from the business. Years later, the Bousloughs expressed no regrets about their time in the restaurant industry, and Doug Bouslough attributed the Newport Café's eighteen-year "winning streak" to the fact that neither of them took shortcuts. "I never took my customers for granted," he said. "It was 'Hello' when they walked through the door, and 'Thank you' before they walked out the door—and that was every single customer."

In 1991, three years after the establishment of the Newport Café, another distinctive South Side business opened its doors when Vietnamese-born restaurateur Can Dao and his wife, Hin, established Tokyo House on South Avenue, not far from Interstate 680. Housed in a former gas station, Tokyo House fit into a long tradition of local eateries whose culinary delights were hidden behind modest exteriors. "When you would drive by, it looked like an old abandoned gas station," recalled Loretta Ekoniak, a former high school teacher who learned about the restaurant through her students. "There was a sign that read, 'Tokyo House,' but it wasn't on the building. It was sitting on the ground, leaning up against the building."

Like most first-time customers, Mrs. Ekoniak assumed the building was empty. Her students advised her, however, that signs of life would eventually appear. "And sure enough, at 4:30, there were people there, standing in line, waiting to get in," she recalled. "At five o'clock, they opened the door, and you'd walk in." Those patrons who arrived on the scene first were seated at one of several large tables that held up to a dozen people. Each table featured a large hibachi grill, where the chef prepared a variety of stir-fry dishes as he moved from one group to another.

Mrs. Ekoniak stressed that, even today, customers need to be patient. Those unable to secure a table bide their time in a waiting room until one becomes available, and after a certain point, no further guests are admitted. "The Tokyo House would continue to serve guests until they ran out of rice," explained Nar Martinez, a longtime fan of the restaurant. He noted that, on one occasion, he drove there with friends "at the spur of the moment," only to find the door locked. "When we knocked on the door, the proprietor popped his head out and said, 'Rice all gone—you go home,'" Martinez recalled. "As long as I live, I'll never forget that."

Can Dao's personality is one of the keys to the restaurant's success. A 2011 *Vindicator* article observed that "from 4 to 8 p.m., he's on stage behind the grills...He combines jokes and theatrics for a night of entertainment— flirting with pretty girls and creating fireballs on

Despite its unassuming appearance, Tokyo House on the city's South Side has developed a loyal following among diners who enjoy traditional Asian cuisine. *Courtesy of Thomas G. Welsh Jr.*

the grill that reach to the edge of the overhead fan."[116] Loretta Ekoniak's husband, Michael, agreed. "People go there as much for the atmosphere as the food," he said. "He has such a genial relationship with his customers."

In the late 1990s, a few years after the arrival of Tokyo House, another South Side destination, Bobby D's, opened on Midlothian Boulevard. Proprietor Bobby DeVicchio had formerly operated Jim Dandy's Tavern on South Avenue, but he was determined to open a full-fledged restaurant. Therefore, in 1995, DeVicchio rented the vacant site of Great Wall Chinese Restaurant, near the corner of South and Palmer Avenues, which became the first site of Bobby D's restaurant. The business thrived, and a couple years later, DeVicchio purchased the former site of Palazzo's, across from Schwebel's Bakery.

To showcase his entrées, DeVicchio offered a special each day of the week. On Mondays, he featured liver and onions, while city chicken was the special on Tuesdays. Wednesdays were devoted to pasta dishes, Thursdays featured burgers and Fridays showcased fish dinners.

The restaurant's most unique offering was grilled chicken with Italian greens, prepared in the traditional manner, with endive and escarole. "We buy it fresh and then steam it until it's nice and tender," DeVicchio explained. "We then prepare a sauté, with a blend of oil and garlic." DeVicchio ran Bobby D's until 2006, when he took a three-year hiatus from the restaurant industry. Along with business partner Carmen Lofaro, he currently operates Bogey's Bar & Grill, in Coitsville, Ohio.

East Side Happenings

A potent symbol of changing times on the East Side was the closing of the Royal Oaks Tavern in July 1991, seven years after it marked its fiftieth anniversary. "I couldn't take it any longer," explained Bobby DeMain, the last member of his family to operate the business. "My overhead was way too high, and there was a lot more going out than coming in," he added. "This is a lot better than filing bankruptcy, but I hope to be back someday."[117]

While Bobby DeMain never returned to the business, the Royal Oaks reopened five years later, in 1996, under new owner George Skrbina, who previously operated a mini-chain called the Ohio Pig House. Like many regular customers, Skrbina was saddened at the closing of the local landmark, and he decided to do something about it. "When the price became right, I bought it," he explained in 1997. "There are no bars on the East Side…I thought I could build up a strong clientele from the old business."

Aware of the tavern's role as a local institution, Skrbina chose not to remodel its interior. "Older Royal Oaks patrons may be surprised to discover the virtually untouched décor," a 1997 *Vindicator* article observed. "Featuring the original, hand-carved, cherry wood bar imported from Ireland and original booths, seats and tables, the bar maintains the tradition that created a Youngstown legend." At the same time, Skrbina expanded the tavern's menu, retaining old favorites like chili dogs but also introducing smoked ribs and widening the selection of beer.[118]

Three years later, in 1999, the tavern was purchased by brothers Lou and John Kennedy, who initially considered buying Boomba's Lounge on the South Side. At one point, however, John Kennedy stopped at the Royal Oaks for lunch and discussed the plan with Skrbina, who suggested they instead consider purchasing the Royal Oaks, their preferred hangout. "So, George

The Royal Oaks has operated on the city's East Side since 1934. In recent years, the local landmark has drawn new customers with its raspberry barbecue ribs and chicken. *Courtesy of Lou Kennedy.*

talked us into buying this," Lou Kennedy explained. "And I will say this: He taught us how to make ribs."

Since then, John Kennedy has done extensive research on traditional barbecue techniques, and the brothers contend that their ribs have won the approval of the most discerning customers. "I have people come in here from all over the world. And I'm always most impressed when we have people from down South come up here, and they like them," Lou Kennedy noted. "I had some guys in here from Texas last week, and one of them said, 'I've been out of Texas for a couple months now, and I have to tell you that this is the most incredible barbecue I've had since.'"

In the fifteen years since the Kennedy brothers took over, the Royal Oaks's Tuesday barbecue nights have become a local highlight, and area food critics Mark Smesko and Michael Vallas credited the tavern with serving "some of the best barbecued ribs you'll ever eat."[119] Meanwhile, the Royal Oaks continues to draw an exceptionally diverse crowd, ranging from polished professionals to underground musicians. "I always direct people to the Royal Oaks," observed local activist Phil Kidd. "When you walk in, you get an almost overwhelming experience of Youngstown's culture and dysfunction, in a setting that has remained virtually unchanged over the years."

Elsewhere on the East Side, the restaurant sector was in a state of transition, as established businesses began to close. In some cases, however, their facilities were purchased or leased by other restaurateurs. This was true of the Beacon Restaurant, a fixture on McCartney Road. In the early 1980s, the property was leased by entrepreneur William Wainio Sr., who reopened the business as My Dad's Restaurant. "It was quaint, and it was homey," recalled Wainio's son William Jr. "It was a family-style restaurant."

A longtime grocer, William Wainio Sr. previously operated an Isaly's outlet at the East Side's Lincoln Knolls Plaza. While he offered a range of Isaly's food products, he expanded the menu to include homemade meals. "We introduced my father's spaghetti sauce and meatballs, which were made from scratch," Wainio's son George recalled. "Then, we offered stuffed peppers, Swiss steak, Salisbury steak—different items that were home-style."

The move to the site of the Beacon Restaurant occurred when William Wainio Sr. learned that the building's current occupant wanted someone to take over the last few years of his ten-year lease. "It wasn't a difficult transition," William Wainio Jr. recalled. "We decided it would be more consistent with our business style." By the early 1990s, William Wainio Sr. had relocated the business to Poland Avenue, where he took over the Flat Iron Café. The new business, called My Dad's Flat Iron Café, promoted many of My Dad's specialties, including a home-style sausage sandwich and a burger called the "Big Daddy."

In the end, the most formidable challenge the family faced was the transformation of the neighborhood itself. "We bought the business knowing that they were going to tear the steel mills down," George Wainio explained. "We were hoping that with the clearing of that area and the construction of the new Center Street Bridge, we would be in the middle of a nice, clean neighborhood." As it turned out, the construction of the new bridge required the razing of My Dad's Flat Iron Café. The neighborhood that emerged from the building and demolition projects of the 1990s was stripped of numerous landmarks, including the nearby Castle restaurant.

Meanwhile, on McCartney Road, the former My Dad's Restaurant was taken over by a young businessman named Dave Mastry, who reopened it as the City Limits. Still in his twenties, Mastry had grown up in the business, given that his father, Raymond, owned a popular restaurant on Market Street.

After Raymond Mastry's death in 1978, his seventeen-year-old son took over Raymond's restaurant and operated it until 1981—an experience he described as "challenging." During its ten years of operation, Dave Mastry explained, Raymond's catered to the South Side's after-hours crowd. "We were known mainly for our midnight breakfasts," he noted, adding that regular patrons gravitated to specialties like baked rigatoni and steak and eggs.

By the late 1980s, Mastry was working as a salesman at a cousin's East Side car lot, and he became a regular at My Dad's Restaurant. When he discovered the business was for sale, he formed a partnership with a friend and cut a deal. After buying his partner's share of the business, he went on to operate the City Limits as sole owner, and within a year, he purchased two additional restaurants: a high-end Italian restaurant called Casa Fino, based in the former Limelighter Club on Market Street, and an East Side barbecue restaurant that didn't even have a name.

Before long, however, the strain of operating three businesses proved overwhelming. "I had my first heart attack at twenty-eight, and I decided to dump it all," he recalled. Chastened by this experience, Mastry didn't terminate his involvement in the restaurant industry. After almost a decade in Erie, Pennsylvania, where he worked at a cousin's Italian deli, he returned to Youngstown, and in 2000, he reopened the City Limits at its original site.

Today, Mastry continually introduces new entrées, but he takes pride in the fact that his menu still features his father's signature omelet and his grandmother's red sauce. He also derives satisfaction from the knowledge that many of his older customers once patronized the Beacon Restaurant as teenagers. For reasons including his commitment to local tradition, Mastry plans to operate the restaurant as long as possible. "I won't leave here," he said. "I can see everything here, right from the top of the hill."

Trends on the West Side

In the wake of Black Monday, a series of restaurants opened on the city's relatively stable West Side. As early as 1984, two couples affected by the economic crisis pooled their resources and opened a Mexican restaurant on Mahoning Avenue. The enterprise, known as La Casita, was the product of a partnership including ex-steelworkers Charles Heiser and George Horvath as well as their wives, Mariana "Mary Ann" and Debby. Sadly, La Casita, like many restaurants of the period, failed to thrive.

Two years later, in 1986, the West Side saw the opening of another small eatery, Mitsi's Cafeteria. Located in the once prosperous Mahoning Plaza, the business had been purchased by Steve Spon, a native of Sharon, Pennsylvania, who opened a branch downtown in 1988. Nineteen months later, however, he was forced to close the downtown branch in the wake of a $2 million road reconstruction project, which was intended to restore two-way traffic on West Federal Street. "The street reconstruction took pretty much everything we had," Spon said.[120] The businessman retained the restaurant on the West Side, which he operated with his wife, Beth, for the next few years.

In June 1993, the neighborhood became the home of a surprisingly upscale business when Armadillo Restaurant opened at the corner of Mahoning and South Bon Air Avenues. Owners Debbie and Cliff Mortimer promoted southwestern-style cuisine, and the interior of their restaurant featured "paintings with western themes, steer horns, brass lamps and table coach lights." Debbie Mortimer noted that all entrées were cooked in a wood-burning stove, and she contended that the restaurant burned "a whole pickup load of hardwood such as oak, cherry, maple or hickory every week."

While the Armadillo was known mainly for its barbecued baby back ribs, the Mortimers introduced dishes less familiar to local diners. "We make a distinctive baked potato soup, our own salad dressing and serve spinach and artichoke dips unlike anything we have sampled," Mrs. Mortimer said. Apart from typical seafood entrées like haddock and cod, the restaurant also featured grilled blue marlin, mahi mahi, shark and walleye.[121] The restaurant closed in the late 1990s, and the building houses Salsitas Mexican Restaurant, part of a regional chain.

One of the most distinctive additions to the West Side's restaurant sector was Casa Ramirez, which opened in 1992, at the corner of Mahoning and Milton Avenues. Owner Carlos Ramírez—a native of Michoacán, Mexico—had established his first restaurant downtown four years earlier. The downtown site, however, was limited to serving lunch, and Ramírez envisioned a restaurant that would offer dinner as well. Therefore, when his lease ended, Ramírez bought an old building that sat a few blocks north of his West Side home. It was there that Ramírez, along with his wife, Celerina "Cele", set out to provide diners with a full complement of regional Mexican dishes.

From the beginning, Casa Ramirez's menu reflected the fact that Carlos and Cele Ramírez hailed from the state of Michoacán. Determined to give customers an authentic culinary experience, the Ramírezes also offered food

Casa Ramirez Restaurant, located on the city's West Side, has offered local diners authentic Mexican food since 1989. The restaurant has previously operated a branch in neighboring Liberty Township. *Courtesy of Thomas G. Welsh Jr.*

items that were familiar to local diners. Their menu featured "Americanized" Mexican dishes (described as "dinners"), while a special section was devoted to "traditional dinners," which were prepared in a style consistent with culinary practices in their native Michoacán. "The way you eat right here is the way you will eat if you happen to go to Michoacán," Carlos Ramírez explained.

Today, Casa Ramirez's signature dish is the "Ramirez Special," a regional favorite called *pollo Michoacano*, which comprises two fried tortillas covered in the restaurant's secret sauce and stuffed with grilled chicken. The couple encountered the dish during a visit to Mexico with their children, and everyone in the family liked it. After returning home, Cele Ramírez replicated *pollo Michoacana* in her kitchen, and she now serves it on holidays and special occasions. To ensure authentic flavor, Carlos Ramírez has resisted pressure to buy food items from big chain suppliers: "We keep telling them, 'I cannot switch with you, because then I'm going to be like the rest of them.'"

Longtime patrons of the restaurant include members of the art community, some of whom maintain studios in the Spring Commons District that abuts the West Side. Artist Robyn Maas often meets with friends at Casa Ramirez

167

A Mexican mariachi band enlivens the celebration of Cinco de Mayo at Casa Ramirez.
Courtesy of Carlos and Celerina Ramirez.

on Friday evenings, and while she respects the restaurant's "consistency," she also appreciates its welcoming atmosphere. "I like the fact that we're practically part of the family," Ms. Maas said. "Carlos and Cele know us by name, and they always come out and greet us; and if we don't show up for awhile, they'll ask if anything's wrong."

For all his success as a restaurateur, Carlos Ramírez envisioned a different kind of career. When he was just nine years old, his father, José, a farmer, sent him away to pursue an education, an option traditionally reserved for those "with means." When he entered college, Ramírez pursued a degree in teaching, and after graduating, he completed a year of service in the Mexican military. Upon his discharge from the military in the late 1960s, however, Ramírez faced a momentous decision. He could accept a guaranteed teaching position in Mexico or join his relatives, who, by that time, had relocated to the United States.

Ultimately, the draw of family proved irresistible. Ramírez chose to turn down the teaching job and relocated from Mexico to Ohio. In time, he met and befriended his future wife, Celerina, whose family had arrived in Youngstown around the same time. Given that the economy was still robust, he was able to secure a good job with a local railroad company. Then, in the late 1970s and early '80s, the steel industry collapsed, and along with thousands of others, Ramírez was laid off. Drawing on his background in education, he became active in a local Hispanic social service agency, rising from a job as a bus driver to a position as youth coordinator.

By that time, Ramírez was already involved in the Mexican Mutual Society, a group organized in the 1930s to provide assistance to members of the Mexican American community. Although the Mexican Mutual Society maintained a hall on the West Side's Midland Avenue, its leaders' fundraising efforts were ineffective. So at one point—along with a brother, two cousins and a friend—Ramírez joined the organization and promoted a new kind of fundraiser. He suggested that the club sell five-dollar tickets for traditional Mexican dinners consisting of rice, beans, a taco and an enchilada. Labor for the event, he noted, would be provided by volunteers, while ingredients were inexpensive.

As the dinners grew in popularity, Ramírez suggested expanding the fundraiser, and by the early 1980s, the dinners were held every Friday and Saturday. The success of the fundraiser, however, fueled disagreements over its future direction. In the early 1990s, Ramírez struck out on his own, establishing his first restaurant in downtown Youngstown. Since then, he said, the local restaurant sector has benefited from the contributions of numerous immigrant and migrant groups. "I think the fact that this town, this area, is composed of different cultures is something very unique," he added.

Elsewhere on the West Side, several established businesses were reinvented under new owners. Among them was the Palm Café, a traditional working-class bar located on Steel Street, a few blocks north of Mahoning Avenue. In 1983, longtime owner Alex Matavich sold the tavern to George Dubic, a former tool-and-die worker looking for a change of pace. "When I was thirty, I decided to do something for myself, and I thought I would enjoy running a bar," Dubic recalled. "I had no clue what I was getting into."

Within weeks, the new owner introduced ethnic food and entertainment. Dubic, who had emigrated from a suburb of Zagreb, Croatia, when he was eighteen, was keenly aware of the city's large Balkan population. "For a long time, we used to have ethnic music every Saturday night," he explained. "The *tamburitza* would come in and play for hours."

Building on the previous owner's practice of barbecuing chicken in the summer months, Dubic also held traditional lamb roasts. "When I took over, I had a lot of Greek painters from Campbell who would come in," he said. "They were very busy during the summer, so they wanted me to cook lamb during the winter months." To accommodate the painters, he built a large cooking facility behind the bar, and by September 1983, Dubic was in a position to barbecue lamb year-round.

In this 2006 photograph, George Dubic, owner of Dubic's Palm Café, helps son John (right) prepare barbecued lamb for his customers. The popular tavern-restaurant maintains its year-round tradition of Saturday outdoor barbecues. *Courtesy of George and Anna Dubic.*

Since then, local demand for traditional entertainment has weakened. "Youngstown isn't what it was thirty or forty years ago," Dubic noted. "The ethnic people are mostly gone, and the young people aren't as interested in ethnic music." At the same time, the Palm Café's traditional Saturday lamb roasts are more popular than ever, and Dubic, assisted by his son, John, barbecues a variety of meats—including lamb, chicken and ham—using traditional Balkan techniques. The slow roasting of the meat over wooden coals takes several hours, but as two local reviewers observed, the result is "[c]rispy skin, perfectly seasoned, mild smokiness, with tender meat that falls off the bone."[122]

Dubic indicated he has no plans to tinker with a successful format. "If it's not broke, don't fix it," he said. "On average, I would say we sell 750 to 800 pounds of lamb on Saturdays, and we sell about 1,300 hams over the Easter holiday." On Saturday afternoons, workers at the Palm Café haul in steaming hunks of meat "right off the spit," and patrons have the option of ordering takeout or dining on the premises. "We have lawyers, doctors, professors and politicians come in, and they never wear suits—it's a picnic-style environment," Dubic explained. On occasion, he added, celebrities stop in. "Ed O'Neill from *Modern Family* comes in," Dubic noted. "Steve Buscemi has been here, and [former Ohio State University football coach] Jim Tressel was in here not long ago."

Over the decades, Dubic's wife, Anne, has come to view the tavern's customers as extended family. "Some of our regular customers first came with their parents or their grandparents," she said. Longtime patron Dave Vasvari, a resident of neighboring Poland Township, swears by the Palm Café. "There are things you can get at these kinds of businesses that you're not going to find in the chains or the so-called high-end places," he said. "A lot of places try to replicate what George does here, but it's just not up to the same standard."

In recent years, younger patrons have included local activist Phil Kidd, who is of partial Croatian ancestry and grew up with holiday lamb roasts. "In many ways, the Palm Café is the kind of place that exemplifies Youngstown's working-class atmosphere and ethnic diversity, but it also transcends generational differences," Kidd observed. "In other words, when you walk in, you're likely to find a young hipster sitting at the bar right next to a middle-aged football fan…It's the kind of social space that, in my view, really characterizes the Mahoning Valley."

During the early 1980s, Molly O'Dea's Restaurant & Lounge, located on nearby Salt Springs Road, underwent a similar transformation. In June 1982, founder Nick Conti sold the business to Jim Precurato, a remote-control locomotive operator who had been laid off two years earlier. Before working in the industrial sector, however, Precurato had received plenty of exposure to the restaurant industry, given that his father had served as a chef at a number of local restaurants, including the Voyager Motor Inn.

Precurato initially operated the restaurant with a business partner, but he soon struck out on his own; and in 1984, he took the final step of purchasing the building. While he renamed the business, shortening the original name to Molly's Restaurant & Lounge, Precurato retained many of Conti's traditional Italian American dishes. At the same time, he expanded the menu. Hiring a full-time chef, he introduced homemade soups and entrées that many would expect to find in a more formal restaurant. "Our signature soups include wedding soup, clam chowder, pasta fagioli and potato soup," Precurato explained. "We have a full-time chef, and some of our other popular dishes include stuffed scrod with Alfredo sauce and fettucine Alfredo."

While the restaurant's Friday fish specials are a perennial favorite, Molly's also features a popular monthly special. "Lots of people come in on the first Tuesday of the month, when we serve black bean soup and pot roast," noted full-time chef Steve Moritz. "On average, we go through about twenty-five pounds of pot roast and about ten bags of black beans." Like most employees, Moritz, the restaurant's third full-time chef, has worked there for years. "Steve has been here, on and off, since he's been a teenager," Precurato observed. "He started off as a dishwasher, so he's been here, in and out, for about twenty years."

For Precurato, who has seen various West Side businesses come and go, there's nothing mysterious about his restaurant's success. "If you offer a good product at a fair price, you're going to keep your customers," he said. "I've got customers that have been coming here for thirty years…and they're actually bringing their grandkids…I feel that's a great accomplishment."

Jim Precurato (left) has operated Molly's Restaurant and Lounge for thirty years, while server Connie Fagnano (right) has worked there for twenty-six years. The restaurant maintains a full-time chef and features entrées including stuffed scrod with Alfredo sauce. *Courtesy of Thomas G. Welsh Jr.*

In 1991, the Open Hearth, located a couple blocks south of Dubic's Palm Café, saw a change in management when Charles Serednesky's widow, Justine, retired and sold off the business. That year, local chef Jeff Chrystal formed a partnership with businessman Mike McCarthy and reopened the establishment as the Open Hearth Grille. With Chrystal's sister, Beth, in charge of the kitchen, the tavern offered a full menu, ranging from appetizers, such as buffalo wings and sauerkraut balls, to entrées, including seared sirloin steak and blackened fish.

Given that McCarthy and Chrystal were actively involved in the local Irish American community, the Open Hearth Grille had a decidedly Celtic atmosphere. Besides domestic beers, the tavern offered Guinness stout and Harp lager, and entertainment featured local Celtic bands such as County Mayo, the Shaffer Brothers and Shillelagh Law (later reorganized as Brady's Leap). In time, the business became a St. Patrick's Day destination.

Despite its initial popularity, the Open Hearth evidently ran into difficulties, and before long, the site was opened to the public only on special occasions. Finally, in 2003, the business was purchased by veteran restaurateur Bill Umbel, then operating the South Side's Pyatt Street Diner. However, not long after opening what he called the Open Hearth Restaurant & Tavern, Umbel was forced to close down because of serious legal problems. Today, the Open Hearth is owned and operated by entrepreneur William T. Matsouris, and despite various changes in management, it remains a significant West Side landmark.

The West Side's tradition of family-friendly taverns was also reflected in the popularity of smaller establishments, such as Dickey's at 27 North Meridian Road. Opened in the early 1980s by entrepreneur Ray Dickey, the tavern gained recognition for its signature Macedonian Stew, which was developed by chef Bertie Zimmerman when a Macedonian American customer requested "something hot and spicy." Still served today, the popular stew features tender chunks of pork loin in a base of potatoes, onions, carrots and celery, "with the addition of Hungarian hot peppers for heat." Over the years, Dickey's has also become known for its chili and sausage tortellini soup.[123]

Longtime customer Marty Pallante, who served as an executive at nearby Standex International Corporation between 1986 and 2000, claimed that Dickey's still serves "the best burger in Youngstown." Pallante lunched at the restaurant almost every day before his retirement, and he recalled that Dickey's atmosphere put him in mind of the popular 1980s television sitcom *Cheers*. "The local businessmen always stopped in for a meal and a beverage," he said, "and everything was good, from the fish on Fridays to the spaghetti and meatballs."

With the exception of short-lived businesses like Armadillo's restaurant, the West Side offered little in the way of upscale dining. Alternatives to neighborhood taverns included coffee shops such as the Donut Oven on South Meridian Road, which offered fresh pastries and reasonably priced meals. In the two decades following the collapse of Youngstown's steel industry, the West Side remained much the same. It was characterized by well-maintained working-class neighborhoods, many of which had grown up around churches. With the passing and relocation of older residents, however, the West Side began to resemble other sections of the city, and its restaurateurs were forced to confront the harsh realities brought on by deindustrialization.

A Pattern of Disappointment

Overall, the period between 1977 and 2000 was one of interminable decline. This pattern, however, was interrupted by developments that held out the promise of renewal. In 1987, for instance, the former site of downtown's Strouss' Department Store was renovated, and in August of that year, the building's third floor became the corporate headquarters of the Youngstown-based Phar-Mor discount drugstore chain, a firm cofounded by local businessman Michael "Mickey" Monus and David Shapira, president and CEO of Pittsburgh-based Giant Eagle Inc.

In time, the historic building became known as the Phar-Mor Centre, and by 1988, its street floor hosted Federal Forum, a large food court whose vendors included Antone's, Jay's Famous Hot Dogs, Plaza Donuts and the Yogurt Exchange. Not everyone was pleased with this development, especially owners of the Plaza Café, a food court located just south of the Phar-Mor Centre. Thomas Berndt, co-owner of the Hasti House on South Phelps Street, also contended that the food court had temporarily affected his business. He added, however, that the larger problem for downtown restaurateurs was a lack of traffic. "Downtown has not recovered one bit," Berndt stated.[124]

For many observers, though, the rise of the Phar-Mor Centre heralded the revitalization of downtown Youngstown, and media reports regarding the discount chain's success fueled such optimism. In 1991, Phar-Mor boasted two hundred outlets across the country, and Monus secured national recognition as a cofounder of the World Basketball League, a minor professional basketball league whose organizers included former Boston Celtics great Bob Cousy. The city even had its own professional basketball team, the Youngstown Pride.

This brief period of euphoria ended in July 1992, when Phar-Mor's board members claimed that financial books stored at the corporate headquarters exaggerated the firm's profits. Amid these allegations, Monus's business partner, David Shapira, contacted federal investigators, alerted investors and fired Monus, along with the company's chief financial officer, Patrick Finn. Court documents later showed that Monus had embezzled $10 million from Phar-Mor, most of which had been funneled into the World Basketball League. The subsequent collapse of the discount chain not only marked the end of Monus's career as a retail magnate but also disillusioned thousands of local residents, who had pinned their hopes on the firm's success.[125]

In the wake of the Phar-Mor debacle, the decline of the city's former hub accelerated. "I can remember how sad it was twenty years ago to walk down

Federal Street," recalled lifelong resident Father John C. Harris. "You'd have to cover your nose because of the stench from the buildings...[from] the mildew, and the false fronts [were] falling off of them."

Not surprisingly, civic leaders argued that the city's deteriorating downtown served as an unwanted advertisement for Youngstown's economic woes, and throughout the 1990s, the municipal government offered generous loans to individuals and corporations that promised to turn downtown landmarks into novelty restaurants that would attract suburban patrons.

Notable efforts included Anthony's on the River, an upscale restaurant located on the corner of Oak Hill and Mahoning Avenues, just west of downtown. However, despite subsidies from city council, a beautifully remodeled site, a wide menu and the participation of noted restaurateur Anthony Saadey, suburban diners did not flock to the city center in the numbers that supporters of the project anticipated. Over the years, the restaurant struggled to attract patrons, and in 2008, it finally closed its doors. Around the same time, efforts to turn the neighboring B&O station into an upscale restaurant met with limited success. The site was closed intermittently, and over time, the facility served as an eatery, a brewery and a banquet center.

While projects of this kind flourished elsewhere, there was a growing consensus among civic and business leaders that the time was not yet ripe for investments in downtown Youngstown. After numerous setbacks, the frustrations of downtown restaurateur Thomas Berndt and his wife, Thelma, were shared by many. In November 1994, as the Berndts announced the closing of the Hasti House Restaurant, they complained about the city's ticketing of customers' vehicles, adding that the presence of indigent people had driven away customers. "This town is over," Thomas Berndt stated. "The last guy leaving just forgot to turn out the lights."[126]

Pessimistic assessments of this kind weren't uncommon in the 1990s. Youngstown's population, after all, had continued to fall steadily despite official assurances that the community would stabilize. Eventually, sections of the once prosperous South Side became so depopulated that bus service for entire neighborhoods was discontinued. As the city contracted, scores of small neighborhood restaurants—including the Old German, the Choo-Choo Diner, Effie's Soul Food and Roller's Cafeteria—were forced to close their doors.

Although the presence of banks, law firms and government offices in the downtown area ensured the survival of some restaurants, most of those that flourished were based on the eastern end of the Federal Plaza, an area redeveloped during the era of urban renewal. One of the most popular of the downtown eateries was co-owned by two of Thomas Berndt's children, Paula and John. In 1997, just three years after the closing of Hasti House, the siblings opened JP's Downtown Grill on East Boardman Street. "We did a lot of cockade specialties, a little bit of Cajun food," Paula Berndt recalled. "Every morning, before six o'clock, the whole street department would come in there for breakfast; it was packed during the lunch period."

Almost a decade earlier, the iconic Youngstown Club had moved from its longtime location at the Bank One Building (formerly the Union National Bank Building) to the Commerce Building (former site of Haber Furniture), on East Commerce Street. The deal was clinched when the Ohio One Corporation, owners of the Commerce Building, agreed to add a floor to the four-story structure. This development, once again, reflected the growth of the East Plaza at the expense of its western counterpart.

The modest growth of the East Plaza, however, did little to offset the overall desolation of Youngstown's downtown. In the wake of the community's inexorable decline, particularly between the 1970s and '90s, few residents could have imagined a future in which a refurbished downtown area would host a bevy of glistening new restaurants. Yet over the next decade, the district was practically transformed, and to the surprise of many observers, the majority of the new development occurred along West Federal Street.

Chapter 5

RECIPE FOR REBIRTH

In the early 2000s, Charlie Staples reached a professional crossroads. After moving to Columbus in the 1980s to open a new branch of his barbecue business, Staples placed his Youngstown-based restaurant under the management of longtime friend Carl Young and his wife, Emma. When the Columbus-based enterprise began to falter, Staples relocated with his wife, Margaret "Magg", to Houston, where they became involved in the production of health and beauty aids.

In 2003, however, unsettling trends within the cosmetics industry coincided with the unexpected death of Emma Young, whose husband, Carl, had passed on sometime earlier. Faced with these circumstances, the Stapleses returned to Youngstown, where they operated their cosmetics business at the former site of C. Staples' Bar-B-Que. It wasn't long, though, before they decided to reenter the restaurant industry.

In 2005, the Stapleses tore down the old restaurant on the corner of Belmont and West Rayen Avenues and bought a vacant warehouse across the street. "It was quite an expensive endeavor," Charlie Staples recalled, noting that the building's façade needed to be restored, while the interior required extensive remodeling. Staples eventually spent about $2 million to refurbish the structure.

Bearing in mind the southern origins of his secret barbecue recipe, Staples gave his new business, Charlie Staples' Bar-B-Que, a regional theme. "I just didn't know what part of the South I wanted to use," he recalled. "I always loved New Orleans, and it just hit me like a ton of

Charlie Staples and his wife, Magg, join another couple for a carriage ride during his barbecue restaurant's annual celebration of Mardi Gras. *Courtesy of Charlie Staples.*

bricks." Staples also recognized that the building's high ceilings made it an ideal setting for the project. "We could turn this [place] into Bourbon Street," he explained.

Staples envisioned the restaurant's main dining area as a theme park–style reproduction of New Orleans's main drag. Designed with the help of a local architect, the dining room featured balconies with wrought-iron railings; and its centerpiece was a two-story mural showing Charlie and Magg Staples at the head of a Mardi Gras parade. "[E]verybody told me that I was nuts to… put that kind of investment over here," he explained. "They said: 'This place is dead. It's never coming back.'"

Yet Staples framed his decision to open a business just north of downtown Youngstown as a calculated risk. The city, after all, was changing. "Anyone that knows anything about what's going on in the rest of the country, and especially up in the Rust Belt, they would have to say that Youngstown is a beacon," he said.

Seeds of Redevelopment

Staples had a point. In recent years, the city's leadership had moved in the direction of comprehensive planning. In December 2002, municipal leaders unveiled "Youngstown 2010," a citywide plan developed in partnership with YSU and community leaders, some of whom participated in workshops and public forums. "Youngstown 2010" was designed to address the community's postindustrial realities, while also developing strategies to cultivate new businesses. By 2008, the *Vindicator* noted that economic development incentives put in place three years earlier had "helped secure $9.5 million in new investments in the city."[127]

Tangible results of the renewal effort were most evident in the downtown area, where aging buildings were either razed or restored. In 2005 (the same year Charlie Staples reopened his restaurant), a high-tech convocation center known as the Chevrolet Centre (now the Covelli Centre) opened on the site of a closed steel mill.[128] At the same time, the Youngstown Business Incubator (YBI), which had begun supporting business-to-business software companies five years earlier, redeveloped a once-decaying block of the downtown area.

The YBI eventually established three state-of-the-art facilities, where it pursued its mission "to accelerate the formation, cultivation, and success of technology-based business innovators."[129] The organization's star tenant was Turning Technologies, which developed leading assessment delivery and data collection solutions for learning environments. YBI also oversaw the National Additive Manufacturing Innovation Institute (NAMII), located just south on West Boardman Street.[130]

The cumulative effect of these developments was startling. By December 2012, the *Vindicator* reported that downtown was experiencing "growing pains," as commercial rents skyrocketed. Tom Humphries, president and chief executive of the Youngstown-Warren Regional Chamber, observed that, in the late 1990s, downtown rents "were among the lowest in the nation," and he framed the current situation as "the difference between night and day." The *Vindicator* placed this development in a national context, noting that "a trend toward urbanization is occurring nationwide that mirrors the growth of downtown Youngstown."[131]

Not surprisingly, the redevelopment of the downtown area, along with the gradual stabilization of certain urban neighborhoods, opened opportunities for restaurateurs seeking alternatives to a crowded suburban market. As it turned out, Charlie Staples's substantial investment in a business located at the northern rim of the downtown area was a taste of things to come.

The Continuing Draw of the Suburbs

In the late 1990s and early 2000s, however, a trend toward urbanization was less than apparent to most observers. Some business leaders were heartened by the fact that locally owned restaurants had persevered, despite the growth of national chains. In 1998, for instance, the *Business Journal* presented the success of restaurants like the Dutch Haus (Columbiana), Charly's (Austintown and Boardman) and Caffe Capri (Boardman) as evidence that "not all locally owned establishments were being eaten alive."[132] While this was true, it was difficult to ignore that all of these restaurants operated in outlying communities.

Moreover, even some locally owned restaurants that flourished in urban neighborhoods eventually relocated to the suburbs. This was true of Johnny's, which opened on Midlothian Boulevard in May 2000. The

brainchild of third-generation restaurateur John Berndt, the restaurant offered upscale cuisine, including specialties like South African lobster and Chicken Queen Victoria, described as "chicken sautéed with scallops and lump crabmeat in a creamy sherry wine sauce."

Johnny's Restaurant, originally located on Youngstown's South Side, benefits from the experience and creativity of owner and head chef John Berndt, a third-generation restaurateur. *Courtesy of Paula Berndt.*

With its exotic safari theme, Johnny's targeted the community's evening crowd. Dinner was served from 4:00 p.m. to midnight, and the bar closed at 1:00 a.m. The menu itself, however, was a major draw. Berndt had honed his craft at various restaurants, including the Hasti House (once operated by his late father, Thomas), Bobby D's, the Boatyard (once located in Liberty) and JP's Downtown Grill, where he was a proprietor before his sister, Paula, took over.[133]

Within five years, Berndt's business skyrocketed, and he began to look for a larger facility. With assistance from the Mahoning Valley Economic Development Corporation, he leased space at the Flamingo Plaza, located on Market Street in Boardman; and before long, Berndt had increased his staff by ten people, while also benefiting from the assistance of his sister, Paula.

Given the restaurant's offerings, including an upscale menu and popular happy hours, Johnny's continues to draw an eclectic crowd. The establishment's most notable event is its annual Mardi Gras celebration, which features blues bands from around the country. "The tradition of holding a Mardi Gras celebration actually started with the original Johnny's on Midlothian," Paula Berndt explained. "The whole place is decorated, and the food is amazing—po' boys, jambalaya and we've even served alligator."

Johnny's, of course, wasn't the only South Side business to relocate to the suburbs in the 1990s and 2000s. Well before Johnny's opened its doors, Thomas Campana Jr. had reestablished the Fireplace in neighboring Poland. In 2006, one year after Johnny's relocation to Boardman, Bobby DeVicchio closed Bobby D's; and three years later, in 2009, he opened Bogey's Bar & Grill (a business that featured Bobby D's menu) in neighboring Coitsville.

These developments were hardly surprising. The exodus of businesses from the city to the suburbs reflected trends that had gained momentum since the late 1940s. However, by the late 2000s, the local and national media became fixated on a different trend in the Youngstown area: the trickle of businesses from the suburbs to the city.

Origins of a Downtown Renaissance

Around the time that Charlie Staples established his new barbecue restaurant at the corner of Belmont and West Rayen Avenues, a similar scene was unfolding several blocks to the south. In 2005, two young real estate developers, Jeffrey Kurz and Brad Schwartz, opened Imbibe Martini

Bar in a former bank building on West Federal Street. The business, designed to draw younger professionals and graduate students from around the community, offered 121 different types of martinis, along with sixty kinds of beer.

Imbibe joined a handful of other downtown establishments with a comparable target market. Given the district's proximity to the university, along with the fact that it hosted scores of local government and law offices, the downtown restaurant industry had never completely disappeared. Popular downtown watering holes included the End of the Tunnel, Martini's Restaurant, the Core, the Old Precinct, the Draught House and the Cedars Lounge, which operated a café that featured Mediterranean food.

Cedars Lounge, in particular, was a draw for members of the local creative community. "It was the bohemian hangout," recalled local artist James Pernotto. "There were a lot of things going on there, and so many people who became movers and shakers in the art scene were regulars at the Cedars—Nanette Lepore, Bob Savage, Peggy Millard." He added, "Nancy Bizzarri ran poetry readings there."

Young people who weren't strongly attracted to the underground music and poetry scene at the Cedars Lounge had the option of patronizing bw-3 Grill & Pub, located on the northeastern end of Central Square, a stone's throw from the former site of the Palace Theatre complex. Others occasionally stopped at Georgeann's, a popular eatery in the YMCA Building, near the corner of North Champion and East Commerce Streets.

Overall, however, few university students found their way downtown. "I originally came to this area in 1998 to attend YSU, and it wasn't until I was almost in my senior year that I came downtown," recalled local activist and entrepreneur Phil Kidd. "One evening, a friend of a friend had a band that was playing at the Plaza Café, which was located near what was then the East Plaza. The fact is there weren't many reasons to come down here."

In 2004, after graduating and spending time in the military, Kidd returned to find surprising changes in the downtown area. First, he discovered that the long-vacant site of McKelvey's Department Store on the corner of West Federal and North Hazel Streets had been razed to make way for two new government buildings. Then, he became aware of the city's plans to reopen Federal Street, which had been closed off since the construction of the Federal Plaza in the 1970s.

Evidence that bigger plans were in the works surfaced when city officials announced they had secured funds to build a convention center. "The most surprising news was that there were plans to have the state designate

Federal Street as an entertainment district," Kidd recalled. "That seed planning…laid the groundwork for the revitalization of the downtown and the growth of its restaurant industry."

By 2006, the planned revitalization of downtown Youngstown was well underway. In April of that year, the *Vindicator* reported that an $11 million renovation of Powers Auditorium, the former site of the Warner Theater, had been completed. The enlarged complex, known as the DeYor Performing Arts Center (in recognition of major donors Dr. John York and Denise DeBartolo York), had a glistening new western wing; and the twenty-four-thousand-square-foot addition comprised the Ford Family Recital Hall, the Eleanor Beecher Flad Pavilion and Overture Restaurant.

As the *Vindicator* reported, the Ford Family Recital Hall, completed at a cost of $4.8 million, was "the first theater built in downtown Youngstown in 75 years."[134] No less momentous was the opening of Overture Restaurant, which signaled the return of fine dining to the downtown area. "I really think they provide the

INSIDE THE ELEANOR BEECHER FLAD PAVILION AT THE DEYOR PERFORMING ARTS CENTER

best food in downtown Youngstown," said Phil Kidd, who operates a nearby business called Youngstown Nation. "Jeff Chrystal is probably the most established chef in this area, and when I sit down for lunch there, I know I'm going to get excellent food, no matter what I order."

This postcard image of Overture captures the restaurant's airy and upscale environment. The restaurant is located in the DeYor Performing Arts Center, a modern complex that incorporates a historic landmark, the former Warner Theater. *Courtesy of Nora Chrystal.*

James Pernotto, who maintains a studio several blocks to the east of Overture, is also a regular patron. "They have a fantastic lunch that runs from 11:30 to 2:00 p.m.," Pernotto explained. "You get homemade soup, a nice salad, an entrée and homemade bread for anywhere from ten to twelve bucks, and that includes the tip—and we're talking white linen tablecloths and an airy, glass-enclosed space that looks out on West Federal Street."

Given Overture's proximity to Powers Auditorium and the Ford Family Recital Hall, the restaurant helped revive a long-dormant tradition, as more residents chose to dine downtown after an evening of live entertainment. This tradition had received a significant boost one year earlier, in 2005, with the opening of an entertainment complex on East Front Street that later became known as the Covelli Centre. The public's overwhelming response to the center inspired the opening of another fine-dining establishment, Café Cimmento, which appeared on the corner of East Boardman and South Champion Streets in 2006.

Owner George Mager acknowledged that the building of the Covelli Centre was a major factor in his decision to establish Café Cimmento. He recalled that in September 2005, media coverage of Tony Bennett's opening performance at the center included quotes from attendees who complained that there were few places to eat downtown. Mager saw an opportunity. "It so happens that my son, Jonathon, who is a chef, had been living in Charlotte, North Carolina," George Mager explained. "Eventually, every chef wants his own place."

The project was a natural move for Jonathon Mager, who got his start in the local restaurant industry. His interest in cooking traced back to his high school years, when he worked at Nicolinni's Restaurant, in Austintown. After graduating from the Pittsburgh Institute of Culinary Arts in the 1990s, Jonathon Mager returned to the area and worked at Rachel's Restaurant, also in Austintown. Within a year, however, he relocated to North Carolina, where he spent much of the next decade as a chef at TCP Piper Glen Country Club, a major venue for tournament golfers.

Once George Mager confirmed his son's interest in opening a local restaurant, he looked around for potential properties. In the winter of 2005, Mager purchased JP's Downtown Grill, a diner with a small kitchen and seating for about fifty guests. Two years later, he rented space next door, enabling Café Cimmento to expand and seat up to ninety guests.

Café Cimmento's menu featured authentic Italian entrées, many of which were hard to find. The restaurant's signature dishes included *cacio e pepe*, pasta served with cracked black pepper and roasted with butter, cheese and

Café Cimmento's main dining room welcomed diners to Youngstown's revitalized downtown area. Owing to factors that included growing competition, Café Cimmento closed its doors in April 2013. *Courtesy of Thomas G. Welsh Jr.*

water; *pasta al fresco*, angel hair pasta served with bruschetta tomatoes; and *farfalle primavera*, a pasta dish served with fresh vegetables in a combination of traditional sauces. "It was definitely a step up from your average Italian restaurant," said regular patron Robyn Maas. "It was the kind of place I was more likely to go for a special occasion."

The Rebound Continues

Over the next few years, full-service restaurants like Café Cimmento not only benefited from the presence of entertainment venues like the Covelli Centre, the DeYor Performing Arts Center and the Oakland Center for the Arts; they also secured business from residents of upscale apartments that had opened downtown. During this time, the district witnessed the establishment of three upscale apartment complexes: Erie Terminal Place, the Federal Building and Realty Towers. As Phil Kidd noted, "Downtown seems to be developing as a residential as well as an entertainment district, and these developments are all part of the equation."

In January 2008, another high-end restaurant opened in the district when local entrepreneurs Greg Sop and George Lenahan established the Rosetta Stone Café & Wine Bar in a former Woolworth's discount store on West Federal Street. Lenahan said he became interested in the project in 2003, after watching a show at the neighboring Oakland Center for the Arts and walking through a downtown area that struck him as a "clean, safe place." Sop confirmed this impression, adding that West Federal Street was "turning into a nice little entertainment district."

Under the direction of chefs Barry Karrh and Chuck Wolfcale, the restaurant offered what its owners described as "diverse world cuisine." The Rosetta Stone's streamlined interior, the product of a $600,000 remodeling effort, became the site of live musical performances, and local visual artists were invited to display their work. Unlike many other downtown restaurants, which focused on the lunch crowd, the Rosetta Stone's kitchen was open from 7:30 a.m. to 10:00 p.m. on weeknights. During weekends, it served dinner until midnight, and these hours were often extended to accommodate downtown events.[135]

An additional boost to downtown nightlife came in 2009, when the Lemon Grove opened a couple of doors west of the Rosetta Stone, on West Federal Street. Proprietor Jacob Harver had expressed an interest in the space three years earlier, in 2006. "When I first learned of the availability of space downtown, Imbibe had just opened up, and the owners purchased what became the first site of the Lemon Grove," Harver recalled. However, when the space became available for lease, Harver had little money at his disposal. "But I did have a small house on the West Side, and I was able to get a home-equity loan," he noted.

Determined to open a business downtown, Harver was influenced by local establishments like the Cedars Lounge and the Beat Coffeehouse, which served as venues for artists and musicians. "The name of the business was inspired by the fact that I liked the old standard 'Shady Grove,'" Harver explained. Informed that the term "shady" might have unwanted connotations, given downtown's years of decline, he modified the name. "I looked through a dictionary and came across the term 'lemon grove,' which conveyed the idea of something fresh, bright and organic," he said.

Harver's stated goal was to open "a coffee shop that also served alcohol." Live entertainment ranged from lone musicians on acoustic guitars to jazz bands, and the work of local artists was displayed in the galley-like interior. Within months, the Lemon Grove's unique ambiance drew a broad cross-section of the community. "I would say we have a diverse clientele, including rich, poor, young, old, black, white, gay, straight," Harver said in a 2013 interview. "Our customers don't fit into a single demographic."

Despite such developments, downtown's revitalization did not reflect a pattern of consistent growth. Setbacks included the closing of the Rosetta Stone Café & Wine Bar in August 2010, three months after its owners placed it on the market for $2.9 million. Co-owner Greg Sop indicated the restaurant was adversely affected by the national economic downturn, but he also cited the difficulties involved in drawing suburbanites to the city. "We've had to change people's habits," he said.

Even though previous efforts to revitalize downtown Youngstown had proved disappointing, Mayor Jay Williams downplayed the notion that the restaurant's closing was part of a negative pattern. "There doesn't seem to be a domino effect," he said. "The hope is that someone else will step in and see its value and potential."[136] Significantly, the mayor's optimism about the future was supported by the developments of the following year.

In October 2011, V² Wine Bar Trattoria opened in the historic Federal Building, located at the corner of West Federal and Phelps Streets. The new business was established by a group of partners that included Vernon Cesta, owner of Vernon's Café in neighboring Niles; his wife, Janeen; Ed Moses; and members of the Gatta family, who purchased the building.

Cesta's Italian restaurant in Niles had been thriving for more than fifteen years, and the entrepreneur was initially skeptical about the option of opening a business in Youngstown. "I wasn't crazy about it at first, but I came over and took a look to see what was happening down here; and it was different than the vision I'd had of Youngstown," he explained. "YSU was growing and the downtown was starting to make a transition, and it began to make sense."

Shortly after V² moved into the corner of the building's first floor, the Gatta family established new apartments on the floor directly above it. "They were all rented before they even had them finished," Cesta recalled. "In fact, there's a waiting list for them right now." He added that, on top of the growing number of downtown residents, an estimated 6,500 people worked in the district. "We figured we would do this and get a decent lunch, and a little bit with dinner, and a little bit with the happy hour crowd," Cesta observed. "Well, it turned out to be a night spot also."

Given that the downtown business targeted young professionals and university students, its menu diverged from that of Cesta's restaurant in

V², the downtown branch of Vernon's Restaurant, in Niles, Ohio, has benefited from the establishment of apartments in the city's former retail district. The restaurant (located in the second building from the left) has become a popular gathering spot for students and young professionals. *Courtesy of Vernon Cesta.*

NBC reporter Harry Smith (right) interviews Tom Humphries, CEO and president of the Youngstown-Warren Regional Chamber of Commerce, on economic developments within the community. The interview took place at Joe Maxx Coffee Company in the heart of downtown Youngstown. *Courtesy of Mike Avey.*

Niles. "This is fun food," he explained. "It's a lot of small plates, appetizers, pizzas done in a brick oven, salads, sandwiches, burgers—and a lot of great drinks and quality wine." For regular patrons, this is a winning combination. "V²'s has the best burger in town," said one customer, Robyn Maas. "It's tender and juicy, and nothing compares to it." The restaurant, however, is best known for its distinctive meatball salad, which was also a major seller at Vernon's Café.

In November 2011, another upscale business appeared downtown when Joe Maxx Coffee Company opened its doors on East Federal Street, not far from Central Square. Proprietor Mike Avey had been weighing the option of opening a coffee shop for several years, when his research suggested that U.S.-based coffee giants like Starbucks had diverted their attention from domestic markets to explore international markets—a development that left up to ten thousand local markets "underserved."

At the same time, Avey was "intrigued" by news of downtown's revitalization, and he believed that a coffee shop would fill a need. "You're not a downtown unless you have certain things, including coffee shops," he noted. "Those elements complete the infrastructure of a modern downtown." Another "hole" in the downtown market, he added, was access to healthful food choices. "We've kind of built a menu around that premise," Avey said. "We focus on wraps, salads and soups—mostly on the nutritious side."

Joe Maxx's biggest attraction, however, was its wide range of flavored and blended coffees. "We have a signature coffee menu you're not going to find in other places," Avey said, adding that one of the shop's top sellers is its "Black and Tan," which features "real chocolate and real peanut butter." He noted that his talented crew of baristas is continually "venturing out on a limb." One of their more unusual flavors has been "Lavender Mocha," produced with lavender flowers imported from France. "They start with a syrup, which is created by boiling the flowers and straining the liquid," he explained.

In February 2012, in the midst of the U.S. presidential election campaigns, Joe Maxx Coffee Company was the setting of an interview that NBC's Harry Smith conducted with local business leader Tom Humphries. The segment, filmed for the now defunct news program *Rock Center*, was designed to highlight Youngstown's revitalization, and the bustling downtown coffee shop was evidently chosen because it reflected this trend.

The community's economic rebound was especially evident in the downtown area, where two more upscale restaurants were established in 2012. In February, the same month that Harry Smith interviewed Tom Humphries, Roberto's Italian Ristorante opened its doors on the western end of Federal Street. Although owners Robert Faraglia and John Naples had previously considered a suburban location for their business, they ruled out this option. "We wanted to replicate…a restaurant in Little Italy in New York, like on Mulberry Street," Faraglia explained. "You really can't do that out in the suburbs."

In their search for an appropriate property, they settled on two nondescript commercial spaces, which had hosted a pizzeria and insurance company, respectively. Naples's skills as an interior designer, however, enabled them to transform these pedestrian storefronts into a single stylish dining area—one that customers have compared with those found in larger metropolitan areas. "We love Roberto's—very friendly, elegant and good food," said Bernadette Angle, a Youngstown native who now lives in Florida. "I feel like I'm in New York City when I'm there."

A native of the largely Italian American community of Lowellville, Ohio, Faraglia grew up with sumptuous home-cooked meals that were served at his grandmother's house. As an adult, he promoted many of these traditional dishes through Roberto's Taste of Italia, a concession business he continues to operate with Naples. During local and regional festivals, customers who visited the concession trailers routinely asked, "Where's your restaurant?" "After hearing that for years…we just plunged in and did it," Faraglia explained.

Roberto's specialties include veal and eggplant parmesan; *calamari fritti*, a lightly breaded and fried squid served with red pepper sauce; *cavatelli anchovy aglio e olio*, pasta served with anchovy sautéed in olive oil, garlic and red pepper; and *fiocchi*, pasta "purses" stuffed with pear slices and four Italian cheeses. Faraglia noted that the restaurant's handmade pastas are shipped in frozen from Italy.

Beyond its intimate atmosphere and authentic cuisine, the restaurant's greatest asset is its location, Faraglia said. "You come downtown, [and] you can stop here for dinner, walk across the street, have dessert and walk two storefronts down and have a cocktail," he explained. "So you can go from place to place and still be in the same area…That's what's bringing people back to the city."

In July 2012, just six months after the opening of Roberto's, the Lemon Grove moved into the storefront that had been vacated by Rosetta Stone. This development surprised many observers, given that the new site, with its ceramic tile flooring and pastel color scheme, had an entirely different atmosphere. "We needed more space," explained owner Jacob Harver in a 2013 interview. "I've heard people say that the first space made more sense, because it had a grittier atmosphere, but we've made this space more rustic."

Meanwhile, the former site of the Lemon Grove was taken over by O'Donold's Pub & Grille, which had operated a branch in neighboring Austintown since 2005. Owner Christian Rinehart explained that he was drawn to the downtown site because of its unique dimensions. "I love the galley style of this space," he said. "It reminds me of Chicago or New York City, where square footage is expensive."

To accentuate this big-city quality, Rinehart refurbished the interior, doubling the size of the bar (now sixty-one feet in length with forty stools) and running a forty-eight-foot-long padded bench along the opposite wall. With the addition of high-topped tables and backed bar stools, the pub's interior could comfortably seat up to eighty-eight people. Three months after its grand opening, the *Vindicator* described the establishment as "the kind of pub that was once common in the city: long and narrow with a bar that runs almost the full length of the room, and a warm look of craftsmanship in the woodwork."[137]

Rinehart had cut his teeth years earlier in the Mahoning Valley's bustling restaurant industry. He began working at local restaurants at the age of thirteen, one day after his father's death, and gained valuable experience at the Sunrise Inn (Warren), Abruzzi's Café 422 (Niles) and Alberini's (Niles). "The biggest impact was Café 422," he recalled. "When I was seven years old, I walked in there, and Bob Abruzzi Jr. knew my name and where we sat...I thought that was cool, and I told my mother, 'I want to do that.'"

As a marketing major at Ohio State University, Rinehart worked his way through school, taking a job at the original Max & Erma's in Columbus's German Village. He spent most of the next four years as a corporate opener for the growing regional chain. "I opened forty-seven restaurants before the age of twenty," he recalled. "They saw me as too valuable to move up to bartending, so I drove home and worked at Sully's Irish Pub (Warren), which eventually became the first O'Donold's."

When developing the concept for O'Donold's, Rinehart drew inspiration from the TGI Fridays chain, with its initial emphasis on adult recreation. "I think people miss adult entertainment," he said. "We love that families come in here, but fundamentally, we're based for the age group thirty to sixty." The name of the business itself synthesizes his mother's Irish American heritage and his late father's given name. "What distinguishes us is that we have a corporate look and feel, with mom-and-pop prices," Rinehart added. "So you have local pricing with a corporate background."

O'Donold's menu specialties include burgers, Reuben sandwiches and fish and chips. For many customers, however, a major draw is the pub's wide range of beverages, including almost sixty beers on tap. Not surprisingly, O'Donold's has emerged as a major St. Patrick's Day destination. "We have the largest St. Paddy's Day in the state of Ohio," Rinehart said. "In 2012, we had seventy-one thousand people at our event; we sold 211 kegs of Guinness, and we sold 2,753 cases of beer—just outside in tents." He added that this figure does not include the $60,000 worth of business conducted in the pub itself. These events are supplemented with live music featuring Celtic and rock 'n' roll bands. (Encouraged by developments downtown, Rinehart later announced plans to open Susie's Dogs & Drafts, a gourmet hot dog shop and brewery, at the former site of the Old Precinct on North Phelps Street.)

The Irish pub soon had a new neighbor on West Federal Street. In December 2012, as the year came to a close, a local classic was reinvented when Avalon Downtown opened its doors. Significantly, co-owner Anne Massullo Sabella had strong personal connections to the Avalon Gardens, a North Side landmark that had closed in January 2012, four months after the tragic disappearance of its last owner, James Donofrio.

The shuttering of this local landmark provoked feelings of nostalgia among the Avalon's customers, some of whom had patronized the business for decades. The Avalon's demise, however, was also unsettling for Mrs. Sabella. Back in the 1920s, her grandfather Gennaro Massullo had established the restaurant, and her husband's family owned and operated the business between 1970 and 1987.

As owner of a well-situated downtown property, Mrs. Sabella joined forces with business partner Angeline Snyder and set out to revive a family tradition. In the wake of a $180,000 remodeling project, the business partners held a "soft opening" of the restaurant on New Year's Eve. "We originally weren't going to open this week, but then we decided it would be a great day to open, with New Year's," Mrs. Sabella told the *Vindicator* at the time. She added that the restaurant would serve pizza exclusively rather than presenting its full menu.[138]

While Avalon Downtown went on to offer a variety of soups, salads, pasta dishes and panini, pizza would remain its signature offering—and once again, tradition played a role. With the closing of Avalon Gardens, Mrs. Sabella and Ms. Snyder secured the services of Robert "Smitty" Smith, who had spent years preparing the tavern's distinctive pizza after first learning his craft from Nick Lavanty, the originator of "Brier Hill Pizza." "They say that everybody in this world is good at something, and after forty years, I think I'm pretty good at what I do," Smith said.

The restaurant also benefits from an unusual piece of kitchen technology. Avalon Downtown's Astraturri mixer, produced in Verona, Italy, is custom-designed for the preparation of pizza dough. "It has a spiral mechanism that mixes the dough in both directions, and the bowl also moves in both directions—and this makes for lighter, fluffier dough," Smith explained. Mrs. Sabella added, however, that the pizza's quality depends heavily on Smith's strong personal commitment. "When something comes out of the oven, Smitty will say, 'If it's not right, I don't want it to be served,'" she said.

"Shifts and Fluctuations"

If New Year's Eve 2012 witnessed the birth of Avalon Downtown, it also marked the demise of one of the city's most enduring institutions, the Youngstown Club. As the *Vindicator* observed, "For more than 100 years the club played host to the city's industrial barons, lawyers, doctors and other elite factions of the population, who would gather privately there for lunch and dinner, holiday parties and wedding rehearsals, among other things." In the 1970s and '80s, the Youngstown Club boasted a membership of 1,100, but that number had plummeted to 250 by the autumn of 2012.

In November 2012, the club's general manager announced the establishment would close after New Year's Eve.[139] The news saddened Honorable Judge Joseph M. Houser, a longtime member whose offices were located a couple floors below in the Commerce Building. As a weekly patron, he witnessed the club's steady decline. "They had regulars that would come there and use their facilities, and they often used the meeting rooms," he recalled. "The daily trade of the lunch crowd, however, seemed to get smaller and smaller."

When Judge Houser joined the club years earlier, the dining room was so popular that some tables were "practically designated" for the use of individual firms. "There was the Standard Slag table, when they had their headquarters here," he explained. "There was the Dollar Bank [now PNC Bank] table, and some law firms had tables." He recalled that some guests made a game of lunch, rolling dice to determine who would pay the bill. "As time passed, the banks were bought out and the companies sold out, and there were fewer customers the club could rely on," he added.

The Youngstown Club wasn't the only downtown landmark to depart from the scene. On New Year's Eve, the Cedars Lounge & Restaurant—a fixture on North Hazel Street since 1975—prepared to close its doors. Months earlier, in September 2012, the Gallagher Building, which housed

Artifacts from the Youngstown Club, including souvenir plates and a silver ladle, reflect the elegance and exclusivity of a bygone era. *Courtesy of Michele Orostin.*

the Cedars, was purchased by real estate developer Dominic Gatta III, who announced plans to refurbish the ninety-eight-year-old structure. "[Cedars] will not stay there," Gatta informed the *Vindicator*. "With all the upgrades [it needs], including the new stairwell, new sanitary, bringing the building up to code and everything else, it does not fit my vision of the building."

Gatta indicated the building's ground floor would house a high-end burger restaurant and wine/coffee bar, while its second and third floors would be turned into commercial office space and private apartments. "It's a shame the [condition of] the building has gotten that bad," he said. "The roof probably only has a year or two left on it, and it's just a good thing that I was able to buy it at the time I did."[140]

For the Cedars's regulars, however, the news came as a shock. "In the past, when I got done with my work at the end of the day, I'd say to a friend, 'Let's go down to Cedars and have a beer and listen to some jazz,'" recalled local artist James Pernotto. "Now, I don't have that, and I don't feel comfortable in some places that have opened up downtown…There were never fights, and people weren't there to prove anything."

In 1981, six years after its establishment by businessman Tommy Simon, Cedars emerged as a venue for local and regional bands, including the

Bangorillas, Boogieman Smash, Figure Ground, The Toll, Walking Clampets, Slackjaw, the 8 Balls, the Infidels and the Sharkbites. "There were a lot of people that used the Cedars Lounge as a launching pad to careers in New York, Los Angeles, San Francisco and New Orleans," Pernotto noted. "Many remained interested in the community and helped enrich the cultural scene."

In January 2013, Tommy Simon's daughter, Mara, and her business partner, Billy Daniels, announced Cedars Lounge's imminent move to the city's West Side, where it would occupy the former site of County Maigh Eo, an Irish-themed bar on Steel Street. "With the remaining structures left in town that are available, this one best fits our time line," Simon explained. "It has many appealing qualities, from being right off the interstate to having the space to facilitate regional and national acts."[141]

These weren't the only unsettling developments within the downtown restaurant industry. In April 2013, George Mager, owner of Café Cimmento, announced that his restaurant would close after seven years of operation. Mager explained that his son, Jonathan, who served as executive chef, had decided to accept a job he felt he couldn't pass up. Mager said that he had no interest in running the restaurant independently, given that he was close to retirement. He acknowledged, however, that the growth of businesses in the district "took a piece of the pie."[142]

Mager contended that the long-term survival of downtown restaurants would depend on the further development of apartments in the district. "I've talked to some developers, and I think their goal is to attract an older crowd to these apartments they're developing downtown," he said. "Most of the apartments right now are filled with people who are thirty-five or under, and they don't necessarily patronize restaurants with a full dinner menu."

Meanwhile, increased competition took a toll on businesses located in the western section of downtown, including the Lemon Grove, which never regained its former popularity after relocating in June 2012. Within a month of the move, the Lemon Grove's transition to the new space was complicated by a disagreement with former landlord SKA Limited, a real estate development firm established by Jeffrey Kurz and Brad Schwartz, proprietors of Imbibe Martini Bar.

In early September, even before Harver had reached an agreement with SKA Limited, he faced an additional challenge when a shareholder in the business threatened its dissolution.[143] The following month, Harver came to terms with SKA Limited, and he downplayed the significance of the second development.[144] The youthful entrepreneur's problems didn't end there, however, and 2013 was fraught with challenges.

Amid the Lemon Grove's steady decline, Harver struggled to rebrand the business. In the spring of 2013, Guy's Barbecue took over the kitchen, and the establishment was reinvented as Guy's at the Grove. Then, in the late summer, Harver hired a local club manager and rechristened the business as the Knox Building.[145] Each of these strategies failed; and finally, that winter, entrepreneur Dan Martini and chef Nate Dukes signed a contract with the owners to take over the business, which they called Martini Bros. One local journalist wrote that while the Lemon Grove burst onto the scene with an "artsy vibe," it found itself "flailing in the face of new competition."[146]

Under these circumstances, some restaurants experienced surprisingly brief runs. Dooney's Downtown Bar & Grill, which opened at the vacant site of bw-3 in the summer of 2012, was forced to close its doors in April 2013, prompting owner Chris Sammarone to cite growing competition as a major hurdle. Despite these developments, however, his father, Youngstown mayor Charles Sammarone, suggested that downtown was better off than it had been in the recent past, given that "when something closes, usually something else takes its place."[147]

Activist Phil Kidd also expressed optimism about the district's overall direction. "These are the kinds of shifts and fluctuations that I tend to associate with a period of concentrated growth and development," he said. "It's amazing to think that all of this happened in just ten years, and I'm excited to see where things are headed." While critical observers have argued that continual growth could lead to a saturation of businesses in downtown's entertainment district, this doesn't appear to have happened yet.

Within four months of the closing of Café Cimmento, the *Vindicator* announced that the vacant site would reopen as a Mexican restaurant. Local entrepreneur Israel Zambrano launched the first Los Gallos Mexican Restaurant in 2004 in neighboring Boardman Township, and seven years later, he was preparing to open his seventh restaurant in downtown Youngstown. "I was looking on Federal Street," Zambrano told a *Vindicator* reporter, "but I couldn't find the right location."

Zambrano decided that the Plaza Parking Deck, which houses the site, was "a good spot" because of its proximity to the Covelli Centre. "The events there will bring some business," he said. At the same time, Lou Frangos of USA Parking Inc., owner of the Plaza Parking Deck, noted that his company had been negotiating with another restaurant to lease the space but chose to go with one that seemed more established. "Israel's got a good business," Frangos said, adding that "this concept was the best for our building and downtown Youngstown."[148]

More recently, in December 2013, Christopher's Downtown opened at the City Centre One Building, in the former site of the End of the Tunnel tavern. According to the *Vindicator*, owners Christopher and Shauna Bonacci "jumped at the opportunity" to open a restaurant downtown after learning that space was available.[149] The Bonaccis were quickly joined by Mitch Lynch and his wife, Patricia Tinkler, who opened a coffeehouse, Friends Specialty, on the corner of West Federal and South Phelps Streets. The business is a branch of Friends Roastery, a coffeehouse the couple operates in nearby Salem, Ohio.

For those who remember the period of the 1980s and '90s, when sections of downtown were practically abandoned, the economic rebound is refreshing. "I think it's just encouraging to see people downtown at night," Father John C. Harris observed. "During the warm-weather months, it's nice to see people out on the sidewalks." Downtown restaurateur Anne Massullo Sabella agreed, adding that a traditional downtown layout enables people to access a variety of entertainment options at their leisure. "I think many people are tired of an enclosed-mall environment," she added.

It would be unfair, of course, to compare present-day downtown Youngstown to its vibrant post–World War II counterpart. Indeed, even the most enthusiastic observers view the district as a work in progress. "What I see, now, is mostly venues for entertainment—clubs, restaurants," observed Ben Lariccia. "That's not totally bad, but we're missing services." Lariccia added that the downtown area still lacks businesses geared toward daily needs, such as pharmacies, dry cleaners and doctors' offices. These establishments are more likely to appear on the scene as the district's residential population grows, he said.

Meanwhile, some local artists have expressed concern that unregulated commercial development could overwhelm downtown's unique cultural scene, which played a role in the district's revitalization. "With the growth of the arts and entertainment district, I just want to make sure we don't forget about arts and entertainment," said artist James Pernotto. "What happened in the Flats in Cleveland is kind of a cautionary tale. You had a vibrant arts scene, and then when the investors and developers moved in, it became basically a bar scene, and the artists were displaced."

Other observers have found little to criticize in the revitalization process. Lifelong resident Fred Ross, who experienced the downtown entertainment district of the 1940s and '50s, could not be happier about recent developments. "It's a great city, and they're taking some of the restaurants that were down on 'the Strip' in Trumbull County and opening them in downtown Youngstown," he said. "Vernon's is down there, and they can be traced back to Cesta's Golden Gate. You're seeing a whole new generation of people who want to see it come back, and I hope I'm here to see a big positive change."

Developments Elsewhere in the City

While Youngstown's neighborhoods have lagged behind downtown in terms of their economic development, a surprising number of small businesses have persisted. Furthermore, in recent years, a handful of restaurants have opened in various parts of the city. In 2012, for instance, Santa Fe Southwestern Café relocated from downtown to the West Side. Originally housed in the former Strouss' Department Store on West Federal Street, the restaurant moved to Mahoning Avenue not long after it came under the ownership of one-time manager Jamie Szmara.

Mrs. Szmara indicated that, while the business was previously dependent on lunchtime patrons, it now offers a wide selection of dinners. "I wanted a storefront that was actually out on Mahoning Avenue because of all the traffic that has built up on this street," she said. Another attraction was the storefront's location in a building that housed three other businesses. "There're a lot of [pedestrians] around here, and they do come in," she said. "Where else can you get your hair cut, get a computer, get your taxes done and [get] lunch—all in one building?"

Like many local restaurateurs, Mrs. Szmara has been pleased with recent developments in the city. "Youngstown's building," she said. "There were a bunch of empty storefronts up and down Mahoning Avenue, and they all have [businesses] going into them, right now." Some of these businesses have benefited from their proximity to large residential neighborhoods. "We have a lot of families that come in with little kids," Mrs. Szmara observed. "I see a mix of older and younger [customers]…I had a guy in here yesterday who was eighty-six years old."

Santa Fe Southwestern Café's tacos, burritos and nachos are presented in a manner designed to give customers a range of choices—a policy that helps to set the establishment apart. "Here, you build it yourself," Mrs. Szmara explained. "You can choose whatever toppings you want." Regular patrons swear by the restaurant's secret Santa Fe Sauce and distinctive enchilada sauce, which are made in-house daily. The owner's insistence on freshness has led her to eschew all frozen foods. "I get my meat every day," she said. "I pick it up in the morning."

In the fall of 2013, another independent restaurant opened within the city limits—this time on the once-vibrant South Side. Soul Food Sensations on Glenwood Avenue has been the latest venture of Gary DeFrance Sr. and his wife, Lillian, who owned several small businesses over the years. As the *Vindicator* reported, the restaurant was the long-held dream of Lillian DeFrance, who "decided to seize the day and share her cooking with others."

Soul Food Sensations's southern home cooking is served in a space that functions as an informal museum of the 1950s and '60s Detroit music scene. Two of the restaurant's interior walls are dedicated to a "Motown Hall of Fame," while another has been reserved for the couple's extensive collection of record covers. Besides barbecued pork and fried chicken, the restaurant offers perennial favorites like macaroni and cheese, baked beans, corn bread, sweet-potato pie and yeast rolls—all at a reasonable price.

The DeFrances' son, Gary Jr., said that working at his parents' business has given him a fresh view of the community. "The best part of running a restaurant is constantly engaging with that positive part of Youngstown that people rarely talk about," he noted. "We've met hundreds of people who have dreams as big as ours and support us 100 percent." Gary DeFrance Jr. is especially gratified by feedback he has received about his mother's cooking. "My favorite moments are when I answer the phone and there's a customer who calls back just to let us know how much they loved the food," he said.[150]

"A LOT CAN HAPPEN AROUND THE TABLE"

The history of Youngstown's restaurant industry is, to some extent, a story of loss. Those who grew up in the community before the collapse of the local steel industry are inclined to look back nostalgically on an era when Youngstown supported a remarkable variety of restaurants. "For an area our size, I think we had an incredible number of five-star restaurants," said Sherry DeMar, whose father operated the long-vanished Chateaubriand. "Those days are gone."

For Stan Nudell, who worked in his parents' delicatessen, recent changes in the restaurant industry cannot be explained by economic trends alone; they also reflect societal shifts. "People were more hands-on, and they were creative," he said. "I think families may have been closer back then, and this contributed to the success of many family-run businesses." His observations were complemented by those of Wendy Aron, whose family owned the Newport Deli. "People seemed to care more about their customers," she said.

A sense of loss was also evident in the comments of area resident James D. Bennett, who indicated he missed the "homemade food" once provided by local family-run restaurants. "In the past, there was selection and a uniqueness of flavor," he added. "Maybe it was because families owned them and a little more care was taken." This quality food was accompanied by an intangible element that Bennett referred to as the "personal touch." "It seemed as if they cooked as though they were serving family," he said. "It's not that some of the chains don't do a nice job, but it's just not the same."

Despite the changes of the past several decades, however, Youngstown's restaurant industry has maintained a surprising degree of continuity. A handful of local restaurants—including the MVR, Golden Dawn and Kravitz's Delicatessen—have prevailed for generations under the management of the families that established them. At the same time, many Youngstown-area natives who have resided elsewhere speak in glowing terms about the personalized service and quality food they once took for granted. "One thing that distinguishes local restaurants is the friendliness of the people," said Rose Pacalo, who spent decades living in other parts of the country. "I don't think I've ever been insulted in a restaurant around here, and people greet you when you walk in."

Mrs. Pacalo's husband, Nick, indicated that he appreciates the area's authentic Italian cuisine. "If you eat Italian food, you develop a taste for it, and you learn how to judge the quality," he said. "Well, quality Italian food is what I missed when I lived outside the area." Retired restaurateur George Mager agreed. "We have two things that you won't find within sixty miles of here, and that's wedding soup and greens," he said. "You can go to Cleveland, and you won't find wedding soup and greens on the menu—and you won't find those items in Pittsburgh."

Amid Youngstown's ongoing economic revival, the characteristics that made the local restaurant industry outstanding have found new expression. These qualities include the community's rich blend of ethnic and regional traditions. Youngstown's diversity, which was once a source of division, has emerged as one of its greatest commodities. "I think the first real eye-opener was when we started the St. Patrick's Day [promotion], which has become the biggest day of the year at the deli," explained Jack Kravitz, owner of Kravitz's Delicatessen. The annual event, which began as a vehicle to promote the sale of corned beef, has blossomed into a weeklong extravaganza that features local Celtic bands.

In recent years, Kravitz has also reached out to the area's large Polish American community. "Every year, we do…an event…called the 'Klezmer Night,' which is the old Eastern European music," he said. "And we try bringing the Jewish and Polish communities together—reuniting, in some ways."

Kravitz noted that many foods traditionally identified as Jewish originated in Poland. "Bagels were a Polish item…gefilte fish, noodle kugel…potato pancakes, herring…borscht," he explained. "Poland was the heart of the Jewish community for many, many centuries." While the tragic aspects of the

Jewish experience in Poland are well known, Kravitz "wanted to recognize a little bit of that other history." With this in mind, he launched a Polish-Jewish happy hour that features *klezmer*, a musical tradition associated with the Ashkanazi Jews of Eastern Europe.

To a remarkable degree, Youngstown continues to be defined by its unique and eclectic restaurant industry. "It's the fabric of our community," said urban pastor Father Edward P. Noga, who described local restaurants as "special puzzle pieces that...help to fill in the picture." Over the decades, the city's restaurants have functioned as expressions of civic and ethnic pride, while simultaneously serving as centers of cross-cultural exchange. "A lot can happen around the table," Father Noga added. "Today, the challenge is...focusing in on that [interaction], as people's...phones go off...To be able to just sit and talk, as we are now, is almost becoming a luxury."

NOTES

Introduction

1. Marie Aikenhead, "Mural Room to Close Doors," *Youngstown Vindicator*, February 22, 1970, A20.
2. Richard Bruno, *Steelworker Alley: How Class Works in Youngstown* (Ithaca, NY: Cornell University Press, 1999), 149.
3. George Packer, *The Unwinding: An Inner History of the New America* (New York: Farrar, Strauss and Giroux, 2013), 52.
4. Staughton Lynd, *The Fight Against Shutdowns: Youngstown's Steel Mill Closings* (San Pedro, CA: Singlejack Books, 1983), 3–4.

Chapter 1

5. *Youngstown Vindicator*, "Worshippers Turn to God at Cathedral," August 15, 1945, 1.
6. Ibid., "Flags and People Line Long Route: Streets Gay for Distinguished Visitor as Holiday Mood Sweeps Through Valley," October 11, 1940, 1.
7. Ibid., "30,000 Jam Downtown in Wild Celebration," August 15, 1945, 1.
8. Ibid., "Lewis G. Raver Dies Suddenly of Stroke: Popular Restaurateur 'Knew Everybody,' Had National Reputation," July 1, 1949, 1.
9. Kenneth T. Jackson, *Crabgrass Frontier: The Suburbanization of the United States* (New York: Oxford University Press, 1985), 232.
10. Frederick J. Blue, William D. Jenkins, H. William Lawson and Joan M. Reedy, *Mahoning Memories: A History of Youngstown and Mahoning County* (Virginia Beach, VA: Donning Co., 1995), 147–48.

11. *Youngstown Vindicator*, "New Method Brings Growth to Once Tiny Oyster House: Reopens after $25,000 Enlargement—Handles Huge Quantities of Fresh Sea Foods," October 10, 1935.

12. *Youngstown Telegram*, "Oyster House, Remodeled, Is Opened Again: Public, Private Rooms Are Provided Diners at New Food Establishment," October 10, 1935.

13. *Youngstown Vindicator*, "New Method."

14. Ibid., "Moore's Tavern Will Give Way to UR Project," May 18, 1969.

15. Ibid., "'Sky Bar' Restaurant Opens Over Old Moore Tavern Site: Joseph and Leo Moore Add New Unit to Establishment at Boardman and Market," April 18, 1937.

16. Ibid., "Black, Silver Tavern Scheme: Glass and Aluminum Used to Beautify Exterior of Raver's," February 21, 1937.

17. Ibid., "Tavern Color Plan Restful: Interior Decoration Lends Atmosphere of Comfort," February 21, 1937.

18. Ibid., "American Has Big Dining Hall: Restaurant Celebrates Opening of New Rooms at 40 N. Phelps St.," October 1, 1933.

19. Ibid., "Hotel Grill Room Opened: New Dine, Dance Spot Is Part of Remodeled Building," December 19, 1936.

20. John F. Mariani, *America Eats Out: An Illustrated History of Restaurants, Taverns, Coffee Shops, Speakeasies, and Other Establishments That Have Fed Us for 350 Years* (New York: William Morrow & Co., 1991), 9.

21. Brian Butko, *Klondikes, Chipped Ham, & Skyscraper Cones: The Story of Isaly's* (Mechanicsburg, PA: Stackpole Books, 2001), 1.

22. Ibid., 32.

23. Ibid., 7–20.

24. Ibid., 20.

25. Blue, Jenkins, Lawson and Reedy, *Mahoning Memories*, 156–57.

26. Jackson, *Crabgrass Frontier*, 233.

27. Ibid., 238.

28. Ibid., 241.

29. *Youngstown Vindicator*, advertisement, undated, courtesy of David Adams, Youngstown, OH.

30. Ibid., advertisement, August 13, 1952, courtesy of David Adams, Youngstown, OH.

31. Ibid., "James Pappas Dies on Greece Trip; Owned Jay's Lunch," August 8, 1969, 12.

32. Karl E. Schwab, "Hot Dogs, Fish Change Habits of Downtown Youngstown," *Youngstown Business Journal* (June 1988): 24.

33. "Menu: Petrakos Grill and Tea Room," menu, undated, original, Mahoning Valley Historical Society, Youngstown, OH.

34. "Isaly's Fountain Suggestions," menu, March 3, 1935, original, Mahoning Valley Historical Society, Youngstown, OH.

35. "Brass Rail Lunch," menu, November 29, 1933, original, Mahoning Valley Historical Society, Youngstown, OH.

36. Janie S. Jenkins, "Aroma of Fish Lures Diners to Popular Boulevard Tavern: Petrellas in Business 40 Years," *Youngstown Vindicator*, April 11, 1976, B3.

37. Aikenhead, "Mural Room."

38. "Purple Cow," menu, original, courtesy of Joshua Foster, Louisville, KY.

39. *Youngstown Vindicator*, "Aiello's Aid Saves Boys from Jail: Boardman Youths Kick In Club Door, Nabbed by Police, Then Freed," January 1, 1947, 1.

40. Jimmy Gee, "Up and Down the Street," *Spotlite*, August 28, 1948, 4.

41. *Evening Independent*, "Cancels One Liquor Permit; Suspends 18," June 12, 1950, 1.

42. Isadore Blakeny, interview by Michael Beverly, April 29, 1999, transcript, African American Migration to Youngstown Project, O.H. 1921, Youngstown State University Oral History Program, Youngstown, OH.

43. William A. Alkorn, "Chapter Closes on Cherol's: Cherol's, a Fixture on Youngstown's West Side for Decades, Is Changing Hands," *Youngstown Vindicator*, January 12, 2011, http://www.vindy.com/news/2011/jan/12/chapter-closes-cherols (accessed May 12, 2013).

44. Ron Fritts and Ken Vail, *Ella Fitzgerald: The Chick Webb Years and Beyond* (New York: Scarecrow Press, 2003), 85.

45. *Richmond Afro-American*, "Ella Fitzgerald Weds Musician," December 27, 1947, 8.

46. Alkorn, "Chapter Closes on Cherol's."

47. *Youngstown Vindicator*, "Shift to Suburbs Shown in Population Figures," August 1, 1954, A6.

48. Jonathan R. Laing, "King of Malls: Despite His Billions, Edward DeBartolo Remains a Shadowy Figure," *Barron's*, June 12, 1989, 8–30.

Chapter 2

49. Jon Baker, "William R. Stewart Was City's First Black Attorney and State Representative," *Valley Voice*, February 11, 2005, 26.

50. Sean Posey, "Can the South Side of Youngstown Be Saved?" *Rustwire*, June 6, 2013, http://rustwire.com/2013/06/06/can-the-south-side-of-youngstown-be-saved (accessed September 3, 2013).

51. Gail Monaghan, "Screen Siren Cobb Salad," *Wall Street Journal*, June 25, 2011, D5.

52. *Youngstown Vindicator*, "Officials Probe Fire at Mansion," March 5, 1984, 1.

53. Ibid., "Arson Fire Sweeps Courtney's; 3 Hurt," July 16, 1976, 1.

54. Ibid., "Auto Bomb Kills Vince DeNiro: Midnight Blast Rips Uptown," July 17, 1961, 1.

55. Ibid., "'Peculiar Events' Here: A Look at Youngstown," editorial by the *Akron Beacon Journal*, July 23, 1961.

56. *Evening Independent*, "Racket Figure Slain," July 2, 1962, 40.

57. *Toledo Blade*, "Youngstown Aroused by Latest Killings: Child Victims Finally Stir Up Community," November 29, 1962, 4.

58. John Kobler, "Murder Town USA: Youngstown Has Had 75 Bombings, 11 Killings in a Decade, and No One Seems to Care," *Saturday Evening Post*, March 9, 1963, 71–76.

59. *Youngstown Vindicator*, "Cicero's Destroyed by Blaze," July 24, 1969.

60. Eric Schlosser, *Fast Food Nation: The Dark Side of the All-American Meal* (New York: Mariner Books/Houghton Mifflin Harcourt, 2001), 19.

61. Esther Hamilton, "Ross Marino's Dog House Chain Has 221 Outlets in 33 States," *Youngstown Vindicator*, January 16, 1966, A6.

62. Esther Hamilton, "Raffel Brothers Aid Area's Economy by Using Steel in Restaurant Products," *Youngstown Vindicator*, February 10, 1963, A6.

63. Leroy B. Raffel, "I've Got No Beef," unpublished memoir, May 1997, courtesy of the author.

64. Jenkins, "Aroma of Fish."

65. Marie Shellock, "Plans to Replace Bridge Threaten Historic Eatery," *Youngstown Vindicator*, October 1, 1987, 9.

66. *Youngstown Vindicator*, "Gennaro James Massullo, 95: Was Owner of Avalon Gardens," October 6, 1991, 3.

67. Esther Hamilton, "Around Town with Esther Hamilton," *Youngstown Vindicator*, January 31, 1952, 23.

68. *Youngstown Vindicator*, "Dollar Bank Buys Old Victoria Café," January 5, 1972, 14.

69. Jack Edwards, "Lavanty Turns Tavern into 'Class' Restaurant," *Youngstown Vindicator*, May 25, 1980.

70. *Youngstown Vindicator*, "Charles Serednesky Sr.; Owned, Operated Open Hearth Grill," January 11, 1990, 32.

71. *Steel Valley News*, "City Population Drops 2,447 in 4-Year Period," February 28, 1965, 1.

72. *Youngstown Vindicator*, "Area Metro Population Shows 7.7 Pct. Gain," April 7, 1966, 1.

73. Posey, "Can the South Side of Youngstown Be Saved?"

Chapter 3

74. Robert A. Beauregard, *When America Became Suburban* (Minneapolis: University of Minnesota Press, 2006), 85.

75. Sherry Linkon and John Russo, *Steeltown U.S.A.: Work & Memory in Youngstown* (Lawrence: University Press of Kansas, 2002), 43.

76. "Star Oyster House," menu, undated, original, Mahoning Valley Historical Society, Youngstown, OH.

77. *Youngstown Vindicator*, "Pick-Ohio Will Close Purple Cow on Oct. 31," October 17, 1962.

78. Ibid., "Hoodlums at the Purple Cow," editorial, March 21, 1960.

79. Ibid., "Moore's Tavern Will Give Way to UR Project," May 18, 1969.

80. Ibid., "New Firm Buys Sears Building at Boardman St.: Legal Arts Is Silent on Intent," December 19, 1963, 1.

81. Catesby R. Cannon Jr., "Will Raze Palace and Sears Bldg.: Legal Arts Center to Go Up on Market St.; New Theater Set," *Youngstown Vindicator*, April 10, 1964, 1.

82. Ibid.

83. *Youngstown Vindicator*, "Motor Hotel to Be Ready by Aug. 1," June 9, 1963, 1.

84. Ibid., "Snips Steel Ribbon to Open Voyager Motel: Mayor Lauds Baytos for Showing Faith in Downtown," November 22, 1963, 4.

85. Ibid., "Voyager Grand Opening Is Friday: Theme Is Beginning of Progress in Downtown," November 21, 1963, 12.

86. Aikenhead, "Mural Room."

87. Jack Edwards, "New Restaurant Satisfies Demand for Chinese Food," *Youngstown Vindicator*, May 15, 1971.

88. *Youngstown Vindicator*, "Strouss Restaurant Planned in Wick Bldg.," August 8, 1969.

89. Greg Edwards, "Sidewalk Café Set for Federal Plaza," *Youngstown Vindicator*, October 25, 1976.

90 *Youngstown Vindicator*, "Union Bank Fire Loss Exceeds Million: Raging Flames Leave Destruction, Icy Drapes," February 4, 1963, 1.

91. "Federal Street Mall Groundbreaking, Oct. 31, 1973," program, Reuben McMillan Public Library, Youngstown, OH.

92. *Youngstown Vindicator*, "Federal Plaza Opening Brings Out Thousands," October 5, 1974, 1.

93. "20th Century Menu," original copy, Mahoning Valley Historical Society, Youngstown, OH.

94. Robin Erb, "Boomba's Business Booming," *Youngstown Vindicator*, July 29, 1991, B1.

95. Sean Safford, *Why the Garden Club Couldn't Save Youngstown: The Transformation of the Rust Belt* (Cambridge, MA: Harvard University Press, 2009), 146.

96. Linkon and Russo, *Steeltown U.S.A.*, 3.

97. *Youngstown Vindicator*, "District Mills Remain Dark," September 19, 1982, 1.

Chapter 4

98. Thomas G. Feuchtmann, *Steeples and Stacks: Religion and Steel Crisis in Youngstown* (Cambridge, UK: Cambridge University Press, 1989), 42–43.

99. Bruno, *Steelworker Alley*, 113.

100. Feuchtmann, *Steeples and Stacks*, 1–2.

101. Douglas R. Sease, "Closing of a Steel Mill Hits Workers in U.S. with Little Warning: Though They Keep Getting Incomes, Retaining Aid, Creation of New Jobs Lag," *Wall Street Journal*, September 23, 1980, 1.

102. Bruno, *Steelworker Alley*, 149.

103. *Youngstown Vindicator*, "Mahoning Co.'s Census Shows 7.1 Percent Drop," July 8, 1980, 6.

104. *Youngstown 2010 Citywide Plan* (Youngstown, OH: City of Youngstown, 2005), 7.

105. *Youngstown Vindicator*, "Antone's Back with $1.5 Million Facility," October 28, 1984.

106. Dan Pecchia, "Two Purchase Colonial House," *Youngstown Vindicator*, December 9, 1989, 8.

107. *Youngstown Vindicator*, "Colonial House Will Close Its Doors," January 27, 1995, A6.

108. B. David Wolf, "Restaurant in Plans of 'Candidate,'" *Youngstown Vindicator*, November 29, 1985.

109. Betram de Souza and Tin Roberts, "Park Inn Fined Over Deck," *Youngstown Vindicator*, December 13, 1990.

110. George Nelson, "Park Inn Expands, Doubles Business," *Youngstown/Warren Business Journal* (November 15, 1988).

111. Mark Niquette, "Park Inn Closes," *Youngstown Vindicator*, February 10, 1994, A1.

112. "In Chef We Trust," *Ohio Magazine Statewide Restaurant Guide* (1989/90): 22–31.

113. *Youngstown Vindicator*, "Deli to Hold Grand Reopening," May 9, 1988, 20.

114. "Sales Boom at Kravitz Bakery," *Business Journal* (January 1993).

115. Sam Vargos, "Jay's Hot Dogs Is Mainstay on Strip," *Business Journal* (March 1995).

116. Christopher Cotelesse, "Tokyo House Is One of Youngstown's Best-Kept Secrets," *Youngstown Vindicator*, March 25, 2011, http://www.vindy.com/news/2011/mar/25/tokyo-house-one-youngstowns-best-kept-secrets (accessed December 3, 2013).

117. Dan Pecchia, "Landmark Eatery Closes Its Doors," *Youngstown Vindicator*, July 17, 1991, A1.

118. *Youngstown Vindicator*, "Oaks Is Back, with Tradition on Tap," July 28, 1997, B1.

119. Mark Smesko and Michael Vallas, "The Royal Oaks; Royal Character," Signature Dishes, *Youngstown Vindicator*, July 31, 2013, C1.

120. Neil Durbin, "Construction Hurt Business," *Youngstown Vindicator*, March 20, 1990.

121. Margaret Nery, "Wood-Burning Fire Adds Flavor," *Youngstown Vindicator*, October 7, 1993.

122. Mark Smesko and Michael Vallis, "Dubic's Palm Café: Time to Meat Up," Signature Dishes, *Youngstown Vindicator*, December 18, 2013, C1.

123. Mark Smesko and Michael Vallis, "Dickey's: Secret Spicy Success," Signature Dishes, *Youngstown Vindicator*, July 3, 2013, C1.

124. *Youngstown Vindicator*, "Owners Put Hasti House Up for Sale," January 21, 1989, 8.

125. Jolie Solomon, "Mickey's Secret Life: The Mystery Man Behind the Phar-Mor Scandal Was Obsessed with Winning—and Lost Big," *Newsweek*, August 31, 1992, 70–72.

126. Jane Schmucker, "After 15 Years in Business, Owners to Close Hasti House," *Youngstown Vindicator*, November 18, 1994, 1.

Chapter 5

127. Angie Schmitt, "Hope and Gloom: Some 24,000 Jobs Have Been Lost in the Mahoning Valley Since 2000; What Does the Contracting Economy Mean for the Youngstown Revitalization Plan?" *Youngstown Vindicator*, February 13, 2008, 1.

128. David Skolnick, "Sealing the Deal on the Chevrolet Centre," *Youngstown Vindicator*, November 18, 2005, A1.

129. Youngstown Business Incubator, website, http://www.ybi.org (accessed October 17, 2012).

130. White House, "We Can't Wait: Obama Administration Announces New Public-Private Partnership Support," http://www.whitehouse.gov/the-press-office/2012/08/16/we-can-t-wait-obama-administration-announces-new-public-private-partners (accessed October 17, 2012).

131. Burton Speakman and Jamison Cocklin, "Growing Pains: As Downtown Develops, Costs of Business Increase," *Youngstown Vindicator*, December 9, 2012, 1.

132. Michele Ristich, "Locally Owned Restaurants Hold Their Own in Crowded Field," *Business Journal*, mid-November 1998, 29.

133. Karen Simko, "Johnny's: Seasoned Chef Offers Upscale Menu," *Town Crier*, August 3, 2000, A18.

134. Guy D'Astolfo, "DeYor Center for the Performing Arts: Gem of a Theater Downtown," *Youngstown Vindicator*, April 16, 2006, A1.

135. Katie Libecco, "Rosetta Stone Offers Upscale Cuisine, Culture," *Youngstown Vindicator*, January 18, 2008, http://valley24.com/news/2008/jan/18/rosetta-stone-offers-upscale-cuisine-culture (accessed January 7, 2014).

136. Grace Wyler, "Acclaimed Downtown Eatery Closes," *Youngstown Vindicator*, August 27, 2010, http://www.vindy.com/news/2010/aug/27/by-grace-wyler/ (accessed January 7, 2014).

137. *Youngstown Vindicator*, "New O'Donold's Pub Has Old-time Charm," October 11, 2012, http://www.vindy.com/news/2012/oct/11/new-odonolds-pub-has-old-time-charm (accessed January 13, 2014).

138. Ibid., "Downtown Pizzeria Opens for New Year," January 1, 2013, http://www.vindy.com/news/2013/jan/01/downtown-pizzeria-opens-for-new-year (accessed January 14, 2014).

139. Ibid., "Downtown Icon Youngstown Club to Close After New Year's Eve," November 14, 2012, http://www.vindy.com/news/2012/nov/14/downtown-icon-youngstown-club-to-close-a (accessed January 14, 2014).

140. Guy D'Astolfo and Jamison Cocklin, "New Building Owner Plans to Shutter Cedar's," *Youngstown Vindicator*, December 8, 2012, http://www.vindy.com/news/2012/dec/08/owner-plans-to-shutter-cedars (accessed January 15, 2014).

141. Guy D'Astolfo, "Cedar's on the Move: So Long Downtown, Hello W. Side," *Youngstown Vindicator*, January 28, 2013, http://www.vindy.com/news/2013/jan/28/cedars-on-the-move-so-long-downtown-hell (accessed January 15, 2014).

142. Jamison Cocklin, "Near Retirement, Owner Decides to Close Café Cimmento," *Youngstown Vindicator*, April 19, 2013, A1.

143. Jamison Cocklin, "Lawsuit Seeks to Shutter Lemon Grove," *Youngstown Vindicator*, September 5, 2012, http://www.vindy.com/news/2012/sep/05/lawsuit-seeks-to-shutter-lemon-grove (accessed January 15, 2014).

144. Jamison Cocklin, "Youngstown: Lemon Grove, Ex-Landlord Settle," *Youngstown Vindicator*, October 25, 2012, http://www.vindy.com/news/2012/oct/25/downtown-youngstown-lemon-grove-ex-landl (accessed January 15, 2014).

145. David Skolnick and Jamison Cocklin, "Downtown Bar Strives to Make a Name for Itself," *Youngstown Vindicator*, August 21, 2013, A1.

146. Guy D'Astolfo, "New Nightspot Operators Plan to Make Martinis from a Lemon," *Youngstown Vindicator*, December 19, 2013, C2.

147. Jamison Cocklin and David Skolnick, "Downtown's Ups & Downs," *Youngstown Vindicator*, May 5, 2013, A1.

148. David Skolnick, "Mexican Restaurant to Open in Downtown Youngstown," *Youngstown Vindicator*, August 20, 2013, 1.

149. Tom McParland, "Downtown Dream," *Youngstown Vindicator*, December 28, 2013, A1.

150. Erin Kouvas, "Soul Food Sensations: Southern Exposure," *Youngstown Vindicator*, December 25, 2013, C1.

INDEX

Index

ABOUT THE AUTHORS

Thomas G. Welsh, PhD, is an independent scholar and professional writer and editor living in Youngstown, Ohio. He is a member of the advisory board of "Steel Valley Voices," a web-based project to promote awareness of the community's diversity. The project is sponsored by the Youngstown Historical Center for Industry & Labor. He is the author of *Closing Chapters: Urban Change, Religious Reform, and the Decline of Youngstown's Catholic Elementary Schools* (Lexington Books, 2011), which describes factors that led to the collapse of an urban parochial school system. He is the coauthor (with Michael K. Geltz) of *Strouss': Youngstown's Dependable Store* (The History Press, 2012).

Gordon F. Morgan Jr. grew up in Campbell, Ohio, and spent many nights enjoying a double burger (ketchup only) and feeding the jukebox at Gaetano's Airport Tavern, where his mother, Pauline, worked as a waitress in the 1970s. In 2012, he earned his master's degree in professional writing and editing from Youngstown State University. His articles have appeared in

About the Authors

Youngstown-based news publications, including the *Metro Monthly* and the *Vindicator*, and blogs that are dedicated to U.S. history. Gordon also writes for and edits *Drum and Bugle Call*, the newsletter of the Mahoning Valley Civil War Round Table, where he serves as program director.

Printed in the USA
CPSIA information can be obtained
at www.ICGtesting.com
LVHW080825011123
762556LV00006B/139